W9-AUI-547

Hello, **WINE**

Hello, WINE

The Most
ESSENTIAL THINGS
You Need to Know
ABOUT WINE

MELANIE WAGNER

Illustrations by
LUCY ENGELMAN

CHRONICLE BOOKS
SAN FRANCISCO

Library of Congress Cataloging-in-Publication Data available.

ISBN 978-1-4521-1102-5

Manufactured in China

Designed by Albertson Design & Alice Chau.
Cover design by Dinah Fried.
Illustrations by Lucy Engelman.

10 9 8 7 6 5 4 3 2 1

Chronicle Books LLC
680 Second Street
San Francisco, California 94107
www.chroniclebooks.com

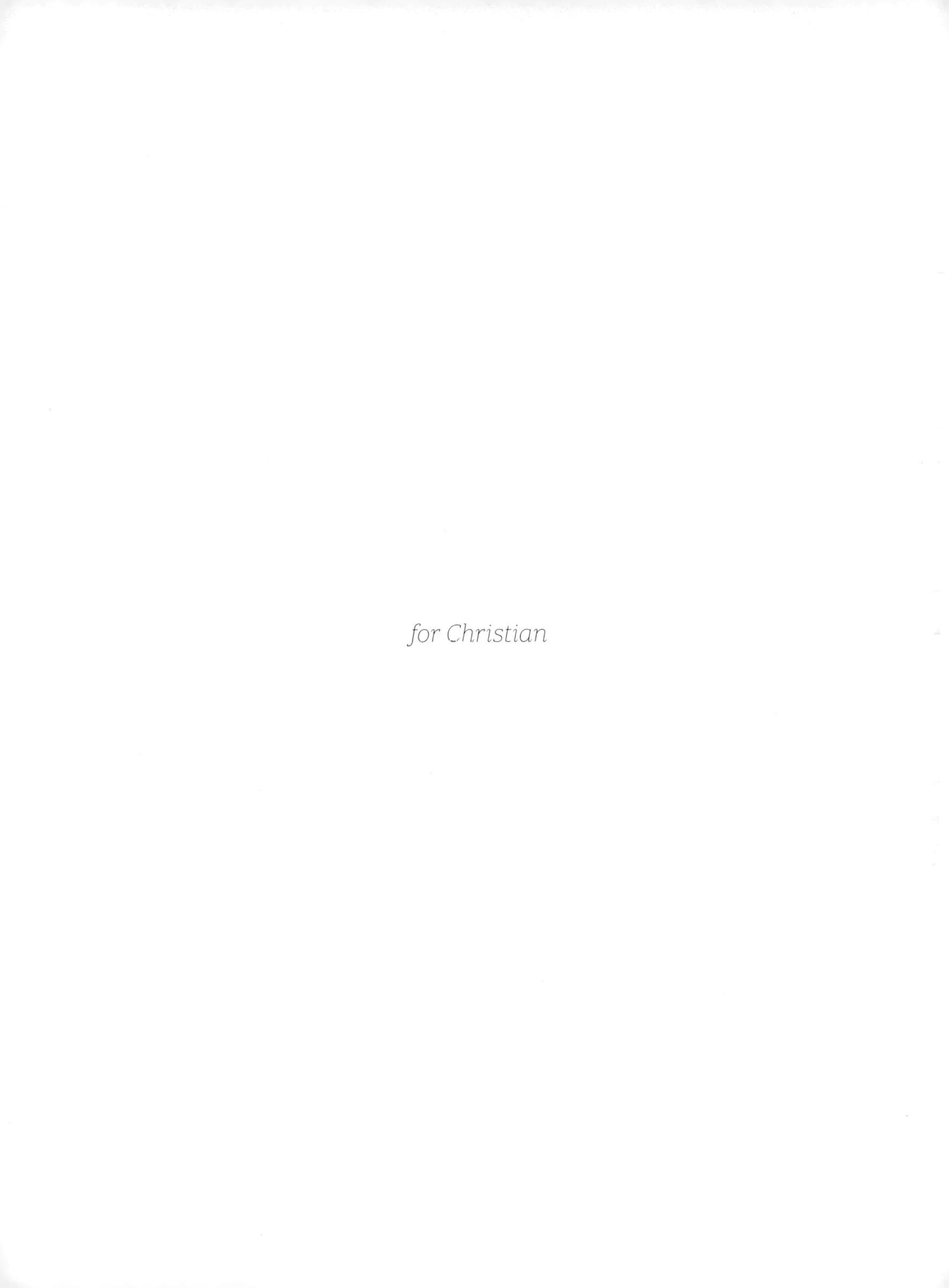

for Christian

CONTENTS

Little Wine Love Notes

I set out to be a teacher; the wine part was a surprise turn. Postcollege, with one psychology degree and two years of teaching adorable but exhausting four-year-olds under my belt, I felt restless. I was living in a dump in San Francisco, scraping by on a steady diet of ramen noodles, when the idea of working with wine entered my consciousness.

One afternoon on the playground I asked the mother of one of my students what she did for a living. When she answered that she sold fine wine, bells went off in my head and my eyes got wide and sparkly. I remember thinking, "Selling wine is a *job*?" It had never occurred to me. I had always loved drinking wine (when I could afford it). A career in wine sounded irresistibly glamorous. I left my preschool gig giddy with the vision of a chic new life. However, my real-world adventures on the way to becoming a wine guru were rarely idyllic.

Promptly after my epiphany, I talked my way into a job I was thoroughly underqualified for—selling fine wine for a top distributor. Seemingly overnight, I was knee-deep in elite circles of the industry, and I knew nothing about wine except that it was wet and it tasted good. If there had been a boot camp for wine, I would have eagerly enlisted; the road would have been more predictable and I would have at least had comrades to suffer alongside. Sadly, I was alone: a misfit. I still remember how embarrassing and uncomfortable it felt to be mocked by the snob sect.

My bumpkin status did come with a perk though. Because I was hobnobbing with top winemakers, importers, and restaurateurs, my aha moments with wine were bittersweet—bitterly humbling as I was constantly reminded of how little I knew, yet sweet because I usually had an incredible glass of wine in my hand. Thankfully, passion and curiosity always seemed to conquer my pride. Maybe it was self-preservation, or the patience I had developed tending to those preschool tots, but I turned frustration with my own ignorance into an unrelenting drive to understand wine, and then to assist others in getting there on a (fingers crossed) less painful path.

During the past ten years, as a Certified Sommelier, writer, speaker, and teacher, I've had the opportunity to educate many wine professionals and connoisseurs. My favorite students, however, are the ones who are just beginning to dive in: people who've had enough experience with wine to know that they are hooked and are eager to learn more. Of course, they want to understand why wine tastes like it does, but they also become empowered when I can provide them with practical, applicable wine info—things like how long a bottle stays fresh after opening, what screw caps say about the quality of the wine, and how much money you need to spend to get a decent bottle of pinot noir. It is my passion and privilege to champion this group on the road to becoming aficionados.

My calling to write this book emerged because my own school of hard knocks left me empathetic with wine rookies, and also because I saw a huge gap in the information being touted as an "Introduction to Wine." Most often in this category, you find beautiful, articulate books that are insightful and accurate, but overwhelming to the beginner. I remember picking up some of them in my early days, and then promptly putting them back on the shelf. They were just too technical, too soon. On the flip side are pocket-size works that do an injustice to wine by oversimplifying it, setting the reader up for disappointment by promising them expert status in one hundred petite pages.

There's a fine line between simplifying wine and reducing it to something less than it is, and also between respecting tradition and getting way too serious. I believe it's possible to enjoy wine, study it in easily digestible chunks, and celebrate its endless intrigue all at the same time.

Think of this book as a gateway to wine. Just as preschool prepares you for the rough-and-tumble world of elementary education, consider this book a precursor to your forthcoming wine adventures.

These pages are the culmination of everything I've learned during my years of mishaps and enlightenment on the wine route, condensed into what I feel are the most essential lessons you need to know *now*—at the beginning of your journey. Think of each chapter as a little wine love note from me to you. Together, they contain the most important nuggets of wine truth that I've learned along the way, the secrets I wish someone had handed me when I was just starting out. I hope this book makes you smarter and more confident. I hope it makes you think and laugh, and that it ignites a desire to always continue learning more, so that your life is rich with the joy of wine.

Welcome to Wine

Maybe you are brand new to wine, or maybe you've been drinking for years and have just decided that it's time to step up your know-how. Either way, I'm glad you're here, and the first thing I want to do is give you a big warm welcome into the wine world. It's exciting and delicious—you are in for a treat.

As I see it, my job is to empower you with meaningful wine information (the stuff you're going to actually use) and to encourage you to feed your passion for learning about wine, so that it far outlasts this book. We begin with a little pre-game prep; the first chapter lays out my plan for how to approach the enormity of the subject, and essential first steps to get started.

WINE IS BIG: GET COZY WITH IT

Wine has a justifiable reputation for being intimidating: there's a lot to know. All that knowledge can seem big and scary, and leave us feeling insecure. It might sound funny, but the first, most essential step to becoming confident with wine is to embrace that vulnerability, and prepare for a lifetime of learning. The sooner you can get comfortable with the magnitude of what there is to know—and content that you, in fact, do not need to master wine to relish it—the more you will enjoy your overall experience. You do *not* need to memorize all the communes in Bordeaux or which grapes are grown in Romania in order to properly swoon over a great bottle; thankfully, the pleasure of wine is not reserved for experts. While I am here to help you develop a sense of intimacy and comfort with wine, I'll also be the first to tell you that getting too technical can suck the romance right out of your glass. As you begin your education, I urge you to celebrate wine's complexity and intrigue, and also to savor the trip. If you fall in love, you will be challenged, as much as you like, for the rest of your wine drinking days.

Here are just some of the ways in which this moving target will keep you curious, once she's captured your heart.

1. WINE IS THE MOST INTERESTING CONSUMABLE SUBJECT IN THE WORLD.

Wine is truly fascinating. I'm not just talking about being intrigued by what's in the glass, but also the way in which it opens doors to learning about so many other things. A single bottle can inspire us to pick up a history book, learn about another culture, contemplate a scientific principle, enthuse over maps, or venture off to a new place. And the best part . . . you drink it!

Wine is one of the only things I can think of that combines intellect with pure, unadulterated sensory hedonism. Reading alone will never make you winewise; no book can duplicate the ultrasexy texture of pinot noir or the purely animalistic aroma of South Africa's signature grape, pinotage. To truly absorb wine, you have to *absorb* it, which is pretty much the best homework ever.

2. WINE IS ALIVE.

Real wine comes from a farm, not a factory. Although some wine companies churn out cases of widget wine so formulated and fixed up in a chemistry lab that it becomes as predictable and tasty as plastic, true wine—artisan wine—is highly affected by the annual cycle of the vineyard, and by the care that is taken in growing the sweet little baby grapes that deliver it. This dynamic beverage, once bottled, still breathes and evolves. It remains extremely sensitive to time, temperature, travel, and context (like what mood you're in when you experience it, who you're with, or what you're eating).

Did You Know? Danish researchers at the Institute of Preventive Medicine say that wine drinkers have a higher IQ than beer and spirits drinkers or abstainers.

Buy a dozen bottles of a stellar cabernet and taste one every year for twelve years. You'll surely notice it keeps changing on you. Like anything with a soul, wine is hard to capture. It is never the same twice, but that's part of its elusive charm.

3. WINE GROUNDS YOU.

You may have already discovered . . . wine has a spiritual side; if you let it, it has a way of brightening your awareness. One of the things that first attracted me to wine was that when I drank it, I noticed that I felt more connected to the earth and to the people I shared it with. In a world where people are increasingly detached—despite, and perhaps because of, a tsunami of technology—wine demands you sit still. It helps you tune out distraction and be more present in the moment. It effortlessly initiates meaningful conversation and carves pathways that link you to the person across the table, even if you start out as strangers. I'm a beer advocate, and I love a handcrafted cocktail, too, but neither seems to have the contemplative trigger that wine does.

Of course, not all wines will change your life and not all of your wine experiences will be thoughtful. But, often, drinking good wine reminds you to be a more mindful human and can make everyday life more vivid.

MORAL OF THE STORY

Wine is big, deep, and mysterious. It's going to take a long time, and a lot of drinking, for you to feel like you really *know* wine. And, typically, as soon as you think you've got it, it surprises you with a fascinating twist. Just keep repeating this mantra: Learning about wine is sexy, not scary.

"WINE MAKES DAILY LIVING EASIER, LESS HURRIED, WITH FEWER TENSIONS AND MORE TOLERANCE."

—Benjamin Franklin

"IN VINO VERITAS. [IN WINE IS TRUTH.]"

—Plato

"WINE IS A PEEPHOLE ON A MAN."

—Alcaeus

BABY STEPS

Now you understand that this adventure will be a long and wonderful one. What next? With wine, as with many things in life, feeling self-assured is half the battle. And, no, that doesn't mean you need to get all snooty—wine is just as at home at a backyard barbecue as it is in the finest French restaurants. Just like if you were learning a new sport, you're going to need some essential equipment, basic vocabulary words, and a few pointers before you take in the subtleties of the game. The following steps will empower you to get your wine on, confidently.

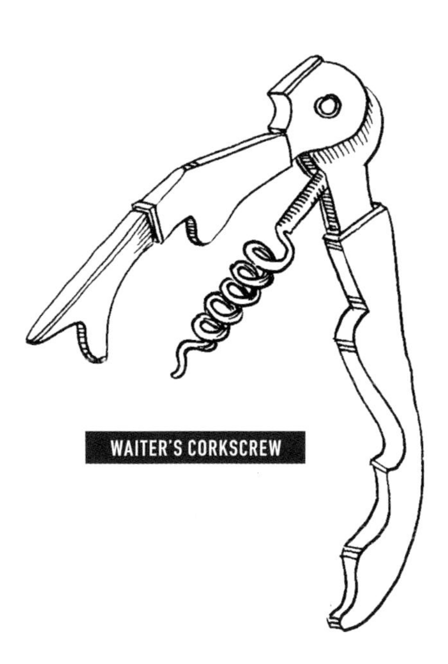

WAITER'S CORKSCREW

GET GEAR

Unlike golf or skiing, starting a wine habit—I mean, hobby—is really not that expensive. You can spend a fortune on wine, but you don't need to. Here are the essentials to get you going.

A TRUSTY WINE OPENER

As long as wineries are using corks to close their wine bottles, you're going to need a device to get that puppy open. You could add drama by sabering the top of the bottle off with a sword. This method may impress dates, but it will inevitably end with a big mess. Since pulling out your sword on the first date is probably not a great idea anyway, the safest bet—however boring it may be—is to stick with a corkscrew. There are many types of corkscrews. Use whichever one you feel most comfortable with.

Basic Corkscrew The basic corkscrew features a handle with a simple, spiraling screw (also called a worm). If your biceps leave something to be desired, I'd avoid this one. Lack of leverage is a real pain.

Waiter's Corkscrew Add leverage and control to the basic corkscrew and you have a great tool. This opener also often includes a handy foil cutter, it's easy to transport, and it's inexpensive. It's my personal favorite, but you may need a little practice to master it.

Did You Know? Only about 50 percent of American households own a corkscrew. / *Barron's*

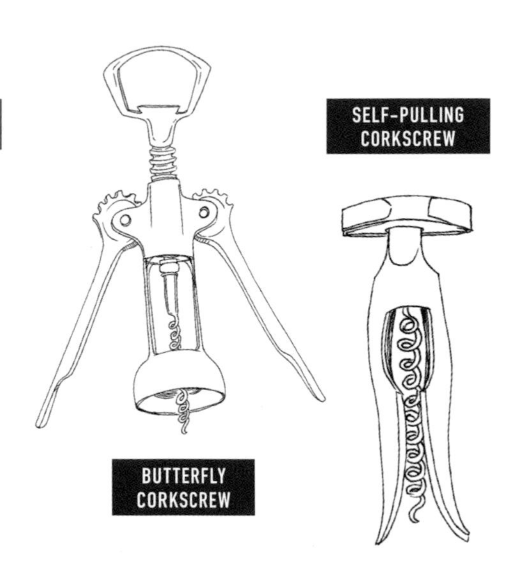

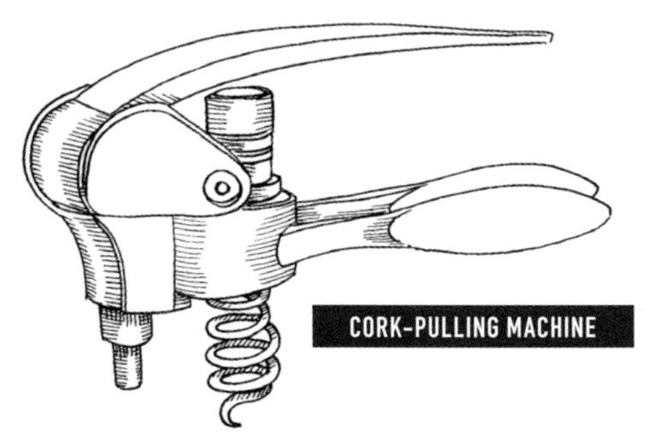

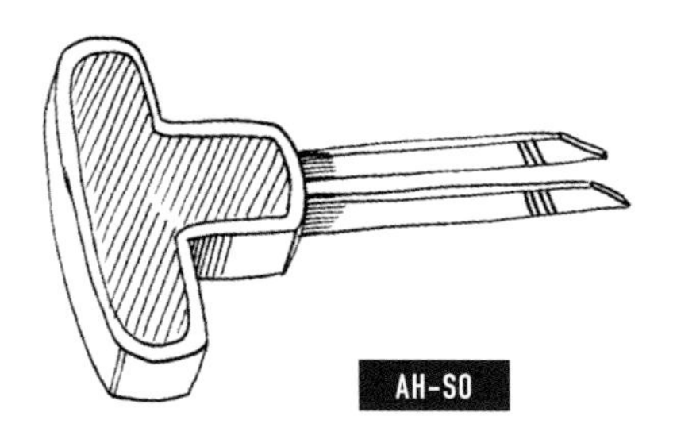

Butterfly or Wing Corkscrew The butterfly combines a corkscrew with a bottle cap opener—a good feature to point out to your beer-drinking friends, who may worry you've abandoned them for a wine-only lifestyle.

Self-Pulling Corkscrew This design consists of a basic corkscrew fitted into a plastic guide. It gets the job done with most corks, but it can be difficult with plastic corks and fragile corks (like the ones you might discover in an older wine, when time has deteriorated the natural material).

Cork-Pulling Machine (e.g., the "Rabbit") This is the Hummer of corkscrews. The Rabbit, and other copycat openers, have two gripping handles that latch on to the top of a wine bottle and a top lever that drives the worm into the cork and pops it out. They are easy to use, but can lack the finesse you sometimes need to remove troublesome corks, and they can be quite a bit more expensive than any of the other corkscrews.

Ah-So You'll find this tool in the pocket of most top sommeliers because it is great for old or injured corks; it won't puncture brittle corks and it can masterfully extract a cork that's been mangled by one of the other tools. The Ah-So is like a cork ambulance—excellent in an emergency, but not necessary or practical for everyday transportation.

FLIGHT RISK When traveling by air, do not leave a corkscrew in your purse, briefcase, or pocket. Apparently, they are a threat to national security. Your tool (weapon) will be confiscated, which is maddening.

GOOD GLASSES

Colorful plastic wineglasses are one of the best inventions ever conceived. Drink wine on the beach, at the pool, or in a boat without the fear of breaking an expensive glass? Brilliant idea. However, for times when you are drinking wine to learn, you need serious glasses. The best are made of thin, clear crystal, with a largish bottom that curves, narrowing at the top.

I promise good glasses make a huge difference—not only in the aesthetic pleasure you can derive from drinking out of a beautiful vessel, but also how it technically affects the taste of the wine. Studies on taste and smell from the Yale School of Medicine have proved that flavors can be perceived as more or less pleasurable based on where they specifically land in your mouth. Glasses designed with that in mind can (at least theoretically) deliver wine optimally. If this is all sounding a little too geeky, it is. Just like serious cyclists can get fanatical about having the lightest possible carbon fiber bike or the golfer who's crazed with the exact angle of his driver, you can get obsessed with having the perfect wineglass for every type of wine. Riedel, one of the oldest and best wineglass-making companies, makes more than two hundred fifty types of wineglasses, many specific to certain grapes or regions. For most people, me included, buying **a nice set of one large size** will do. Admittedly, when I'm at home, I usually drink most wines—white, red, and pink—out of the same glass.

For wines with bubbles, I typically use a **tall flute** with a slightly larger bowl than lip. Tulip-shaped flutes also work well. Again, thin, clear crystal is best.

AN IDEAL ALL-PURPOSE WINE GLASS

AN IDEAL CHAMPAGNE FLUTE

Flutes are gorgeous and elegant, but they are not absolutely necessary to enjoy sparkling wine. Wine professionals sometimes use a regular wineglass to evaluate Champagne or sparkling wine. In fact, I think you can smell sparkling wines better in a glass with a larger opening, but the bubbles fade faster, and it's just not as fun.

The one glass I would never advise for sparkling wine is the Champagne coupe, or Champagne saucer, which legend says was modeled on the breast of Marie Antoinette.

This shallow (sorry, Marie) broad-bowled glass is a horrible vessel for delivering sparkling wine. The best parts of drinking sparkling wine are (a) savoring the aroma and (b) watching all those beautiful bubbles dance around in your glass. The broad surface area of the coupe allows both aroma and carbonation to escape quickly.

GLASSWARE CARE Caring for your wineglasses is easy. It's best to wash them by hand, with a little soap and hot water. Rinse them well and let them air-dry.

OTHER OPTIONAL GEAR

A wine carrier For wine on the go, you can't beat the fun neoprene totes from Built (builtny.com). They make bringing a bottle to a restaurant, the park, or a friend's house convenient and stylish.

Champagne stoppers On the rare occasion I cannot empty a bottle of sparkling wine, I find this little tool indispensable. It's the best way to keep bubbles in the bottle a little longer—in between evenings, or even in between pours.

Charms for glasses Washing wineglasses is decidedly un-fun. One way to ensure less dishwashing duty is to make sure nobody loses his or her glass. There are hundreds of options available for marking your wine territory, ranging from corny baubles to sleek tags.

CHAMPAGNE STOPPER

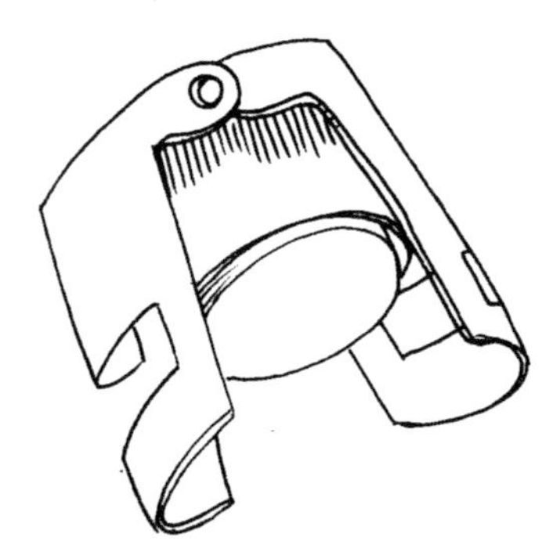

CHARMS FOR GLASSES

DECODING THE POMP AND CIRCUMSTANCE

Wine culture is inextricably linked to a certain ceremonial showiness that can, regrettably, turn people off and alienate them from the otherwise humble beverage. Don't fret. Things have changed and there are really no rules when it comes to imbibing. While some of those little rituals you've seen or heard of are more for show, some are actually useful and have real scientific purpose.

HOLDING YOUR GLASS BY THE STEM

It prevents the glass from getting dirty and ensures you don't raise the temperature of the wine with your hot little hands. Temperature plays a substantial role in how a wine tastes—the hotter the wine, the more we taste the alcohol and the less we taste of everything else. (More on that later. See Temperature, page 130.)

SWIRLING

This practice aerates, or adds oxygen to, the wine. Getting a little oxygen in your wine by swirling your glass allows the wine to breathe, so that it opens up and reveals its true aromas and flavors. The idea is to expose as much surface area of the wine as possible to oxygen. So swirl away!

STINGY POURS

Contrary to what you might think, a large, glass-filling pour is not a good one. When entertaining at home, fill the glass about halfway full, so you have plenty of room for swirling. If you're using a decent glass (see "Good Glasses," page 17), filling it halfway will still provide a substantial serving (3 or 4 fluid ounces).

CORK PRESENTATION

Relax—you don't need to smell or fondle the cork. Proper etiquette is actually to just ignore it. Yes, a moist cork is an indicator that the wine was stored properly: on its side. (If a wine with a cork is stored upright for too long, the cork can shrink, allowing potentially damaging amounts of oxygen to seep into the bottle and ruin the wine.) A cork's condition, however, is no clear indication of the wine's condition. The only way to tell if a wine is happy and healthy is to smell the wine itself. Pristine corks can encapsulate flawed wine, just as you can pull a grimy, moldy, black-and-green mess of a cork out of an otherwise perfect bottle. Save the cork to remember the evening if you so desire. Otherwise, just forget about it.

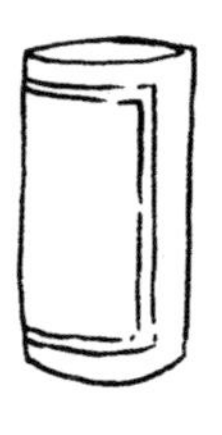

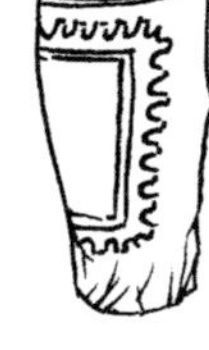

ALL ABOUT CORKAGE FEES BYOB, the acronym for *bring your own bottle*, is music to wine lovers' ears. A restaurant that invites you to bring your own wine not only ensures you'll be drinking a favorite, but also that you'll spend less money, right? Not always. If a restaurant advertises that it's a BYOB establishment, chances are it's because it does not have a liquor license. In this case, there is typically a minimal corkage fee or none at all. A *corkage fee* is the price a restaurant charges for serving the bottle to you; they should open it, provide glassware, and pour it for you. (It also helps them recover the profit they lose by not selling you a bottle.)

Even if a restaurant doesn't advertise as BYOB, practically all of them will allow you to bring in a bottle. Here's the nicest way to do that.

Call ahead and ask if there's a corkage fee, and look on the restaurant's website to make sure you're not bringing a bottle that is already on the wine list.

Limit it to one bottle.

The general rule of thumb is that if you bring a bottle, you also buy a bottle from the wine list.

Be prepared to pay the corkage fee. This may seem obvious, but some restaurants will waive the fee when you buy a bottle from their list. (It's a nice surprise if it happens—just don't expect it.) Corkage fees can range from $10 to $100. Don't be shocked if you are charged a significant fee at a top-notch restaurant, especially one that is noted for its wine selection. A high corkage fee is how a restaurant gracefully encourages you to order off its list.

KNOW YOUR ABTS

The language of wine can be especially intimidating. From "malolactic fermentation" to "volatizing esters," there's a lot of sophisticated wine lingo rolling off the lips of those in the know, not to mention all the descriptors for tasting . . . *roses* and *tar* in your wine? Take a deep breath. It's easy to get so bogged down in wine's daunting vocabulary that you forget why you were interested in the first place—because it tastes good! Don't worry. In time, you will master the vernacular. For now, if you have a good grasp of your ABTs—acidity, body, and tannin—you'll be smarter than most.

ACIDITY

Acidity is the razor-like tang running sharply through the core of wine. Acidity makes your mouth water. It's a wine's verve, zest, and vitality.

All fruits have acidity, some substantially more than others. When imagining acidity, think of fruits that make you pucker . . . the most iconic acidic fruit is a lemon, but other high-acid fruits include grapefruit, lime, and green apple. All wines have some measure of acidity. It comes naturally from the grape. As grapes ripen, acidity drops and sugars rise. The longer the sunbathing session and the warmer the weather, the lower the acidity in the finished wine. That's why, no matter what the grape, warm places like southern Australia create wines with lower acidity, and cool regions like Germany and Austria generally produce wines with higher acidity.

Too much acidity can taste harsh, like it's stripping the enamel off your teeth. Inadequate acidity makes wine taste flat, dull, and lifeless. Although you may prefer the tang of high acidity or the lush mouthfeel of wines that have very little acid, higher (but balanced) acidity is generally considered best. It tastes more refreshing, and it makes wine much more pleasant to drink with food. It is also a natural preservative that can add years to a wine's shelf life.

Wines with Exceptionally High Acidity

» Champagne and other sparkling wines
» German wines (red and white)
» Austrian wines (red and white)
» Sauvignon blanc
» Italian reds

BODY

A great body is a wonderful thing—when it comes to people *and* wine. But as with the human form, "great" is subjective. A wine's body refers to its weight or viscosity. The more alcohol a wine has, the more body it will have. What exactly does a light-bodied wine *feel* like as opposed to a full-bodied wine? Like skim versus whole milk. A light-bodied wine isn't quantifiably any better or worse than a full-bodied wine; it's all just what you and your tongue prefer.

Here's a guide to the body in some popular wines. Keep in mind that where the wine comes from, how it's handled, and the weather of a given year can make a big difference in a wine's body. (Some chardonnays seem light and airy, others heavy and thick.) And, for clarification purposes, grape names are lowercase and appellations (or place-names) are capitalized. This gives you an idea of where wines generally fall in relation to their peers.

LIGHT

WHITES

- pinot grigio and many other Italian white wines
- riesling
- Champagne and sparkling wines
- sauvignon blanc
- Chablis
- albariño
- grüner veltliner
- white Burgundy
- viognier
- chardonnay

REDS

- Beaujolais
- red wines from Germany and Alsace, France
- Rioja
- dolcetto
- red Burgundy and other pinot noirs
- Chianti
- Côtes du Rhône
- barbera
- Chinon
- cabernet franc
- red Bordeaux
- merlot
- primitivo
- brunello di Montalcino
- Barolo and Barbaresco
- syrah/shiraz
- malbec
- dry Portuguese red wines
- cabernet sauvignon
- zinfandel

HEAVY

TANNIN

Wine that dries out your mouth? That's tannin in action. If you've ever tasted oversteeped tea or can recall the bitter aftertaste of a walnut, you already know how tannin tastes and feels. In the case of grapes, tannin is a compound that comes mostly from the skins and seeds. (Some additional tannin can be derived from an extended stay in oak barrels.) It is most evident in red wines made from small, thick-skinned grapes, which equate to more tannin per volume of juice. Tannin not only dries out your mouth, but also provides a skeletal structure for the rest of the wine.

Like acidity, tannin is a natural preservative, and wines that are born with hard, massive tannins typically have a long life. Over time, those harsh, stiff-feeling tannins soften, feeling silkier. Instead of dominating the wine, they integrate with the other components. Catching tannins at their prime—when they are still present enough to provide backbone, but have mellowed enough to be drinkable—is more a game of luck than skill.

Wines That Generally Have High Levels of Tannin

» cabernet sauvignon
» Barolo and Barbaresco
» Bordeaux
» brunello di Montalcino
» Hermitage and Côte Rôtie
» malbec
» petite sirah

Did You Know? Wine's calories come from alcohol, so a wine with more body has slightly more calories. Usually wines range from about 80 calories (light-bodied) to 120 calories (full-bodied) for a 4-ounce pour. / *The Wine Institute*

BECOME A SAVVY SHOPPER

Whether perusing the aisles or scanning an unfamiliar restaurant list, these tips will help you make smart wine choices.

FIND A WINE STORE YOU LOVE AND COMMIT TO THE RELATIONSHIP

A wine store can make or break your love for wine, especially in the beginning. The worst wine stores are dusty, dispassionate places that care only about profit. Or they are havens for self-important wine clerks who know just enough about wine to make you feel inadequate. The best shops are vibrant places with an interesting selection, an impassioned slant on wine, and a knowledgeable, friendly staff that goes out of their way to help you choose wines that are right for your taste buds. I can't emphasize enough how important it is to find a wine store you love and trust to help you along your wine journey. Once you find the right spot, committing to wine shop monogamy will give the resident experts the opportunity to get intimate with your palate.

How to Gauge the Integrity and Enthusiasm of a Wine Shop

Do they write about wine? Newsletters and blogs are a great way to judge a shop's passion and position on wine. Does what they write ooze with excitement? That's a good sign.

Do they host regular tastings, classes, or seminars? Providing opportunities for customers to taste and learn is another indicator of a shop's fervor; it means they are eager to share and interact with their customers.

Are the bottles in the store clean, well organized, and well cared for? Just as you wouldn't buy strawberries covered in dusty plastic, an unrefrigerated pork loin, or potatoes that were strewn across a supermarket floor, you want to make sure you're buying wine that has been loved up.

It's a wine store's job to care for and mindfully market wines. They should put time and thought into it. The easiest way to judge wine care is to touch a bottle. It should be cool and clean. If bottles are warm and dusty, or the shelves lack organization, it's probably best to shop elsewhere.

IF YOU DON'T ASK, YOU DON'T GET

It's a saying I live by, and it's as true for wine shopping as it is for anything else. Get better at asking for what you want. It should be the driving factor for learning and understanding wine vocabulary. Even before you're comfortable talking about particular flavors and aromas, just line up bottles and say, "I liked this, this, and this, but not this." That information holds valuable clues to decoding your preferences. Anything you can communicate to your trusty wine shop clerk or sommelier—good or bad—will make the wine whizzes

---

Did You Know? Women buy about 70 percent of the wine purchased in U.S. grocery stores, yet women account for less than 20 percent of the customers in fine wine shops. */ Vineyard and Winery Management*

more useful to you; they'll have the ammo they need to make good predictions of what you'll enjoy next.

BUY IN BULK

Most wine stores offer a discount if you buy a case of twelve bottles at a time—and many don't require that it be a dozen of the same bottles. Some shops offer discounts on six bottles.

BE CAUTIOUS OF PRETTY LABELS AND TOO-CLEVER NAMES

Within the wine industry, it was once standard knowledge that the prettiest labels adorned the worst bottles of wine. They were heartless, profit-driven eye candy with catchy names and colorful images meant to grab your attention on deep, crowded wine shelves. More money was spent on marketing than on the wine. Authentic wines—those that spoke of a place and were crafted by loving hands—most often had the most innocuous labels. Boring and forgettable on the outside, marketing was an afterthought for these gems.

I am happy to say that all of that is changing now. The evil wine-marketing militia is still out there peddling a smorgasbord of brightly colored rainwater, but now the farmers and families realize that you need a little panache on the outside to compete.

The lesson? There are lots of cute labels out there; some of them actually contain decent wine. Let that trustworthy wine retailer guide you, especially if you're going to spend a good deal of your hard-earned bucks on a bottle. Retailers should taste every wine that comes in the door. If they're really good at what they do, their buying decisions should shelter you from the lackluster stuff.

Did You Know? Per capita, the United States has a lot of catching up to do when it comes to wine consumption. We only drink about two gallons each annually—compared with fifty-four gallons of soft drinks per person per year! Europe drinks us under the table; countries like Italy, France, and Portugal consume closer to thirteen or fourteen gallons of wine per person annually. / *The Wine Institute*

WHEN HUNTING FOR SOMETHING SPECIAL, LOOK IN THE "SWEET SPOT."

I have a theory that the best bang-for-your-buck bottles are in the thirty- to fifty-dollar range. This is the slowest category in wine retail, because consumers usually enter a wine shop knowing they want to spend a little (usually under twenty dollars) for everyday wine or a lot (more than seventy-five or one hundred) for a special occasion. Wine marketers know these stats, and price their wines accordingly, avoiding the dreaded no-man's land in between the two price points. Wines priced in between that range are typically made by folks who are less concerned about the perception of price point (and how it affects sales), and are just charging what it actually costs them to produce the wine. Imagine that. Truth be told, I'm much more often blown away by forty- and fifty-dollar bottles than the ones that cost two hundred dollars.

MY TWO CENTS Throughout the book, you'll find specific wine recommendations. These are some of my personal, perennial favorites, and they're widely available at fine wine shops. No matter the price, these are wines that I believe are overachievers—they consistently outshine their peers with superior quality and value.

STEALS	$	less than $15
CLASSIC EXAMPLES	$$	$16 to $25
THE SWEET SPOT!	$$$	$26 to $50
SPLURGES	$$$$	$51 to $150

LABEL LANGUAGE

Appellation: An *appellation* is the specific place that the wine comes from. For example, California is an appellation. So is Napa Valley. It is implied, and often true, that the more specific the appellation, the higher quality the wine.

Château: *Château* is French for "winery." Other fancy-sounding foreign synonyms for "winery" include *domaine* and *mas* (also French), *tenuta* (Italian), *weingut* (German), and *bodega* (Spanish).

Cuvée: *Cuvée* has no official definition, but it loosely means that the wine is a blend. It may signify a blend of grapes, of vintages, or of batches of wine.

Estate Bottled: Most of the time—but not always—the phrase *estate bottled* is a sign of quality. *Estate bottled*, or the French equivalent of the saying, *mis en bouteille au château*, signifies that the wine has been made entirely on the property, allowing the winemaker more control over the process.

Old Vines: (also *Vielles Vignes*, *Vigne Vecchie*, or *VV*) Another term with no legal definition, *old vines* typically connotes grapevines that are more than thirty or forty years of age. Grapevines this old say more with less. That is, they produce a lot fewer grapes, but the grapes they do produce have more concentrated and complex flavors, typically resulting in more deeply flavored wines.

Unfiltered: Most wines go through some amount of clarification and filtering before bottling. This process is like straining; it removes unwanted particles from the wine, leaving it bright and clear. Some winemakers, the purists, feel passionately that fining and filtration of any sort potentially strips the wine of its true character. If a winemaker chooses not to filter, he'll typically announce it proudly on the label.

Variety: *Variety* refers to a specific type of grape. Chardonnay is a variety.

Vintage: If a year, or *vintage*, is stated on the label, it means all, or almost all, of the grapes were harvested in that year.

NINE SECRETS FOR ORDERING WINE ON A RESTAURANT LIST

Although streamlined, shopping for wine at a restaurant can be even more intimidating than at a store: sometimes the list can be esoteric, leaving you without the comfort of familiar favorites. Also, on a wine list, you can't study the labels for more information, and you're usually considering how it will pair with your food (or everyone's food). To make matters even worse, there's the added pressure of making a quick decision. Here are some tips to ease the potential discomfort.

1. CHECK OUT THE LIST AHEAD OF TIME.

Many restaurants post their wine lists on their websites, providing an excellent opportunity to get familiar with pricing, how the list is arranged (usually by region, grape, style, and/or price), and to study the available options. Word to the wise: wine lists can change daily, so setting your heart on the perfect bottle can be dangerous, because it might not be there when you arrive. Most fine dining establishments will eagerly set aside the bottle(s) you desire ahead of time, if you call and speak to the manager.

2. ASK FOR A TASTE.

Any bottle that is available by the glass is already open (or will be soon). Most restaurants are more than happy to offer you a sneak preview before you commit to a glass.

3. STEER CLEAR OF "HOUSE WINE."

Unless you're in a quaint European village, where the wines of the house are traditionally decent quality, house wine is synonymous with "the absolute cheapest stuff we can get our hands on." Yes, I did say earlier that wine quality is not solely dependent on price point (there are plenty of good and inexpensive wines out there), but most restaurants that offer a "house wine" look for a passable wine to sell at the lowest price possible, knowing that the customer who typically orders this category of wine values price over flavor.

4. BOTTLES AND HALF-BOTTLES OFFER MORE BANG FOR YOUR BUCK.

With by-the-glass wines, most restaurants try to recoup the entire cost of the bottle on the first glass. Full-size bottles (750 ml) and half-bottles (375 ml), if available, are usually a better deal. I adore half-bottles because they allow you some variety during dinner—you can order a half-bottle of white and then a half-bottle of red, or two half-bottles of red, or even three. You get the picture.

5. PRACTICE POINTING.

If you're on a hot date, ordering for a large group, or entertaining clients or business associates, it can be awkward to talk money at the table. But you can communicate your price range without uttering a number. Just hold the wine list up to the waiter and let him know you'd like a white or red wine like *this* (point to a price) and ask for his suggestion. Similarly, if you can't pronounce a wine or a producer's name, just point to it.

6. LEAN ON THE WINE GURU.

If you're staring at a daunting leather-bound tome or an unfamiliar list of oddities, don't be afraid to ask for help. Higher-end, wine-centric restaurants will often have a sommelier (som-el-YAY, the French word for wine steward) on staff. It's a sommelier's job to choose wines for the list and make recommendations to guests. Luckily, most sommeliers aren't elitists; making you comfortable and happy is their top priority. You can ask for the sommelier, the resident wine expert, or the manager, or you can enlist your waiter for his thoughts on certain wines or his suggestions for pairings. I'd advise first just telling your waiter that you'd like some help with wine and would love to speak with someone who knows the list well. If the waiter perks up with pride and tells you he's your man, he likely is. If he runs away to get someone more senior, he's not, and you've just made things easy for him by taking the pressure off. Just like in the wine shop, anything you can communicate about wines you like is extremely helpful.

7. TAKE A POLL, BUT THEN TAKE CHARGE.

When you're ordering bottles for a group, it's always good to first ask: what does everyone like? Anything people can't stand? If no one likes white wine, don't order it. If they are merlot superfans, that's probably your best bet. Don't wait around forever for a consensus though; you want to make sure the wine arrives at the table well before your meal.

8. IN A PINCH, CHOOSE PINOT NOIR.

When you're ordering bottles for a group and everyone is having different food, choose a highly versatile wine. Pinot noir's silky texture and light tannin make it an extremely adaptable red that can go well with everything from fish to filet mignon. (See "Great Wines for Pairing," page 156, for more information on table-friendly suggestions.)

9. ACKNOWLEDGE SERIOUS BUSINESS.

In addition to the preceding tips, if you're out to dinner on business, it's best to stick with a midpriced wine and also to defer to the top dog if there is one. You don't want to look cheap or reckless, and you don't want to steal any thunder if you can help it.

THE TASTE TEST

Once you've ordered, here's what happens:

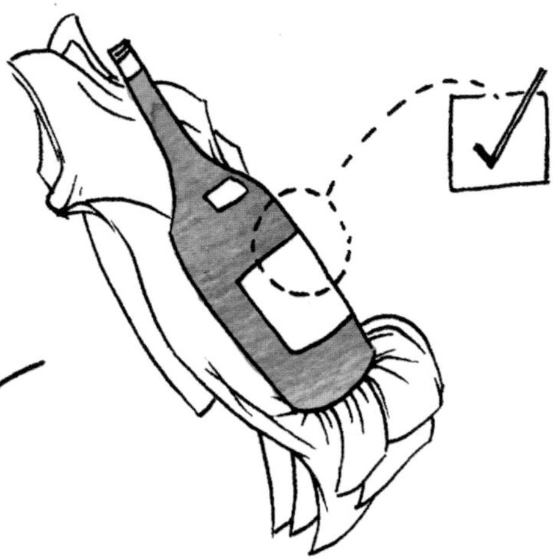

1 The server or sommelier presents the wine. **Check the label** to make sure it is indeed the wine you ordered. If it is, an approving nod is all that is needed to urge the server to go on with the show.

2 The server then removes the cork and presents it to you. Remember: **ignore** it.

3 The server pours a tiny taste into your glass. Take a **smell** (see page 67) and a **quick sip** and let the server know the wine is okay. (See "Awful Aromas," page 70, for a list of aromas that indicate something has gone wrong with the wine.)

5 The server will then **proceed pouring** for your guests (usually ladies first), finishing up with your glass.

4 If the wine smells bad, now is the time to **send it back**. If it smells good, nod and smile, or say something to the effect of "it's good" or "yeehaw."

Little Wine Lies

Santa. The Easter Bunny. The value of calculus in adult life. Life is laced with viciously innocent lies: those spun with good intentions, but capable of leaving scars. Similarly, wine myths are little mistruths proliferated by naïveté. Like old wives' tales, the fiction becomes pervasive, despite a lack of substance. Sure, no wine lie will ever hurt as badly as finding out that the people you trust the most have deceived you about a fairy who trades money for your lost teeth, but it's still best to know the truth. Let's set the record straight on a few of the wine world's most prevalent fabrications.

#1: EXPENSIVE WINE IS GREAT WINE

It is easy to assume a wine's quality is directly correlated to its price. Generally, folks trust that each incremental dollar spent gets a more exciting and delicious wine. While it is true that most esteemed wines are costly—because they are expensive to produce and also sometimes scarce—just because a wine is expensive does not mean it is better.

There's an inner-industry assertion that all superpremium wines (those that retail at one hundred dollars or more per bottle) cost about ten dollars a bottle to produce, and anything a winery charges above that is pure profit. Do I agree with this sweeping generalization? Not totally. There are so many factors that go into pricing a wine that a "typical profit" is impossible to deliver. For example, some wineries may own their properties outright, bringing the cost to produce wine down drastically. Some may owe millions, and thus need to charge more to recoup their investments.

There is some truth to the smoke-and-mirrors pricing theory though. Given the right set of circumstances, wine prices are sometimes falsely inflated. For example, a cabernet blend that just won't sell at thirty-five dollars a bottle is jacked up to seventy-five because the brand manager believes it will sell better if it is perceived as a more costly and thus exclusive wine. The wine and the packaging remain the same, and the wine actually does sell better at the higher price point. Is it a "better" bottle because the price changed? Not a chance. This is unfortunately all too common.

Conversely, sometimes bottles are subjectively great because they overdeliver for the price. I can appreciate an expensive, legendary wine any day. But a "better" bottle, for me, is finding something I love that I can afford to buy on a regular basis. More wine = happier Melanie.

#2:
SCREW CAPS ARE FOR CHEAP WINE

Screw caps rock. I'm a big fan. The reason? There are many things that can cause a bottle of wine to go bad. Too much heat, too much light, bacteria, chemicals, and simply old age can turn the best wines downright rotten. The thing that goes wrong most often is that the wine is "corked." A corked wine has been contaminated with Trichloroanisole, or TCA, a funky, musty compound. TCA contamination, interestingly a by-product of the bleaching process most wineries undertake to keep things clean, is one of the biggest problems in wine, affecting as many as one in every twelve bottles.

Corked wine exists on a spectrum. Sometimes it's overt, and that insidious, musty, wet cardboard smell is pervasive. Other times it is much more discreet, and wine pros debate its presence. However apparent, it won't make you sick, but the wine certainly won't taste the way the winemaker intended. (All that mustiness mutes fruit, leaving the wine tasting dirty and flat.) The worst part is that most wine drinkers have never even heard of TCA. They drink a wine that tastes musty, or maybe just "off," and make a mental note not to buy that wine again. How sad.

The solution? There are a number of enclosures that eliminate the possibility of TCA cork contamination. Zorks, glass tops, synthetic or plastic stoppers (unfortunately hard to open), and screw caps are all promising options. You'll find the majority of these alternative enclosures on wine from the industry's youngest and most innovative regions, like New Zealand. The real reason why most wineries don't switch to cork alternatives and fix the problem of TCA right now is perception—they think you'll think their wine is cheap.

Now, to be fair, there is some validity to the argument that the teeny-tiny amount of oxygen exchange that happens with natural cork plays an important role in the evolution of fine wine over decades—*decades*! But most people are drinking the wine they buy today, today. So for all but the most enduring wines, this argument is moot.

There are plenty of people who lament the potential loss of the tradition, romance, or pop of a true cork. However, I can assure you there is nothing romantic about a corked bottle of wine. My advice? Screw corks whenever possible; buy wines with screw caps.

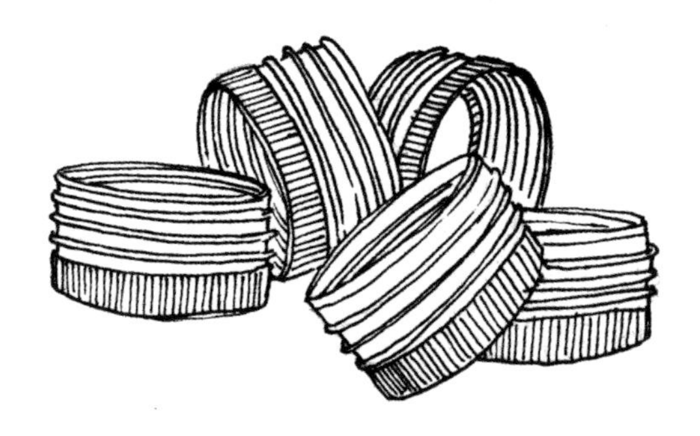

#3: YOU'RE ALLERGIC TO THE SULFITES IN WINE

Sulfur, a natural chemical element, has been used to preserve wine for centuries. Sulfur dioxide, the most common form of sulfur used in winemaking, inhibits yeasts and acts as an antioxidant, keeping the wine fresh in the barrel and bottle. Chances are, you are not allergic to it. Only about 1 percent of the population—typically severe asthmatics—are truly allergic to sulfites, which is why the Food and Drug Administration requires wineries to print "contains sulfites" on their labels. If you were allergic to sulfites, you'd be on a heavily restricted diet. Many processed foods contain much higher levels of sulfites than wines do. Some of the things you wouldn't be able to eat include dried fruits, fruit toppings, shrimp, corn syrup, pickles and relish, maple syrup, avocado dip and guacamole, and many fruit juices and soft drinks.

So if you're not allergic to sulfites, why do you get:

A HEADACHE, ESPECIALLY WHEN YOU DRINK HEARTY RED WINES

Big, hearty red wines have a lot of alcohol. There's always the chance that you drank too much wine and didn't eat enough food or drink enough water and you have a good old-fashioned hangover. Another probability is that you could have sensitivity to tannin, in which case you should try drinking white wines. If you're a red-only lover, switch to lighter red wines, like pinot noir, which have less tannin.

Some light red wines to try if you suspect you're sensitive to tannin:

pinot noir: a light and silky red with aromas of earth, raspberry, and cranberry

Beaujolais: a juicy, light French wine made from the gamay grape

barbera: a fruity and refreshing (but still rustic and earthy) Northern Italian red

A FLUSHED FACE, ITCHY BLOTCHES, OR CONGESTION

According to the National Institute on Alcohol Abuse and Alcoholism, some people, especially those of Eastern Asian descent, are genetically predisposed to this reaction.

If you're not East Asian, and you find yourself with a stuffy nose or covered in itchy red blotches when you drink some wines, you may be allergic to (A.) the histamines that are a natural by-product of fermented beverages; (B.) the histamines that live inside the grapes themselves; or (C.) other environmental allergens (like dust and mold) that are carried on the skins of the grapes. In any case, there's no way to know which particular wines will trigger your allergy. Until we fully understand the science of allergies, you are in for hit-or-miss drinking.

Did You Know? Red wines contain fewer sulfites than white wines. Tannin, most present in reds, is a preservative, and makes sulfur dioxide use less necessary.

#4:
BLENDS ARE BETTER

A *blend* is a wine made from a mix of grapes, as opposed to a *single-varietal wine*, which is made from only one. (Well, theoretically one; different regions have different rules, but with most single-varietal wines, anywhere from 75 to 100 percent consists of that one grape.) For some reason, many new wine drinkers feel drawn to conclude that one is distinctly better than the other. Let me tell you, in no uncertain terms, that you don't have to, nor should you, declare a winner in this fictitious contest. Some blended wine is better than wine made from a single grape. Some single-varietal wines are superior to blends. There are many factors that go into evaluating if a wine is good or not—most important, do *you* like the way it tastes? The sheer nature of a wine's blended or non-blended status should not influence your feelings in the slightest.

So why blend? Sometimes winemakers blend two grapes together because they complement each other (e.g., Winemaker Sam's cabernet is particularly bitter and tannic, so he balances it by blending in some soft, fruity merlot). Sometimes blending is used to compensate for farming challenges. A notable example of this kind of blending happens in the Bordeaux region of France. The weather there stinks. Rains at harvest are probable and can be devastating. As an insurance policy, Bordeaux winemakers have traditionally used up to five different grapes in the blend. All five grapes ripen at different times. If the rain destroys one grape's harvest, they can make up the difference with the other four.

Blending can help compensate for shortcomings, adding complexity and depth to the flavor of the wine, if done in the right way. Blending can also go awry, and a wine can end up tasting like soup: a homogeneous mix in which nothing distinctive stands out. To blend or not to blend—there's no right answer. You're just going to have to enjoy them both.

WHAT'S A MERITAGE WINE? Good question. *Meritage*, pronounced like "heritage," signifies a blended wine made in the traditional style of Bordeaux, France. That is, wines that use some or all of the grapes traditionally grown in that region: cabernet sauvignon, merlot, cabernet franc, petit verdot, and malbec for red; sauvignon blanc and semillon for white. The word first appeared in the late 1980s after a group of American vintners selected it from more than six thousand entries in an international contest. *Meritage*—the winning word—combines "merit," implying the quality of the grapes, with "heritage," signaling the centuries-old tradition of blending. In order to use the word *Meritage* (it's a registered trademark), a winery must obtain a license from the Meritage Association.

#5:
VOLUPTUOUS LEGS ARE RAVEWORTHY

"Legs," or "tears," are the drips that you see running down the inside wall of your wineglass after you swirl a wine. The first wine lie I remember digesting was that thick legs were the sign of a good wine. I can just hear my know-it-all uncle's voice: "Oh yeah, when you see big legs like that, it means the wine is top-notch." I, of course, believed him—until I learned otherwise. In truth, thick drips are not an indication of quality. But don't take your investigative goggles off just yet; they do give clues about the wine.

If drips are thick and slow-moving, you can be assured the wine you're about to consume is heavy in alcohol and body. The texture will be thick in your mouth (like whole milk or cream). The wine will likely taste full and very rich. If it's hard to see any drips, you've got a wine that is light in body (like skim milk). It will taste thinner and have less alcohol. The flavors will likely be more delicate and fine.

If you dig a substantial, heavy wine, then voluptuous legs in your glass are an indicator that your mouth is about to get happy. If you like a more delicate wine, that might not be the case. Ah, yet another totally subjective wine debate. Are you sensing a trend here?

#6:
IT'S OK FOR ANYBODY TO USE THE C-WORD

We often hear the C-word, *Champagne*, used universally to talk about any sparkling wine, but that's a mistake. Here's the skinny: sparkling wine is an umbrella term meaning any wine with bubbles made anywhere in the world. Champagne is a *type* of sparkling wine. It just so happens to be the original and most iconic type of all.

SPARKLING WINE HAS MANY NAMES...

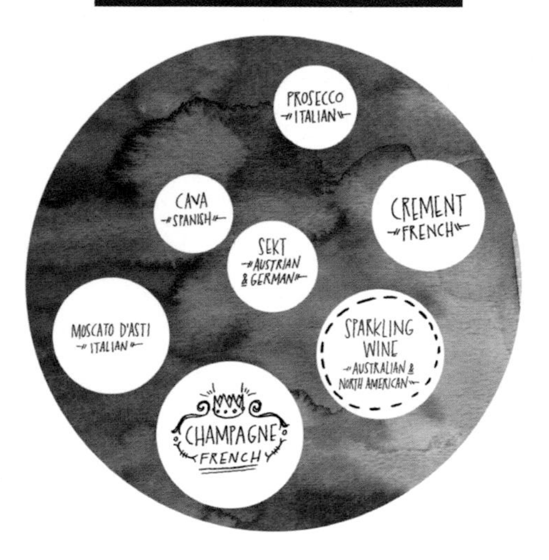

I love bubbles. Whether it's the hiss and pop of all that pent-up pressure, the delicate strand of pearl-shaped air dancing in the glass, or the signature sophisticated tang, there's just something different—something sexy—about wine with sparkle. There's no denying that a glass of great Champagne will magically make you stand straighter, speak more eloquently, and smile more often. This curious behavior is likely due to all the cachet attached to Champagne, the world's most expensive, extravagant sparkling wine.

What makes Champagne so special? True Champagne comes only from Champagne, France. Champagne is one of the coldest and most northerly winegrowing regions on the planet. In fact, the only reason grapes can survive the chilly temperatures (and constant threat of frost) is that there's usually ample sunshine during the growing season thanks to the northern latitude. (I say usually, because sometimes there isn't, in which case entire vintages can be ruined.) Grapes that are able to straddle this fringe climate retain a laser-like acidity that ultimately creates intensely focused, precise wines. When the weather is perfect, this is the best place on the planet to grow the grapes destined for sparkling wine.

The dirt here is special too. Apparently, the Champagne region used to be underwater, and the subsoil is rich with marine fossils. What this means is that the best wines from the area take on a chalky, minerally aspect that you can actually taste in the wines.

THE PURPOSE OF THE PUNT The punt, or large indentation at the bottom of sparkling wine bottles, is there for a purpose other than aesthetic. Bubbles create a lot of pressure (up to about ninety pounds per bottle in some cases); the punt allows for a more even distribution of that pressure, thereby decreasing the chance that the bottle will explode.

In addition to the unique attributes of the grapes, climate, and soil, Champagne (the sparkling wine) abides by strict laws that govern how it is made (the most labor-intensive process possible) and how long it is aged before it is released (longer than any other sparkling wine, which gives it complexity and depth). The most important process, and the primary distinction between how Champagne and other types of sparkling wine are made, is that the secondary fermentation (the process by which bubbles are born) happens in the bottle, as opposed to another, larger vessel.

Champagne's glamour is undeniable, and that has proven an irresistibly shiny target for imposters. In Europe, there are laws in place that protect the name *Champagne*. No other producers in the European Union can make sparkling wine and label it *Champagne*. Making wine in Spain and labeling it with a French region would be as preposterous as calling a bottle from France "Napa." However, outside the European Union, anyone, unfortunately, can steal the name. This is why you sometimes see "Australian Champagne" or "California Champagne" printed on a wine label.

It is worth noting that typically only sub-par wineries do this in an effort to cash in on the reputation of the most famous and high-quality sparkling wine. Well-respected producers wouldn't think of using the C-word illegitimately. They know that although they will never be able to produce Champagne, they can still make a gorgeous sparkling wine. They don't need to borrow a name to get your attention.

THE MYSTERIOUS NV What does that little NV on bottles of sparkling wine stand for? It means nonvintage, or not from a single year. This tradition began in Champagne, France, as insurance against the unpredictable weather. Blending multiple years of wine created a consistent "house style" for winemakers; even if the weather one year totally bit and the grapes didn't ripen, they had enough juice from other years saved to be able to compensate and produce a wine that tasted pretty similar to other years. As an added bonus, vintners seemed to like the complexity of a multiple-year blend and, thus, the tradition stuck. Now many regions outside of Champagne make NV or MV (multivintage, which means the same thing) sparkling wines. Vintage sparkling wines (those that state a particular year on the bottle) are made in outstanding years only, with a winery's best grapes. As you may have already guessed, vintage sparkling wines cost more.

Beyond blending vintages, Champagne producers also love to artfully mix still wines to create the ultimate blend each year. Most Champagne bottles contain thirty to sixty different base wines!

Did You Know? More than 25 percent of all sparkling wine is sold during the two weeks before Christmas. / *Oakland Tribune*

MY FAVORITE CHAMPAGNE PRODUCERS

Easier to Find

- Billecart-Salmon
- Bollinger
- Deutz
- Krug
- Laurent-Perrier
- Philipponnat
- Roederer
- Taittinger

Harder to Find

- Egly-Ouriet
- Gaston Chiquet
- Henri Billiot
- Jacques Selosse
- Michel Turgy
- Pierre Peters

MY FAVORITE NON-CHAMPAGNE SPARKLING WINES

California Sparkling Wines

Many parts of the Golden State are just too warm to grow grapes destined for sparkling wines. A few very-cool-climate regions, however, are perfect, especially for wines from these producers.

- Iron Horse Vineyards
- Roederer Estate
- Schramsberg Vineyards

Cava

When it comes to bang-for-your-buck bubbles, it doesn't get much better than cava, Spain's sparkling wine. Dry, citrusy cava is cheap and cheerful, simple and straightforward, and should be paired with equally laid-back foods. The following are some of my favorites.

- Avinyo brut reserva
- Jaume Serra Cristalino
- Castillo Perelada
- Raventós i Blanc

Prosecco

Most prosecco, which hails exclusively from several regions in northern Italy, is light, frothy, and much fruitier than Champagne. Less pressure in the bottle translates into less aggressive bubbles, making prosecco dangerously easy to drink. (The average price tag of around fifteen dollars a bottle doesn't hurt either.) Try bottles from the following producers.

- La Marca
- Nino Franco
- Zardetto

Moscato d'Asti

There is perhaps no more aromatic sparkler than moscato d'Asti, the famously sweet and floral wine from Piedmont, Italy. Moscato d'Asti is sweet enough to pair with light desserts, and comes alive when paired with berries, citrus, and stone fruits. Below are some recommended bottlings.

- Ceretto S. Stefano
- Saracco

Sparkling Shiraz

Not only does this wine's appearance spark conversation (a dark purple wine with bubbles!) but its myriad interesting flavors will have your guests talking too. The best have a strange yet beautiful bouquet of cranberries, pomegranate, chocolate, and smoke. Sample the wines listed below for a taste of this unusual sparkler.

- Molly Dooker
- The Chook

#7:
PINK IS PASSÉ

This is a book about uncovering truth, so I'll admit it: The first wine I ever drank was Boone's Farm Strawberry Hill. It was pink and sweet and I distinctly remember an awful hangover. I bet many of you reading this may have a similar memory of your first experience with wine. Consequently, when most people think pink, this is what is etched in their mind—syrupy sweet wines like Boone's Farm, "blush" wines in a jug, or the slightly more respectable white zinfandels of California. Although these saccharine beverages are *technically* wine and they serve as a sort of gateway substance to the more genuine stuff, the truth is that they taste more like a Jolly Rancher than real, grown-up wine. However, as you may have gleaned by the ironic heading "Pink Is Passé," serious pink wine exists. And if you're turning up your nose to all wines with a rosy hue, you are missing out.

Dry pink wines are collectively called rosé (ro-ZAY). They are made all over the globe, but most notably stand out in southern France and Spain. Rosés can be made from a variety of grapes, most often grenache, syrah, mourvèdre, cabernet franc, and tempranillo (or a combination of any of these). They are made in a few different ways: **(1)** by blending red and white wines together, **(2)** by leaving the grape skins in brief contact with the juice before fermentation, or **(3)** by a technique called *saignée*, where not-quite-red-yet juice is "bled" off of red wine destined to continue its own fermentation.

Good rosé can be delectable in a way no other wine can; it can be simultaneously juicy and tart, robust and delicate. They are best drunk very fresh and young (don't buy last year's vintage on clearance) and are best served well chilled, outside, in warm weather. Seriously. These are not winter wines. Rather, they are wines that exude the laid-back charm of a summer cookout or a day at the beach.

THREE WAYS A ROSÉ IS MADE

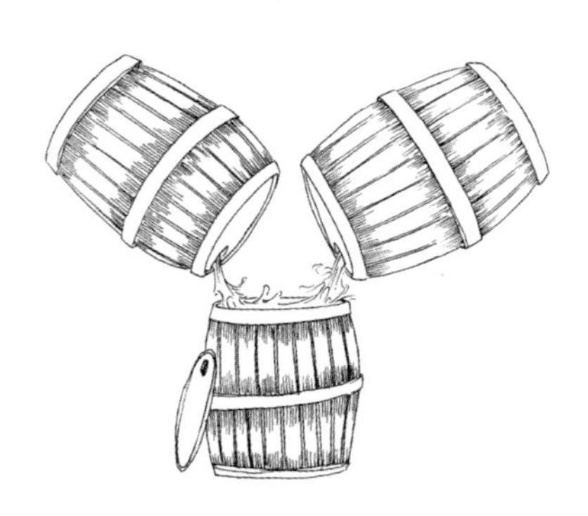

(1) blending red and white wines together

(2) leaving the grape skins in brief contact with the juice before fermentation

(3) a technique called saignée, where not-quite-red-yet juice is "bled" off of red wine destined to continue its own fermentation

MY FAVORITE ROSÉS

$

- Bonny Doon, Vin Gris de Cigare */ Central Coast, California*
- Château Pesquié Terrasses */ Côtes du Ventoux, France*
- Crios de Susana Balbo, rosé of malbec */ Mendoza, Argentina*
- Domaine de la Mordorée "La Dame Rousse" rosé */ Côtes du Rhône, France*
- Mulderbosch rosé of cabernet sauvignon */ Coastal Region, South Africa*
- Parés Baltà, Ros de Pacs */ Penedès, Spain*

$$

- Castello di Ama rosato */ Chianti, Italy*
- Domaine de Terrebrune rosé */ Bandol, France*
- Domaine Ott, Les Domaniers de Puits Mouret rosé */ Côtes de Provence, France*
- Domaine Tempier rosé */ Bandol, France*

ASSIGNMENT:

ROSÉ

Check out "Rosé Sampler," page 185, for a homework six-pack. These six wines are a great way to begin experimenting with serious pink wines.

ROSÉ WITH BUBBLES

I can't justly conclude a pink passage without at least mentioning the fabulousness of sparkling rosé. My desert-island wine, pink Champagne (and other rosé sparkling wines) can be powerful and profound, and extremely elegant at the same time. The following are some of my favorites.

$

- Jaume Serra Cristalino brut rosé NV cava */ Spain*

$$

- Gruet brut rosé NV */ New Mexico*
- Roederer Estate brut rosé NV */ Mendocino, California*
- Lucien Albrecht Crémant d'Alsace brut rosé NV */ Alsace, France*
- Taltarni brut Taché */ Victoria, Australia*

$$$

- Schramsberg brut rosé NV */ Napa, California*

$$$$

- Billecart-Salmon brut rosé NV */ Champagne, France*
- Egly-Ouriet Grand Cru brut rosé */ Champagne, France*

Grape to Glass

Winemaking is a beautiful marriage of science and art. Like science, the growing of grapes and their eventual transformation into wine is explicitly natural, yet fascinatingly complex when you break it down. Like art, it is infinitely wide open to interpretation—both the winemaker's interpretation of what the land gives him and, ultimately, the taster's interpretation of the finished work.

This chapter follows the life of the grape—both the science and the art—from the vineyard to your lips.

GROW, BABY, GROW

Viticulture is the science and study of all things that happen in a vineyard—and a lot can happen there. Most winemakers would tell you that how a grape grows is the single most important factor in determining the quality of a wine. With today's technology, a winemaker can compensate for many faults, but truly awful grapes are an insurmountable obstacle.

Viticulture: the science and study of grape growing.

Oenology: the science and study of wine and winemaking. (What happens once the grapes are harvested.)

When it comes to viticulture, there are thousands of choices a winemaker makes. All of them combined have a serious impact on the finished wine.

Site Establishment: Where to plant? Which grapes to plant? Which clones to plant? How to arrange spacing of the vines? How to trellis the vines? Stay on budget? Install an irrigation system? If so, what kind?

Farming: How to manage pests and diseases? How to manage frost? How to manage irrigation? Hiring a great crew? Managing the crew? Stay on budget? Fertilize? Farm organically? Farm biodynamically? Plant cover crops? Green harvest? How to prune? When to harvest? How to harvest?

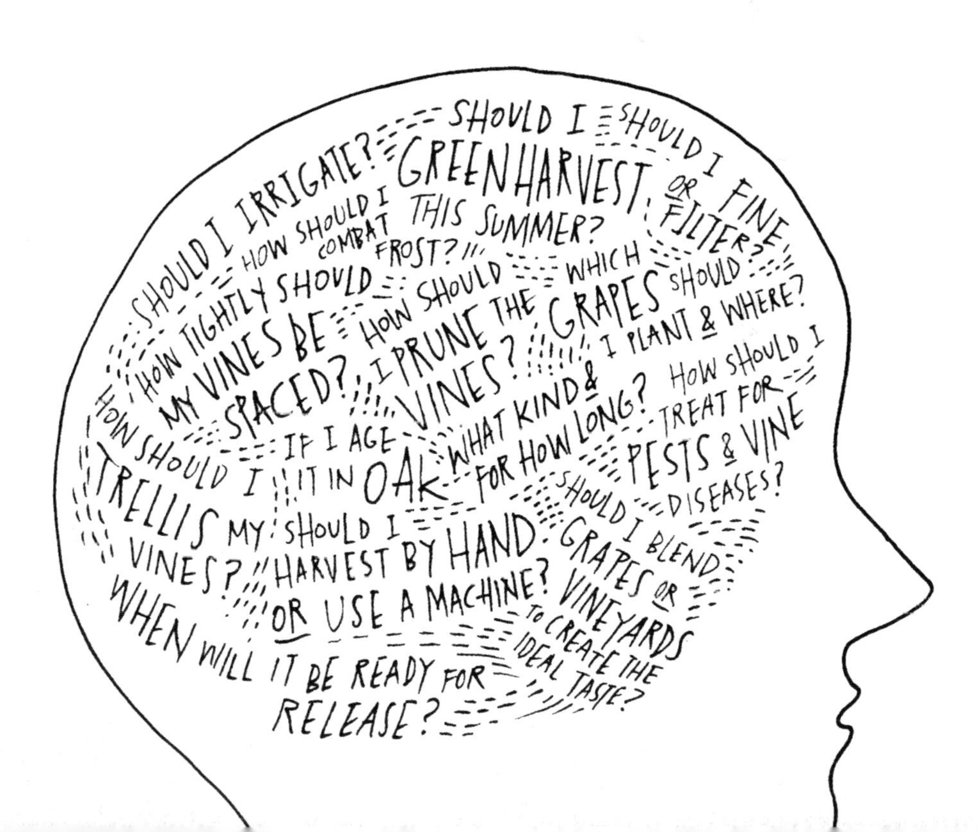

VINEYARD VOCABULARY

Clone: Grapevines are ambitious plants that mutate easily, readily evolving their genetic code to adapt to the environment. This is awesome for the vine's survival, annoying if you're trying to produce a consistent style of wine. Grape clones are cuttings from an existing vine that share identical genetic information. Planting clones not only affords a grape grower more predictability, but it also enables him to select grapevines with DNA specifically suited to his environment (or *terroir*, see page 60) or even with certain characteristics or flavor profiles. For example, here are three of the most popular pinot noir clones, and what they bring to the party.

Pommard: Wines from this clone are sometimes known for having a meaty, gamy edge.

Clone 113: Perhaps the most elegant of pinot noir clones, with perfumed aromatics.

Dijon 828: Noted for its large, long, and skinny clusters, this clone contributes deep color, focused sweet berry fruit flavors, and excellent retention of acidity.

Brix: The Brix scale is the U.S. system used to measure the sugar content of grapes and wine. The Brix (sugar content) is determined by an instrument called a hydrometer, which indicates a liquid's specific gravity (the density of a liquid in relation to that of pure water).

Trellis: Trellising is how a grapevine is trained to grow on wires and/or posts. There's no "best" way to trellis a vine; each vineyard comes with its own requirements. A grape grower can use trellising to manage factors like sun exposure and vine vigor, and also to make harvesting easier.

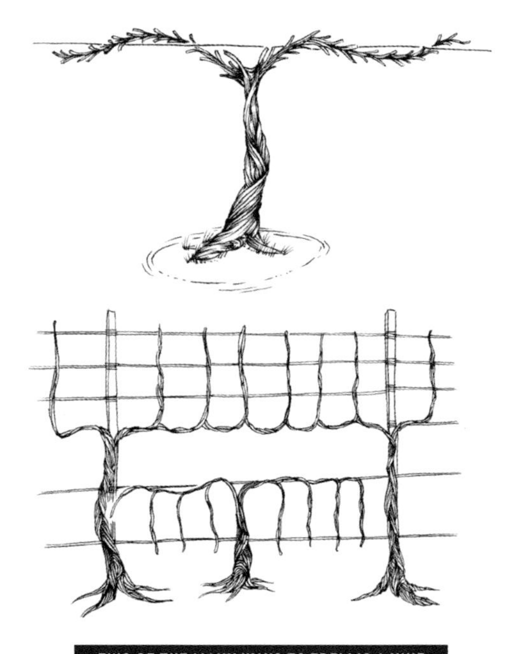

TWO OF THE MANY WAYS TO TRELLIS A VINE

Green Harvest: Green harvesting, or "dropping fruit," is most often used in the production of fine wines. Workers strategically cut off some of the tiny, immature grapes at the beginning of the growing season. This is costly, as less fruit always equals less wine, but a worthwhile investment. The vine inevitably focuses all of its energy on ripening and developing the flavor of the remaining grapes, whose quality rises dramatically as a result.

Organic: Organic wine, in its most broad sense, is wine made without synthetic chemicals: fertilizers, pesticides, herbicides, or fungicides. Organic certification is complex and varies by country. The current U.S. certifications include the following.

100% Organic carries the United States Department of Agriculture (USDA) organic seal and indicates the wine is made from 100 percent organically grown ingredients.

Organic also carries the USDA organic seal and indicates the wine has 95 percent organically grown ingredients.

Made with Organic Grapes or *Made with Organic Ingredients* means the wine is made from at least 70 percent organic ingredients. (It does not have the USDA organic seal.)

Biodynamic: Biodynamic farming principles are based on a concept originated by early-twentieth-century Austrian philosopher Rudolf Steiner. Beyond being 100 percent organic, biodynamic farming aims to balance nature, and views the vineyard as a cohesive, interconnected ecosystem. There is a mystical, spiritual aspect to this type of farming as well, which believers swear by and critics lampoon. For example, biodynamic grape growers plant, prune, and treat vineyards according to the cycle of the moon, and utilize a number of strange-sounding but effective "preparations" to invigorate the vineyard. (Preparation 500—cow manure—is buried in cow horns in the soil during the winter. The horn is then dug up and its contents stirred in water and sprayed on the soil.)

Diurnal: In very warm winegrowing regions (most of California comes to mind), grapes love the roller-coaster ride of a strong diurnal shift. Diurnal (dye-UR-nal) shift is fancy talk for the up and down of temperatures from day to night. If you've ever visited the San Francisco Bay Area you've felt this rapid transition firsthand—you can be downright hot during the day, but still have to pull out your sweater for the chilly evening. On any given day, the temperature range can vary as much as 20 to 30 degrees! In regions like Napa and Sonoma, the diurnal shift helps grapes retain their bright acidity over the growing season. It also ensures a longer growing season, which results in more developed flavor maturity.

PICTURE-PERFECT SEASONS

WINTER

Cool, wet winter provides ample groundwater

SPRING

Lack of rain or frost after the first warm days of spring

SUMMER

Mild days and cool nights all summer long

FALL

Warm, dry days preceding harvest

“WINE IS SUNLIGHT, HELD TOGETHER BY WATER.”

—Galileo

“WINE IS MADE IN THE VINEYARD.”

—Old wine-industry adage

THE ANNUAL CYCLE OF A VINE

WEEPING

Temperatures rise in early spring (approximately February for the Northern Hemisphere and August in the Southern Hemisphere). When they hit about 50 degrees Fahrenheit, sap begins to concentrate where the canes were pruned. This leaking of sap, called *weeping*, is the first signal that the vine is waking up after a long winter sleep.

BUD BREAK

Twenty to thirty days after the vine begins weeping (typically March to April in the Northern Hemisphere and September to October in the Southern Hemisphere), tiny buds on the vine start to swell and open. This is commonly known as bud break. It is a joyous albeit tense time for vintners. Late spring frosts can be devastating, killing the tender baby buds, and thus the potential of the harvest, in a single evening.

EARLY GRAPE DEVELOPMENT

In mid-April (in the Northern Hemisphere) and mid-October (in the Southern Hemisphere), shoots, leaves, and eventually teeny green clusters begin to emerge on the vine.

FLOWERING

The vine continues to grow. About eight weeks after bud break those green clusters form flowers, which, after blooming, eventually become grapes. Flowering lasts only about ten days, but it is an extremely sensitive time in the vine's life cycle. Climactic conditions like frost, heat, wind, and rain can wreak havoc on the delicate flowers.

FRUIT SET

From June to July in the Northern Hemisphere and December to January in the Southern Hemisphere, each fertilized flower develops into a grape. If desired, weeding, spraying for pests and diseases, and summer pruning (see "Green Harvest," page 46) all happen during this time, as the grapes continue to mature.

VERAISON

Sometime around August in the Northern Hemisphere and January in the Southern Hemisphere, the grapes finally plump up and change color from green to yellowish white (grapes destined to make white wines) or black (grapes that will make red wine). This is known as veraison. During veraison, the vineyard workers sometimes prune some of the leaves around the grapes (to increase the circulation of air, thus reducing rot) and also continue green harvesting. Prior to veraison, the grapes still taste sour and are immature; but once it begins, sugars in the grape start to rise dramatically.

HARVEST

Traditionally, harvest occurs about one hundred days after flowering (August to October in the Northern Hemisphere, February to March in the Southern Hemisphere), but many factors are considered—especially the sugar and acid levels of grape samples, and the tannin maturity. White grapes are

50 THE ANNUAL CYCLE OF A VINE

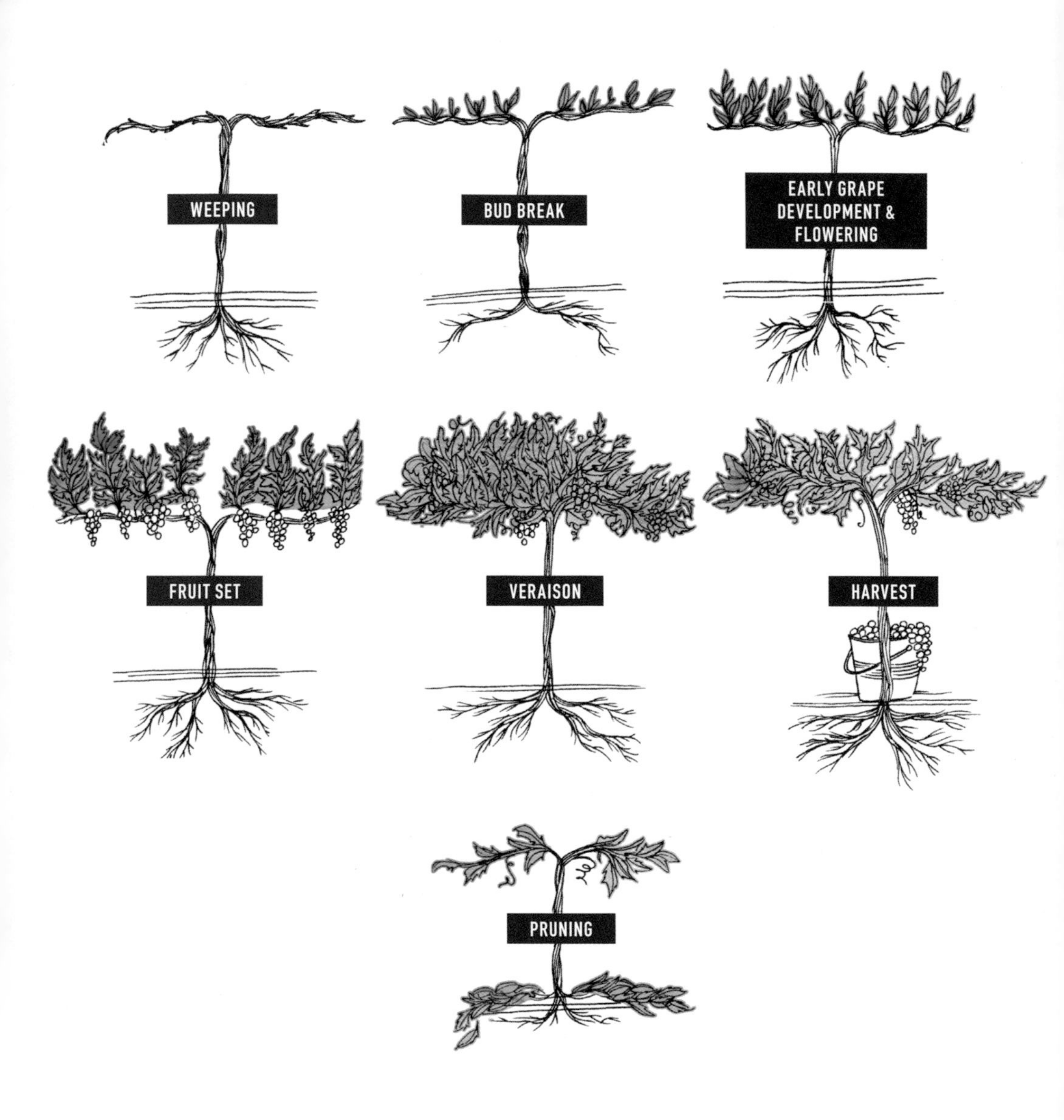

generally harvested before black ones to help retain higher acidity in white wines. Grapes are picked by hand or by a machine. Handpicking is more expensive, but is considered superior because it is gentler and more accurate. Also, occasionally it's the only option (e.g., if your vineyard is on a steep slope).

PRUNING

After harvest, leaves turn yellow and fall off, and the vine is pruned. Pruning helps protect the vine from cold winter temperatures and also ensures that it saves as much energy as possible while in the dormant phase. How a vine is pruned, in part, determines how it will come back to life in the spring.

RAIN KILLS FLAVOR Rain at or around harvesttime can be a grape catastrophe. All year long, vineyard workers have toiled and tended to the precious grapes. They are juicy and just about perfect for picking. If it rains at this stage, the grapes will eagerly soak up the water, and the flavor that has slowly matured all season can be lost in an instant. Fat, bloated, watered-down berries result.

What can be done? In developing vineyard regions, people avoid planting grapes where autumn rains are common. However, some long-standing regions, like Bordeaux, France, aren't going anywhere, even given their propensity for harvesttime rain. The Bordelais have two options—they can pick slightly ahead of schedule (immediately upon spotting that first rain cloud) or they can risk losing an entire crop of grapes (it happens). Rain in Bordeaux is the main reason why there are big differences in the taste of wines from one year to the next. And early picking is why you can sometimes taste slightly green, underripe flavors (like green pepper) in these wines.

FIGHTING FUNGUS HAS AN UPSIDE

There has been a lot of buzz in the last decade about wine's health benefits. One of the most studied, potentially happy-health compounds in wine is a powerful antioxidant called resveratrol (rez-VARE-ah-trahl). Although human studies are still in their infancy, scientists have done extensive animal testing and are claiming that resveratrol can significantly reduce heart disease, lower the risk of Alzheimer's, and help regulate cholesterol, and has anti-cancer and even antiaging properties.

Once resveratrol was isolated, Cornell researcher Leroy Creasy decided to compare resveratrol levels in different wines, in an attempt to better understand how and why the compound is produced. After sampling dozens of wines from all over the planet, he made a couple of discoveries. First, across the board, resveratrol levels were highest in red wines. This is logical: antioxidants are found in grape skins, and red wines spend much more time in contact with their skins during the winemaking process than white wines do (more on that in a minute). Secondly, and more curiously to Creasy—pinot noir, and specifically Oregon pinot noir—had much higher levels of resveratrol than other wines.

What's the magic resveratrol recipe? It turns out resveratrol is produced by plants protecting themselves against environmental dangers—most commonly pathogenic organisms, temperature extremes, and fungi. Pinot noir is a temperamental, thin-skinned grape that tends to thrive in cool, damp climates (where these dangers are more common). Therefore, pinot noir grown in the extremely moist climate of Oregon's Willamette Valley has to produce loads of resveratrol just to survive. It seems the grape's natural life-saving defense could end up saving human lives as well. I'll drink to that!

Resveratrol Rock Stars

My Favorite Oregon Pinot Noir Producers

- Adelsheim
- Bergstrom
- Bethel Heights
- Domaine Drouhin
- Domaine Serene
- St. Innocent
- Soter

A HICCUP IN HISTORY: THE DEVASTATOR STRIKES

In the history of wine, one vineyard pest has proven more vicious than any other—*Phylloxera vastatrix*, alias "the Devastator."

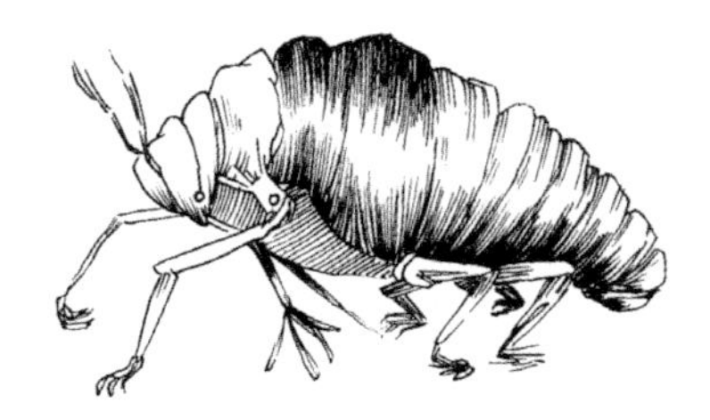

This tiny vampire aphid, native to the United States, first began its course of destruction when it hitched an unwelcome ride to France in the mid-1800s on some American grapevines. At that time, both America and France were experimenting with crossbreeding different species of grapevines to improve characteristics like vine vigor, flavor, and color. French winemakers were eager to study the American vines. They had no idea what was coming.

In 1865, the first American vines arrived in Bordeaux and were promptly planted. Two years later, vines in this prestigious region started to get sick with an unknown disease, and many died. The mysterious ailment spread quickly; within a decade, a reported two-thirds of all French vines had completely vanished. Scientists were baffled, and the French government even offered a reward (the equivalent of about $1.5 million today) to anyone who could figure out what was killing their vines, and how to stop it.

Eventually, the root louse was identified as the culprit, and an American came up with the solution: to graft, or attach, European vines to American (phylloxera-resistant) rootstock. This simple fix sounded crazy, but it actually worked. Today, almost all the fine wine vineyards in the world are planted with American rootstocks on the bottom and European grapevines on top (illustrated below).

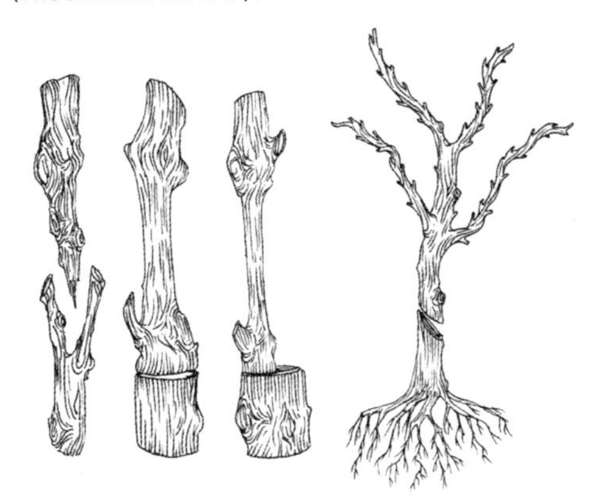

Did You Know? Besides disease and insects, some of the most destructive vineyard pests include deer, birds, wild hogs, wild turkeys, and kangaroos.

WINEMAKING 101

A season in the vineyard is over. Vines have done their work and the precious fruit has been harvested. Now the process of winemaking (or vinification) begins. Although there are many different schools of thought on how to best convert grapes into wine (many of these philosophies are region- or grape-specific), there are basic stages that all wine must go through in order to be born. Here are the most essential.

PHASE ONE: CRUSH

Juice is extracted from the grapes. Free-run juice is the coveted liquid that literally drips out of the ripe grapes before any crushing begins. Some wineries may use free-run juice to make a separate, extra-fine bottling, but most of the time it is just mixed in with subsequent pressings. The grapes are crushed (a.k.a. pressed) so that the liquid nectar can be separated from the skins, seeds, stems, and other stuff (see "MOG," following). Ages ago, people used their feet to press the grapes. Now, winemakers use a variety of less romantic but more efficient (and sanitary) machines.

Skins are removed from white wines immediately to ensure a clear, bright color. Skins are left in contact with the juice of red wines; prolonged exposure provides color, flavor, and tannin. Red grapes with thick skin and/or small berries will have a higher ratio of juice to skin during this process, which will mean more color, flavor, and tannin in the finished wine.

Petite sirah is an example of a very thick-skinned grape with small berries. If you're a petite sirah fan you already know that this grape packs loads of big jammy fruit flavor, a ton of mouth-drying tannins, and enough color to turn your teeth a bright bluish purple.

MOG *MOG* stands for "material other than grapes." The more careful the harvesting and winemaking operation, the less likely that stems, leaves, bugs, and even the occasional lizard make it into the wine. Disgusting, absolutely. Avoidable altogether, usually not.

PHASE TWO: FERMENTATION

Once the juice has been pressed, it is allowed to come in contact with yeast. Yeasts are like little ravenous monsters, chomping up the natural sugar in the grape juice and leaving the by-products of alcohol and carbon dioxide. In the old days, everybody just waited for naturally occurring yeast in the air to begin eating the sugar in the juice. These days, we're not so patient. Many winemakers intervene by adding yeast strains that jump-start and move the fermentation along. Fermentation typically takes place in stainless-steel tanks, where temperature (and thus the speed of fermentation) can be monitored and controlled, or oak barrels, which impart flavor and texture to both white and red wines.

Did You Know? With only a couple of obscure exceptions, all red grapes produce white juice. The color in red wine comes from contact with the skins.

PHASE THREE: AGING

A final, and optional, winemaking step is aging the wine—in or out of oak barrels—before release. Aging usually lasts anywhere from six months to two years, although some fine wines age longer than that. In Europe, the length that fine wines are aged is mandated; in most other areas it is not. Aging in stainless steel is neutral—it gives nothing to the wine, except a place to hang out and get a little more complex and integrated before it's bottled. (Like lasagna or beef stew, most wines taste better when flavors have a chance to meld.) Oak aging, however, can play a considerable role in how a wine tastes and feels; it can add tannin and a textural creaminess, and also impart aromas and flavors like toast, nuts, vanilla, butterscotch, caramel, nutmeg, cinnamon, smoke, and coconut.

There are many choices when it comes to oak barrels. First there's the origin of the oak, which, believe it or not, plays a huge role in the flavor. For example, American oak is less expensive but more porous. It adds an aggressive oak taste (and often the telltale aromas of dill pickle and coconut!). French oak is generally preferred for its tight grain and, thus, more subtle, slow integration of oak flavor (more like butterscotch and vanilla). It is also much more expensive. The second choice is the age of the wood. New oak barrels give a more prominent flavor than oak that is a year or two old. Last, there's the option to char (or toast) the inside of the oak staves, and if so, how much. Winemakers can specify that they want a light toast, medium toast, or heavy toast to their barrels; the heavier the toast, the more dominant the flavor of the barrel will be.

Additionally, winemakers may opt to age a wine *on the lees*—in contact with the dead yeast cells leftover from fermentation. This practice, widely used in Champagne and chardonnay production, adds a creamy texture and aromas of freshly baked bread.

Did You Know? If you ever want to engage a winemaker, casually ask him which yeast strains he uses. His eyes will light up and a big geeky smile will appear. Don't plan on going anywhere in a hurry. However glamorous their jobs may appear, all winemakers are science nerds at heart; they love to talk biochemistry.

WINEMAKING 101

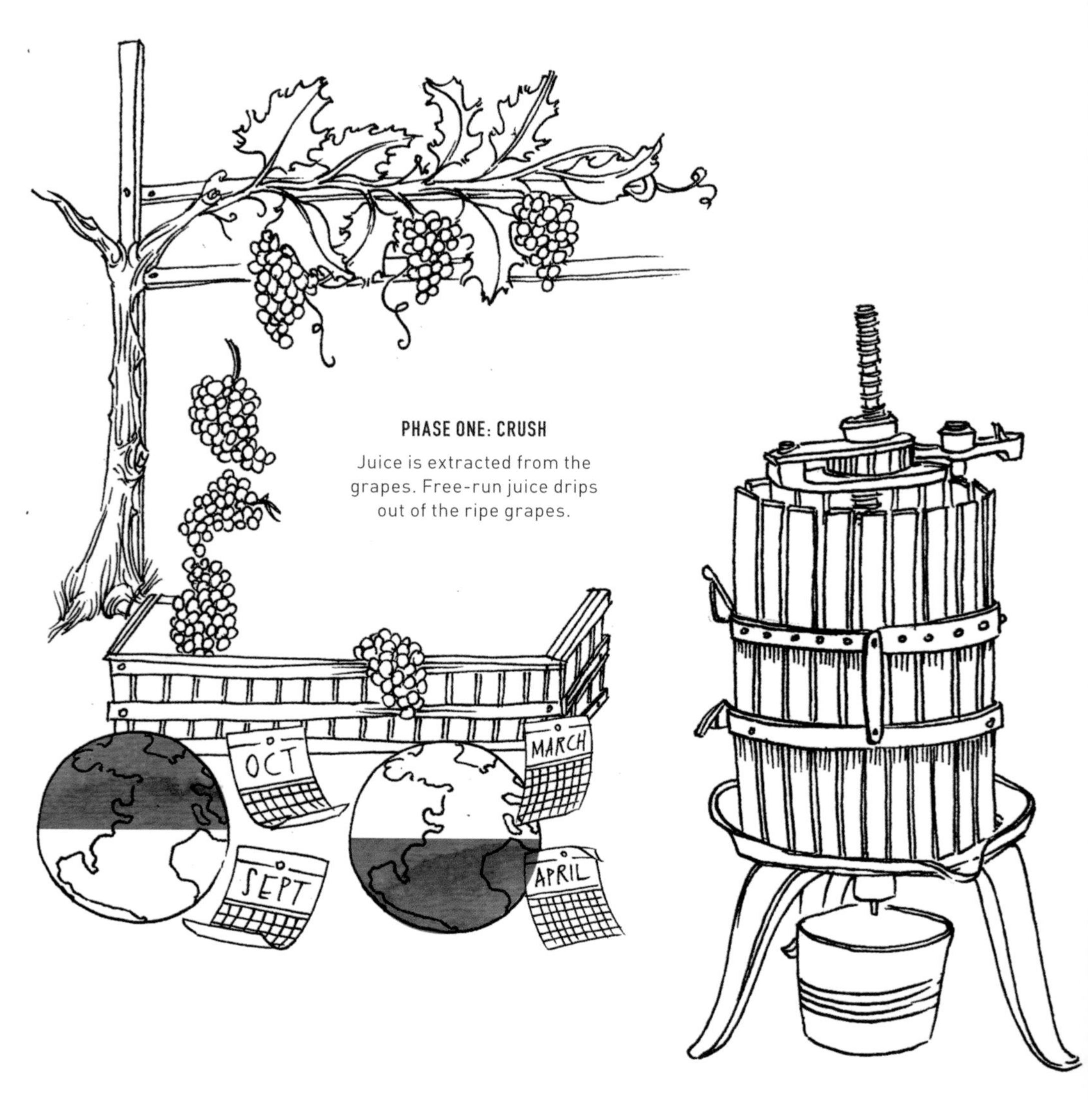

PHASE ONE: CRUSH

Juice is extracted from the grapes. Free-run juice drips out of the ripe grapes.

The grapes are crushed (a.k.a. pressed) to separate the liquid from the skin, seeds, and stems.

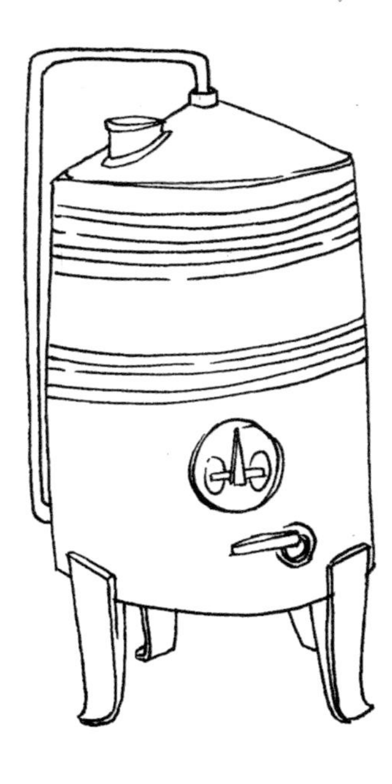

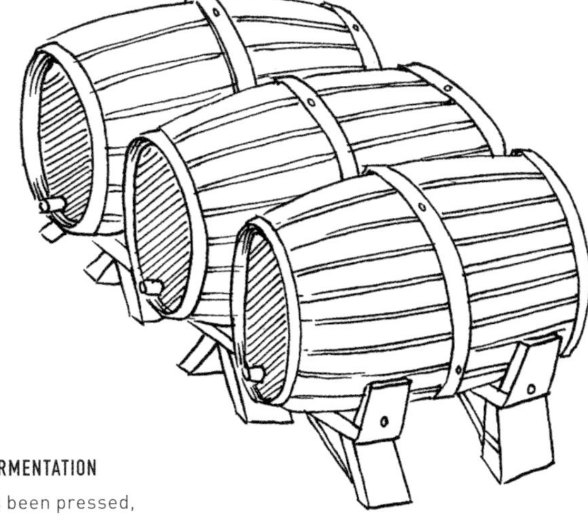

PHASE TWO: FERMENTATION

Once the juice has been pressed, it comes in contact with yeast and fermentation begins. Fermentation typically takes place in stainless-steel tanks or oak barrels.

VINE MATH

59
GALLONS

25
CASES

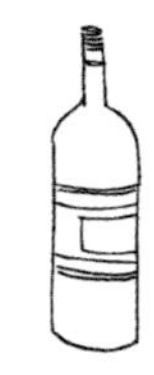

300
BOTTLES

1
BARREL

2 the number of grams of carbohydrates in the average glass of wine

3 the approximate number of years it takes for new vines to start producing wine-worthy fruit

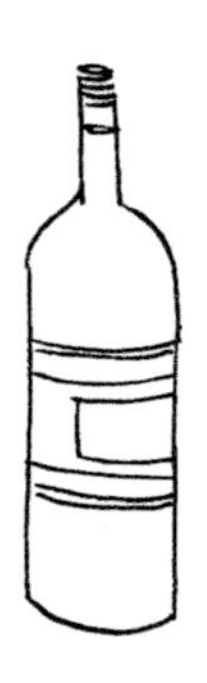

4 the approximate number of grape clusters in a bottle of wine

5 the average number of glasses of wine in a bottle

30–50° latitude

In both the Northern and Southern Hemispheres, these are the most important regions of the planet for grape cultivation

900–1,300

the approximate number of vines that live on one acre of land

1,300

the minimum hours of sunshine required by any vine during the growing season

3,000

the approximate number of bonded wineries in California—about half of those produce less than 5,000 cases annually

77,000

the number of acres of cabernet sauvignon planted in California

120,000

the number of new wine labels (one winery can make multiple labels of wine) that were approved by the Alcohol and Tobacco Tax and Trade Bureau in 2011

NAKED BABY WINE

One wine that does no aging before its release is Beaujolais nouveau (bo-jho-LAY new-VO), from Beaujolais, France. Beaujolais nouveau is made from the gamay grape and is released just a few weeks after harvest—the third Thursday in November to be specific. It's a fresh, fruity, and short-lived wine. It's typically very inexpensive and is meant to be consumed immediately. Because of the unique way it's made, typical aromas and flavors include raspberries, candied fruit, grapes, bubble gum, and banana.

The style, originally promoted by wine producer and marketing genius George Duboeuf as a way to create some buzz and generate cash flow, became wildly popular in the 1970s; Beaujolais producers would literally race to Paris with fresh juice (and a great excuse to drink!). The party spread to other European countries, and then America, where it was adopted as a traditional Thanksgiving wine. Over the years, and with so many other choices available, the hype and demand of Beaujolais nouveau has shriveled. It's still worth drinking, and as long as you keep your expectations low, you'll likely enjoy the fresh fruitiness of nouveau. Just remember to buy the current year's release, chill it, and drink it within a few weeks.

Best Bets for Nouveau Producers

» Bouchard
» Drouhin
» Duboeuf
» Jadot

An Important Distinction

Because of Beaujolais nouveau's popularity, most people only think of these super-cheap, quaffable wines when they think of Beaujolais, and thus pooh-pooh any mention of the region. But, one of wine's best kept secrets is *cru Beaujolais*. There are ten superior wine-producing Beaujolais towns, called *crus*. They are capable of producing some surprisingly beautiful, graceful wines that can have the sensual aromatics and supple texture of pinot noir from northern neighbor Burgundy, at a fraction of the price. If you love earthy wines, ask your favorite wine retailer for its best cru Beaujolais wines. I think you'll find their taste, and their price (usually fifteen to twenty dollars), refreshingly delightful.

Did You Know? Oak barrels are a major expense for wineries. If you are drinking a ten-dollar bottle of chardonnay that brags about oak flavors on the back label, chances are it didn't come from a barrel. There are several far less expensive—but far inferior—ways to impart an oaky aroma, namely dipping "tea bags" of oak chips in large vats of wine. Often, this type of oak flavor can come off as coarse, harsh, or out of balance with the rest of the flavors in the wine.

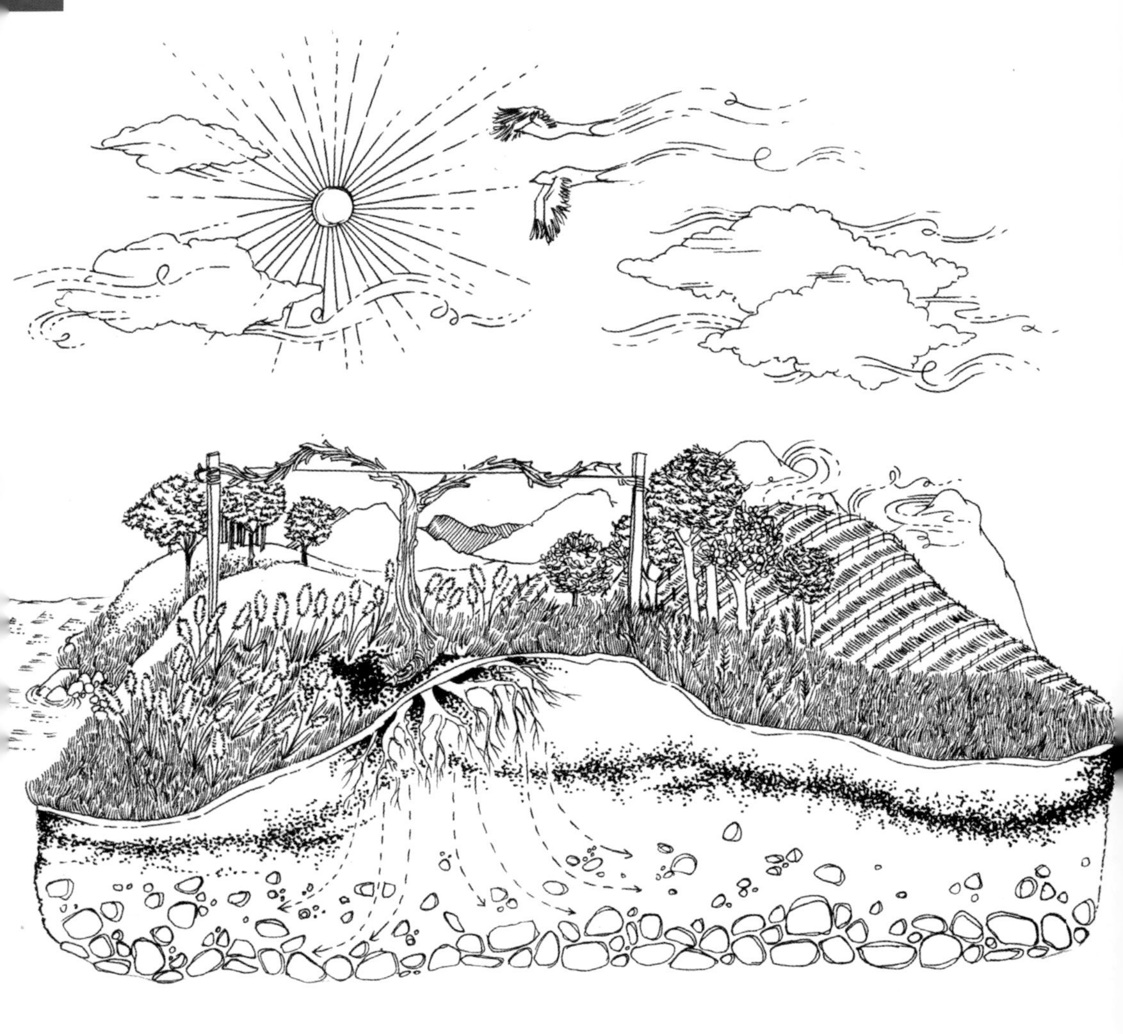

TERROIR: THERE'S NO PLACE LIKE HOME

Besides the grape variety, the most important factor in how a wine will taste is the environment it grows up in—its *terroir*. There is no direct English equivalent for *terroir*, the fancy French word that you are certain to hear time and time again in wine circles. It's pronounced "tare-WAH." Go ahead. Practice saying it. Tare-WAHHHH. Many people mistakenly oversimplify terroir, and think of it as soil. It is so much more.

Terroir is the essence of a particular place. As it applies to a grapevine, terroir encompasses the soil, subsoil, aspect, slope, nuances of weather, orientation to the sun, the ocean, the river, humidity, neighboring plant species, elevation, and, ultimately, human intervention. Each vineyard—each grapevine—is said to have its own unique terroir, which is ideally recognized and appreciated in the finished wine. Terroir is ultimately what makes pinot noir from Germany taste different from the same grape grown in Sonoma, California. As with human development, the impact of environment can be even more influential than genetics.

The French may have been the first to coin the term, but terroir is no new concept. From the very first Greek and Roman vintners to Eskimo fisherman and ancient Chinese rice farmers, humans have always been innately programmed to identify, gravitate toward, and then dissect specific places that produce exceptional food. Georgia's Vidalia onions taste sweeter than onions from a neighboring state. Florida oranges are the juiciest. Coffee beans planted in the shaded mountains of Colombia are especially rich in flavor. Fresh yellow corn from Farmer Ned's patch bursts with just a bit more bright, corny flavor than Farmer Joe's next door. The list of examples could go on and on.

As intangible as it is, terroir is real. Ancient winemakers embraced it. Modern winemaking has used science to try to outthink it. But, today, thoughtful wine farmers everywhere agree: Terroir is what gives a wine its soul, and it cannot be concocted, no matter how hard we try. Terroir is nature's magic.

GRAPES LOVE A GOOD FIGHT

Whether you're talking to a Buddhist monk or a solicitous winemaker, one universal truth is clear: A little suffering is good for everyone. A life without challenge is a half-life, and only through enduring adversity is one presented with the opportunity to fulfill the depth of their capacity for truly being alive. Suffering might be an uncomfortable subject, but I doubt you could find many who didn't regard some sort of suffering as an integral part of the formation of their character. Often the most interesting and evolved people are those who have managed to persevere—and surprisingly to thrive—through hardships. In short, suffering is good for us. It produces strength, resiliency, and character. Incredibly, it is the same with grapes.

Unlike most plants, grapes are human-like when it comes to character development. Grapes that are given everything they ever want and need grow up fat and lazy. The resulting wines lack character and depth. The finest wines are made from grapes that struggle.

HOW DOES YOUR GRAPEVINE GROW?

The coddled vine results in megagrowth—big fat grapes and lots of them. More grapes per acre is always better for profit, so large wine companies work their vineyards like factories, pumping out the most volume possible. There is a consequence; wines made from coddled grapevines are generally watery, flat, and lacking in character. Many times these wines taste so boring that the wine scientists feel the need to add chemicals to boost flavor. Additionally, since the coddled grapevine does not have to dig deep to find water or nutrients, its root system is thin and shallow, and it is utterly dependent on receiving these things from humans, forever.

In contrast, the vine that struggles produces much less fruit. Take, for example, that some of California's most prolific vineyards are producing more than ten tons of grapes per acre, while some of its highest-quality vineyards produce a scant one ton or less per acre. Not only are there far less grapes as a result of struggling vines, but these survivor grapes are much smaller in comparison. The vines dig deep into the soil to find water and nutrients. They develop an extensive root system, allowing them to tap into the complex, natural mineral flavors of the earth and giving them a natural resiliency in times of drought. Struggling vines are stronger, more independent, and produce profoundly better quality and more interesting grapes, which in turn, make for better wine.

CODDLED

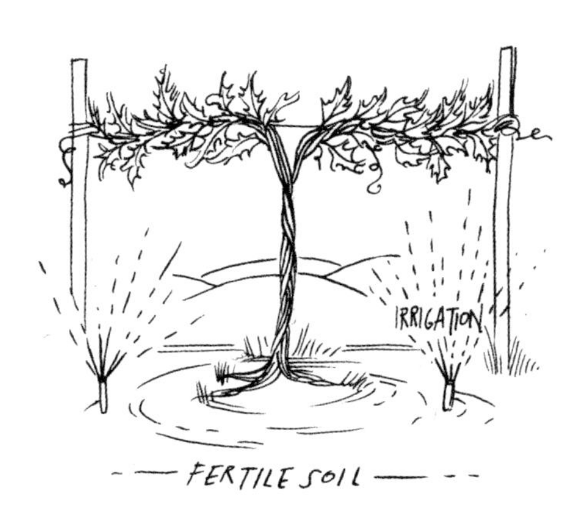

» rich, fertile soil, like a valley floor
» irrigation
» protected from elements (such as pests, diseases, rot, wind, and drought)
» plenty of room to grow (little competition for water and nutrients from other vines and plants)

STRUGGLING

» poor, nutrient-deficient soil, like a mountaintop
» no irrigation, or extremely limited irrigation
» exposure to harsh environmental elements
» tight spacing (competition with other vines for water and nutrients)

Evaluating What's in the Glass

Becoming a better taster—that is, more easily identifying and talking about what's in your glass and why you like it—takes practice. Remember, this is not like hammering out piano exercises or algebra homework. This is wine; to practice is to analyze pleasure.

SEE

Observing wine in the glass is the first step to investigating it. Here are some things to consider when you are getting a visual.

Is the wine **clear and bright**? (It should be.)

What is the **color**? Color can give many clues about a wine's origin, the grape variety used, and the age of the wine (see "Color Confidential," page 66).

Are there thick, viscous **legs** when swirling the wine? If so, the wine is likely to be full-bodied, and to have come from a warmer growing region. If not, it is likely to be lighter-bodied and come from a cooler region.

WINE AND BLINDFOLDS I once announced to a class of beginners that the following week we'd be practicing blind tasting. A young woman came up after class and asked for a suggestion of the best place to buy a blindfold. I explained that although it would definitely make class more interesting to require blindfolds, we weren't going to need them. *Blind tasting* is, simply, tasting without knowing what the wine is and trying to guess where it's from, what grapes are in it, and how old it is. It's good practice in analytically thinking about wine, and it's fascinating to see how perception changes when there are no preconceived notions of what a wine is or should be.

Typically, blind tasting is facilitated by placing wine bottles in bags, so the labels and bottle shapes are unknown to the tasters. It sounds crazy, but there are some talented wine people who can name an exact wine—grape(s), location, producer, and the vintage year—all without ever seeing the label!

Did You Know? White wine gets darker in color as it ages. Red wine gets lighter.

COLOR CONFIDENTIAL

	WHITE WINES	RED WINES
LIGHT	**Color:** pale straw, perhaps with hints of green	**Color:** lighter garnet or brick red, perhaps with orange tinges; can see through the glass 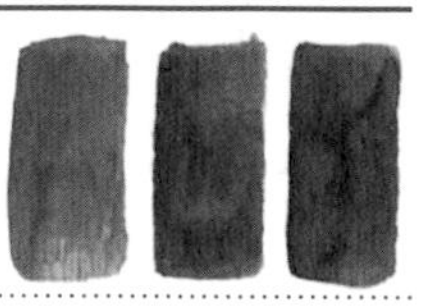
	Legs/tears: barely visible drips, more like sheeting	**Legs/tears:** thin, quickly moving drips
	Interpretation: The wine is probably relatively young, comes from a cooler growing region, has minimal (if any) oak aging, less alcohol, and has a lighter, sheerer body.	**Interpretation:** The wine is probably from a cooler growing region and/or is older. The wine probably has lower alcohol and a lighter, thinner body.
MEDIUM	**Color:** more of a true, rich, lemon yellow 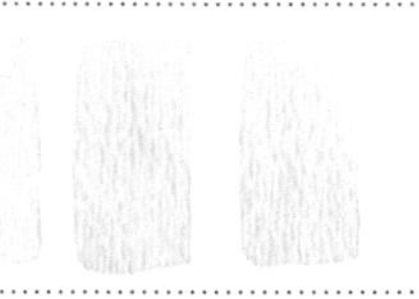	**Color:** medium garnet or ruby color 
	Legs/tears: more visible, viscous drips; wine seems to have a little weight	**Legs/tears:** more visible, viscous drips; wine seems to have a little weight
	Interpretation: The wine is of average age, has a medium amount of alcohol and body, may have had some oak aging (but not too much), and comes from a temperate growing region.	**Interpretation:** The wine is probably of average age, has a medium amount of alcohol and body, and comes from a moderate growing region.
DARK / FULL	**Color:** rich, golden 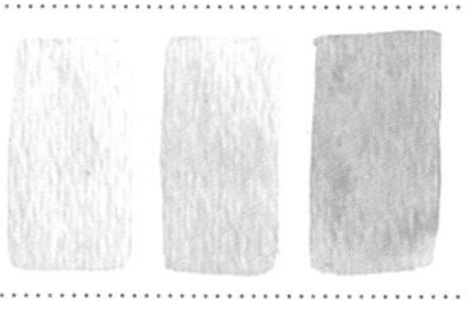	**Color:** deep, dark, opaque purple color, perhaps with tinges of pink or red 
	Legs/tears: well-defined, thick, slow-moving drips	**Legs/tears:** well-defined, thick, slow-moving drips
	Interpretation: The wine may be from a warmer growing region and/or have been aged in oak and/or may be an older wine. The wine probably has a higher level of alcohol and a richer, fuller body.	**Interpretation:** The wine is probably relatively young and comes from a warmer, or even hot, growing region. It is likely the wine has higher alcohol and a richer, fuller body.

SMELL

Among the first, very logical, questions I get from my students is . . . how does a wine end up smelling like cherries (or lemon, tobacco, or wet rocks)? Do winemakers add those things to the wine? The short answer is no. The extended version: grapes naturally contain thousands of aromatic compounds. Different grapes contain different compounds, and the same grape grown in different places can take on more or less of the genetically predisposed compounds. In addition to natural compounds from the grape and the ground, chemical reactions between those compounds and acids, sugars, and alcohols take place—during fermentation and as wine ages in the bottle—creating secondary aromas. The act of smelling wine takes in all of these vaporized compounds. Many of these are also found in other things we smell—like fruits, vegetables, and flowers. For example, here are two compounds found in many pinot noirs.

COMPOUND	SMELLS LIKE	ALSO FOUND IN
raspberry ketone	raspberries	raspberries
beta-Damascone	roses	roses

THE NOSE KNOWS

If you've ever had the kind of stuffy head cold where you just can't taste anything, you already understand the importance of smell when it comes to tasting wine. It's so critical, in fact, that in professional blind tastings, some top tasters can determine a wine accurately on sight and smell alone.

When you're smelling wine, be brave. Stick your nose way down into the glass and get a big whiff. Certain grapes and certain places have unique smells, which you will come to recognize as you taste more often. The most essential duty of that first sniff, though, is to ensure that the wine is in good condition—that it smells like wine (fruit, earth, etc.) instead of something funky. (See "Awful Aromas," page 70, for help with decoding bad smells.) Once you know the wine is in good condition, you can try to identify some aromas.

THE AROMA WHEEL

A supremely helpful way to hone your ability to articulate what you're smelling is to look at a list of possible suggestions. Ann C. Noble, a professor at the University of California, Davis, came up with an ingenious aid she deemed the Aroma Wheel. It helps tasters take broad smells (like fruit) and pin them down into more and more specific aromas (tree fruit, and then peaches).

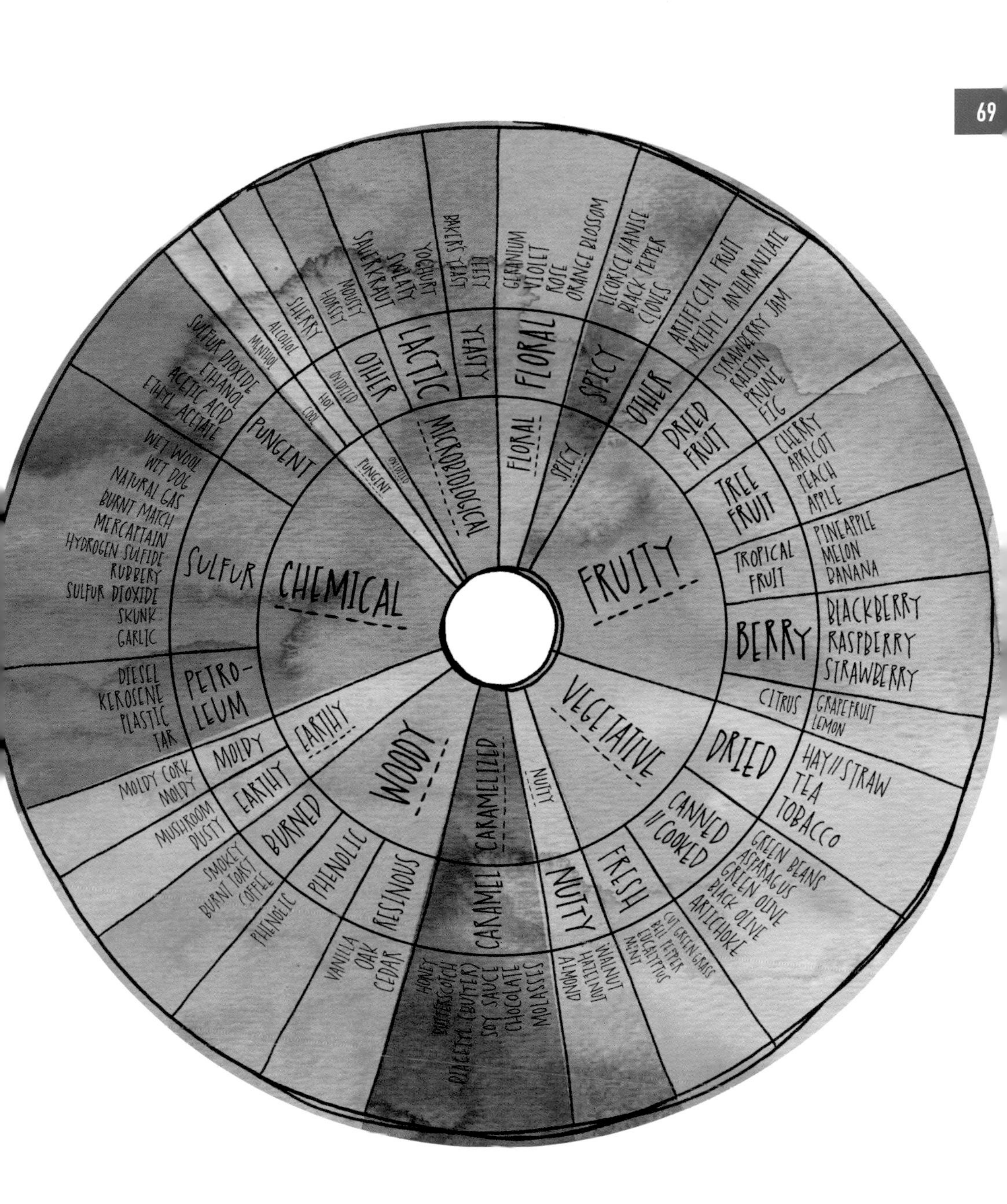
CHEMICAL
FRUITY
VEGETATIVE
NUTTY
CARAMELIZED
WOODY
EARTHY
PUNGENT
OXIDIZED
MICROBIOLOGICAL
FLORAL
SPICY
FLORAL
SPICY
OTHER
DRIED FRUIT
TREE FRUIT
TROPICAL FRUIT
BERRY
CITRUS
DRIED
CANNED // COOKED
FRESH
NUTTY
CARAMEL
RESINOUS
PHENOLIC
BURNED
EARTHY
MOLDY
PETRO-LEUM
SULFUR
PUNGENT
COOL
HOT
OXIDIZED
MENTHOL
ALCOHOL
SHERRY
OTHER
LACTIC
YEASTY
GERANIUM
VIOLET
ROSE
ORANGE BLOSSOM
LICORICE//ANISE
BLACK PEPPER
CLOVES
ARTIFICIAL FRUIT
METHYL ANTHRANILATE
STRAWBERRY JAM
RAISIN
PRUNE
FIG
CHERRY
APRICOT
PEACH
APPLE
PINEAPPLE
MELON
BANANA
BLACKBERRY
RASPBERRY
STRAWBERRY
GRAPEFRUIT
LEMON
HAY//STRAW
TEA
TOBACCO
GREEN BEANS
ASPARAGUS
GREEN OLIVE
BLACK OLIVE
ARTICHOKE
CUT GREEN GRASS
BELL PEPPER
EUCALYPTUS
MINT
WALNUT
HAZELNUT
ALMOND
HONEY
BUTTERSCOTCH
DIACETYL (BUTTER)
SOY SAUCE
CHOCOLATE
MOLASSES
VANILLA
OAK
CEDAR
PHENOLIC
SMOKEY
BURNT TOAST
COFFEE
MUSHROOM
DUSTY
MOLDY CORK
MOLDY
DIESEL
KEROSENE
PLASTIC
TAR
WET WOOL
WET DOG
NATURAL GAS
BURNT MATCH
MERCAPTAIN
HYDROGEN SULFIDE
RUBBERY
SULFUR DIOXIDE
SKUNK
GARLIC
SULFUR DIOXIDE
ETHANOL
ACETIC ACID
ETHYL ACETATE
MOUSEY
HORSEY
SAUERKRAUT
SWEATY
YOGHURT
BAKER'S YEAST
LEESY

AWFUL AROMAS

THE SMELL	THE CAUSE	WHAT TO DO
MUSTY WET CARDBOARD FUNKY BASEMENT	**Trichloroanisole** (TCA) is the most common wine fault. Affected wines are dubbed "corked." TCA most likely originates as a metabolite of mold growth on chlorine-bleached wine corks and barrels.	Approximately one of every twelve wine bottles encapsulated with natural cork will be corked. If you suspect your wine is corked, save the bottle and return it to the shop where you bought it. At a restaurant, politely send it back and order a different wine.
VINEGAR	**Ethyl acetate** is a compound occasionally produced when ethanol alcohol and acetic acid (both present in all wines) combine with oxygen.	Save the bottle and return it to the shop where you bought it, or politely send it back at the restaurant and order a different wine. Alternatively, you can use it for salad dressing.
BARNYARD WET HORSE MOUSE DROPPINGS	When a **yeast** called *Brettanomyces*, or "brett," grows in wine it produces an array of metabolites that sometimes smell horsey or gamy. Some winemakers welcome it, and some wine drinkers love the smell and believe it gives the wine character.	If you like it (at lower levels, many do), drink it. If a wine smells too much like horse or mouse to you, it is because of brett. It is technically a flaw, so you have every right to send the bottle back at a restaurant or return it to the shop where you bought it.
CARAMEL BUTTER BUTTERSCOTCH RANCID BUTTER AT HIGH LEVELS	**Diacetyl** is produced by lactic acid bacteria. The process of converting harsh malic acid (like the acid found in a green apple) to smooth lactic acid (like the acid found in milk) is called malolactic fermentation. Some white wines and most red wines undergo malolactic fermentation.	If you like it (at lower levels, many do), drink it. If a wine is too buttery for your taste, this is why. If it smells like rancid butter, you can certainly send it back at a restaurant or return it to the shop where you bought it.
MATCHSTICKS BURNT RUBBER MOTHBALLS	**Sulfur dioxide**, a common wine additive for centuries, is used as a preservative and antioxidant. When used excessively, or not managed well, it can overpower the wine's aromas.	Decant the wine, or swirl it in your glass (sulfur dioxide smells can dissipate quickly). If the smell persists, save the bottle and return it to the shop where you bought it, or send it back at the restaurant.

THE LANGUAGE/SMELL DISCONNECT

Communicating what you smell and taste can be a real challenge. It turns out that getting your sense of smell to work with the language center of your brain is an awkward task, and there's a logical evolutionary explanation.

The earliest humans relied primarily on their sense of smell to obtain information about the environment. As we moved out of caves and into huts, olfaction became less and less important. Dr. Joseph LeDoux, professor of neuroscience at New York University and author of two books on the brain, explains how and why smell has taken a backseat to other senses. "As primates went from ground dwellers to tree dwellers, smell became less important and vision, especially color vision, became more important. The relative amount of the brain devoted to olfaction was reduced while the amount devoted to vision has vastly increased."

As language and other higher functions emerged, brain real estate continued to morph. However, it seems the ever-shrinking sector for smell remained relatively isolated from the areas responsible for forming words. According to Dr. Richard Robertson, professor of neurobiology at the University of California, Irvine, "The brain systems that handle language were formed many millions of years after those that control olfaction, and there are relatively few connections between the parts of the brain that process smell and those that control language." This probable theory makes perfect sense; it's why you can smell something familiar but still have such a tough time naming it. So don't sweat it if you don't smell wild truffles and roasted suckling pig in your wine when your neighbor does—they've probably just been practicing a little longer.

“THE DISCOVERY OF A WINE IS OF GREATER MOMENT THAN THE DISCOVERY OF A CONSTELLATION. THE UNIVERSE IS TOO FULL OF STARS.”

—Benjamin Franklin

TASTE

Now the really fun part—putting the wine in your mouth. Learning to communicate what you taste is as challenging as talking about what you smell, but practice makes progress. The more wines you've tasted and have under your belt as a reference point, the better you'll get at this too.

There's not one singular, standard tasting method that all wine professionals use when evaluating wine, but the following are a few key components on everyone's mind.

Acidity: How tart, or acidic, is the wine?

Balance: Are all the flavors of the wine harmonious?

Complexity: Is it interesting? Or one-dimensional?

Finish: What is the finale of the wine like? Is it short or long? Elegant or harsh? Does it leave you wanting more?

Tannin: Is there mouth-drying tannin in the wine? If so, is it pronounced or subtle?

Typicity: Does the wine taste like the grape and/or the region it comes from?

v

SPIT OR SWALLOW? After a moment or so of holding the wine in their mouth, pro tasters usually spit it into buckets, especially when they have a long lineup of bottles to evaluate. Staying sober ensures that the last bottles get the same level of focus and unbiased opinion that the first ones did.

Three-step guide to professional spitting:

STEP 1
Insert wine in mouth.

STEP 2
Gently roll the wine around the mouth.

STEP 3
Locate spittoon, aim, and fire.

Did You Know? A supermarket chain in England insured the tongue of its chief [wine] buyer for a reported 17.3 million dollars. / *Wine Spectator*

WINE TALK

Just like with the aroma wheel, having a handy vocabulary list of tastes helps you convey how you feel about a wine's personality. Here are some of the most commonly used descriptors and what the heck they actually mean.

acidic. A wine with high, but balanced, acidity tastes tart and crisp—with echoes of lemon or grapefruit in white wines and cranberry in reds. *Acidic* can have a negative connotation, if the acid seems too harsh.

angular. A wine that is tough and harsh-feeling in your mouth. The opposite of round and supple. A bed of nails vs. a pillow-top mattress. Crunchy vs. creamy. Young, tannic wines can sometimes be described as angular—they haven't had the benefit of time to soften all the rough edges.

appley. A wine that tastes and smells like apples.

approachable. A wine that seems friendly and easy to drink.

aromatic. The wine has obvious and pleasing smells.

austere. The wine is lean and lithe, and ripe fruit is *not* the main focus. Graceful and elegant, but somewhat closed. The subtle, lean and mean wines of Chablis, France, are often called austere.

baked. The wine tastes like cooked or reduced fruit. It could be a sign of a very hot vintage, when the grapes came in overripe, literally baked from the sun, or of heat damage to the bottle sometime after vinification.

balanced. All the aromas and flavors of the wine are harmonious; nothing sticks out.

beefy. Similar to *big* and *brawny*. A bold, manly wine.

big. A full-bodied, mouth-filling wine with a lot of flavor and alcohol.

bitter. Most likely a wine tastes bitter due to high tannin levels.

brawny. A weighty, substantial wine with an unpolished edge.

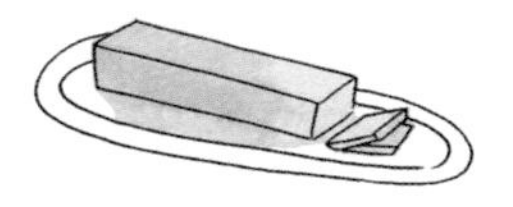

buttery. The wine has the flavor of butter or cream; apparent most often in some chardonnays.

chewy. The wine has a thick texture; it almost feels as though you could chew it.

cloying. The wine is offensively sweet and syrupy, and lacks acidity to balance the sugar.

complex. The wine is interesting; it has a lot going on. There are many aromas and flavors to talk about, and it keeps changing.

creamy. Implies a lush, rich, cream-like texture; the opposite of *thin* and *tart*.

deep/depth. Similar to *complex*. Wine with depth has layers of flavor.

delicate. A wine with mild manners and fine, focused flavor; the opposite of *brawny*, *beefy*, and *big*.

dry. A word used often to describe wine. A red wine can taste dry because it has a lot of tannin (like the kind of dry you taste in unsweetened iced tea); it can also taste dry because it has an absence of ripe fruit flavor, or sugar.

earthy. The wine smells or tastes like earth, manifested in aromas and flavors including barnyard (or farm animal smell), chalk, dirt, dust, forest floor, granite, gravel, limestone, meat, moss, mushrooms, peat, and salt.

fat. A derogatory term meaning that a wine lacks acidity. It's all flesh, with no bone or spine.

flat. A dead-tasting wine. It lacks life and vibrancy, most often because it lacks acidity.

floral. A wine that smells like flowers. Common flowers include rose (especially in gewürztraminer, pinot noir, and Barolo), gardenia (in viognier), and citrus blossom (in chardonnay).

fruit-forward. Fruit flavors dominate the smell and taste; less earthy.

fruity. Much the same as *fruit-forward*, with a connotation of a very ripe fruit flavor, bordering on slightly sweet.

full-bodied. A wine that has significant weight and viscosity. Full-bodied wines feel thick, as opposed to light-bodied wines, which feel thinner. Body is directly related to alcohol; more alcohol equals more body.

funky. Some might prefer a little earthy funk in their wine, but for the most part this is a negative descriptor of wines that smell rotten. (See "Awful Aromas," page 70, to find out what this can tell you about your wine.)

grassy. A wine that smells or tastes like freshly cut grass.

green. A wine that tastes underripe. Cabernet sauvignon grapes that don't fully mature can taste green—like green bell peppers or even jalapeños.

hearty. A substantial wine with lots of flavor, power, and intensity.

herbal. A wine that tastes like herbs; basil, mint, sage, rosemary, lavender, chamomile, and white or black pepper flavors are all commonly found in wine.

hot. A negative descriptor. It means that the alcohol is out of balance; there's so much that it's the dominant flavor in the wine.

inky. A wine with deep, saturated color. Typically it will look and feel thick, like ink.

jammy. A wine that tastes like fruit jam.

lean. A wine that is light and muscular, as opposed to *big* and *brawny*. Think ballet dancer as opposed to sumo wrestler; sushi as opposed to pot roast.

light-bodied. A wine that feels light and silky in your mouth.

lively. A vibrant wine with a good deal of acidity; similar to *acidic* and *tart*. A lively wine will certainly make your mouth water.

lush. Similar to *creamy*, a lush wine feels rich and viscous, like velvet.

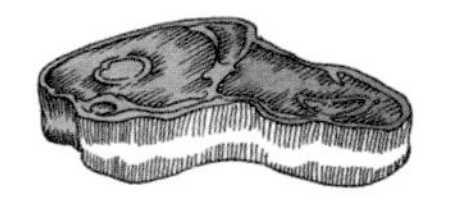

meaty. A wine that smells or tastes like meat. It can also refer to a wine's texture, meaning that it is substantially chewy and viscous.

medium-bodied. A wine that falls somewhere in between light-bodied and full-bodied.

oaky. A wine that smells or tastes like oak, or any of the aromas or flavors that oak can manifest as, including toast, nuts, vanilla, butterscotch, caramel, nutmeg, cinnamon, smoke, dill, and coconut to name a few.

perfumed. A wine with an alluring and prominent smell; pretty much the same as *aromatic*.

plump. A juicy, fleshy wine with lots of soft fruit flavor. A positive descriptor, whereas *fat* is *plump* gone bad.

powerful. A strong, substantial wine. Typically wines described as powerful have high alcohol and lots of tannin.

racy. A tart, lean wine with lots of zest and vibrancy; a high-acid wine.

rich. A wine with a full, rounded flavor.

ripe. A wine that tastes like ripe fruit.

robust. A substantial wine with big flavor and lots of power.

rough. Generally a negative descriptor. Implies the wine feels coarse, like sandpaper, as opposed to smooth, like velvet.

round. A ripe, fleshy wine that is more about fruit than tannin or acidity; the same as *smooth*.

rustic. A wine that lacks polish and is generally pretty earthy. Not necessarily a negative term; some rustic wines can be very charming.

smoky. A wine that smells like smoke.

smooth. A wine that is texturally seamless and velvety feeling on the palate; the same as *round*.

sour. When acidity is overwhelming and out of balance, it can make a wine taste sour.

spicy. A wine that tastes like spice (for example: cumin, curry, black or white pepper).

stemmy. A wine that tastes green and underripe, like the stem of a tomato vine.

tart. Crisp and vibrant, like fresh citrus; the same as *acidic*.

thin. Negative term denoting a wine that lacks body or substance—so much so that it tastes watery.

tight. An introverted, closed-down wine that doesn't have a very generous aroma. The wine can seem like it's under tension—like a wound spring that's ready to release. Typically a wine is tight because it's dominated by young, hard tannins. In time (either time in the bottle or time exposed to oxygen once the bottle is opened—or both) the tannins will soften and you'll be able to smell and taste other characteristics of the wine.

toasty. A wine that smells or tastes like toasty oak; the same as *oaky*.

vegetal. A wine that smells or tastes like vegetables—green peas, asparagus, black or green olives, and beets are common.

vinegary. A wine that smells like vinegar (usually due the presence of ethyl acetate)—never a good thing.

WHAT MAKES A WINE EXCEPTIONAL?

By now, you can probably predict my answer to this question: If you like it, that's all that matters. Everyone—even wine ninjas—cannot help but be swayed by subjectivity. Taste is highly personal.

Wine critics have perspective and can be a good source for suggestions. They taste exponentially more wine than the average person, and have a broad sense of how the wine compares to its peers. Critics can also tell their readers if a bottle is a good value and if it seems to have something special going on. Here is a list of some of wine's most influential critics, magazines, and websites.

» Robert Parker's *The Wine Advocate*, erobertparker.com
» Jancis Robinson, jancisrobinson.com
» Stephen Tanzer's *International Wine Cellar*, wineaccess.com
» *Wine & Spirits*, wineandspiritsmagazine.com
» *Wine Enthusiast*, winemag.com
» *Wine Spectator*, winespectator.com
» Allen Meadows' Burghound.com
» *Connoisseurs' Guide to California Wine*, cgcw.com
» *Decanter*, decanter.com
» James Halliday's *The Australian Wine Companion*, winecompanion.com.au
» JamesSuckling.com
» *Pinot Report*, pinotreport.com

THE PROBLEM WITH NUMBERS Practically everyone who rates wine assigns a number to it. Some use a twenty-point scoring system, but most use a one-hundred-point system. I completely understand the necessity for deeming one wine a seventy-eight and another a ninety-two, but philosophically disagree that a bottle of wine can be quantified. After all, as we've already discussed, wine changes over time. A rating is not only biased to the preference of the taster, but also just a snapshot in time—one person's brief encounter with one bottle at one stage in its evolution. Look at the numbers, but don't fixate on them. Instead, read the taster's narrative. How they describe a wine should be even more important than the numerical score attached to it.

VINTAGE VARIATION

Okay, the last thing I'm going to say about evaluating wine is that vintages matter less than you think. In Europe, weather is unstable and consequently its vintages vary more than in places like California, New Zealand, and Australia, where the weather is milder. However, even in Europe, winemakers now have the technology to better predict, prepare for, and adapt to seasonal differences. Most of the time, different vintages end up tasting more like a subtle variation in character, as opposed to the extreme disparities that the media likes to propagandize.

Remember, the press is always hungry for a story. Media sensationalizing vintages by boldly declaring that an entire year is doomed or, on the other end of the spectrum, that it is the "vintage of the century!" (a claim curiously made many times during said century) serves only to sell more newspapers, magazines, and advertising space on websites. Nuance does not have the same effect. Take any all-encompassing clichés about a region's vintage with a grain of salt. If you're buying an expensive wine from a place where weather can be tricky (especially Bordeaux and Burgundy in France), look to the producer, the importer, or the person selling you the wine for his personal take on how each individual wine compares with others of that year.

The Great Divide

Taking a broad view can be dangerous with a subject as expansive as wine, but there is one generalization that is so obvious and helpful when you're beginning to dissect information that I don't mind making it. Begin this chapter knowing you'll find exceptions along the way, but that this one simple assertion will put a lot of things in perspective . . .

The entire wine world is split into two camps: the Old World and the New World.

They couldn't be more different, in both philosophy and execution. Luckily for us, both worlds can be stunning.

HOW OLD IS OLD?

So just what qualifies as the Old World? Think old . . . really old. These are the places that have been making wine since the happy accident of fermentation first happened. Consider that one of Italy's oldest wineries, Ricasoli, is still owned and run by the founding family, nearly one thousand years after its establishment in 1141. And two-thousand-year-old vineyards in Burgundy, France, were once operated by Cistercian and Benedictine monks, who took copious notes on viticulture: how to best plant, prune, pick, crush, etc. Vineyards, and intimate knowledge of them, have been handed down over generations in the Old World. With experience comes expertise. The Old Worlders have been in the game for a long, long time.

By comparison, New World regions are relative babies on the wine scene. In the late seventeenth century, European settlers brought high-quality grapevines to South Africa, Australia, and North and South America. From there, the grapevines and the craft of winemaking spread, and today wine is made on every continent except Antarctica. From New Zealand to New York, Argentina to China, exciting wine regions continue to pop up around the globe. They emerge with passion, determination, and much greater marketing savvy than any of their predecessors. However, all of them lack one thing the Old World has in its well-worn back pocket: a road map.

California is a great example of a New World region that is proudly and painfully carving its own path. California is responsible for most of the wine production in the United States, and its top wines garner worldwide acclaim. And yet, compared with their European counterparts, the Californians are just getting started.

Technically, the state has been making wine for about a century. Unfortunately, in the early 1920s, just as things were starting to get interesting, Prohibition obliterated almost all of California's 713 bonded wineries. The handful that remained survived only by acquiring a license to make shoddy wine for religious purposes. Prohibition was, of course, eventually repealed (thirteen excruciating years later), but it left a deep scar on America's perception of wine and on the country's wine consumption. The California wine industry did not truly emerge until the 1970s. It took nearly half a century to restore the number of operating wineries back to pre-Prohibition numbers.

Most New World winemakers and grape growers will admit they have a lot to learn. Despite the challenges of forging industries on their respective continents, they are enthusiastic pioneers. In fact, if you were to visit any New World winery today, I'm certain you'd hear them say they are experimenting with growing this grape variety or that, that they are correcting some huge mistake they recently made in the vineyard, or that they are excited about a new technology or technique they are trying. In other words, they're still figuring out what works. Fifty years is but a blip when it comes to wine. California, and other New World regions, will certainly evolve considerably in another millennium.

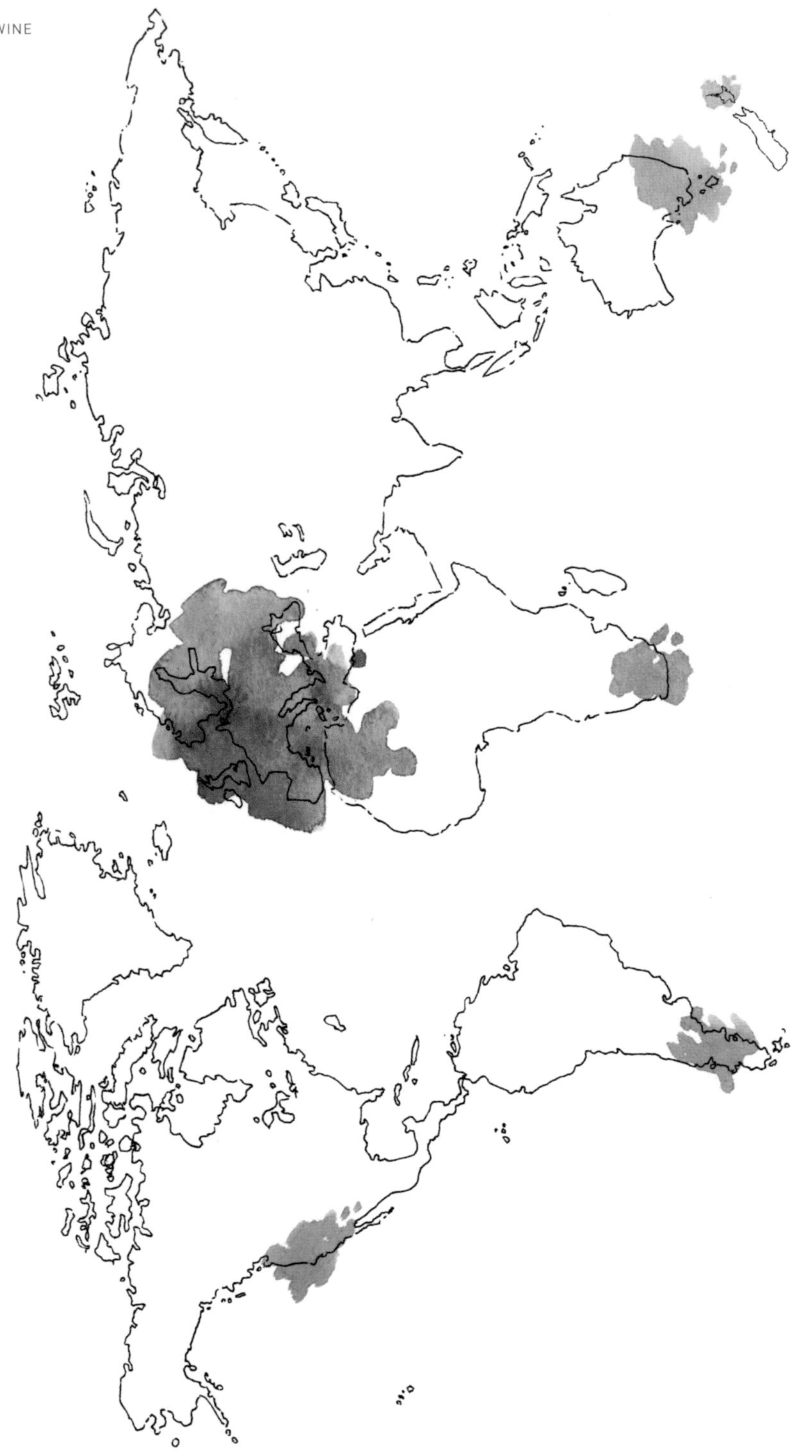
NEW WORLD
OLD WORLD

RULES AND REGULATIONS

Sometimes a map can be restricting. Sometimes, the best discoveries are made when you're a little lost. Is it better to follow a proven path or to blaze a trail?

The Old Worlders don't have much of a choice because quality winemaking in the Old World is strictly regulated. In Europe in the early 1900s, wine fraud was rampant. Unethical winemakers would make a wine and label it with a more prestigious region's name. France cracked down by establishing an intricate system of laws for winemaking, deemed the Appellation d'Origine Contrôlée, or AOC, system. It also created a governing body to ensure that the rules were followed: the Institut National des Appellations d'Origine (INAO) or, as I fondly refer to them . . . the wine police.

The AOC system is based on tradition, and many of the laws are unique to each region. The guidelines set forth cover everything imaginable: yield per acre, permitted grapes (and even percentages of permitted grapes), vineyard practices, labeling, winemaking procedures and techniques, and aging requirements, to name a few. Most of these made and still make perfect sense, serving to protect the integrity and tradition of places making stellar, classic wines. However, some are archaic and have been overhauled. (For example, most French wine regions were not allowed to put grape names anywhere on the labels of their wine until 2006, when this wine law was abolished.)

Other European countries witnessed France's AOC system emerge, and they, too, wanted to ensure quality and protect winemaking traditions. Italy created its own copycat system, the Denominazione di Origine Controllata—or DOC—and the rest of Europe soon followed.

New World regions are a free-for-all in comparison. They have very few guidelines or restrictions, and that has pros and cons for consumers. For example, let's take the word *reserve*. European wines have specific standards for using the word *reserve* on a wine label. The standards vary by country and even by region, but they generally include things like the requirement of better-quality grapes, restricted yields, and longer aging before release.

However, in California and other U.S. states, anyone can put the word *reserve* on any bottle of wine, free of restriction or scrutiny. Most New World wineries use the word *reserve* for their best selections, but some lowbrow wines use it arbitrarily (e.g., Two-Dollar Blah Blah Reserve).

If an Old World winery is suspected of using the word *reserve* illegally, a covert wine-police SWAT team raids the unscrupulous winery with a fleet of unmarked surveillance vans, equipped with night vision goggles and military-grade wine openers. (Or, more likely, they send a letter involving a hefty fine. Needless to say, it's taken very seriously.)

The flip side of the lack of rules is that New World regions revolutionize and propel the science of wine forward. New Zealand, a true innovator, was the birthplace of not only screw-cap enclosures, but also stainless-steel fermentation—a game-changing practice that allows winemakers to control the temperature, and thus the length (slower is better), of fermentation. Now wineries everywhere, including many in the Old World, use stainless-steel tanks for fermentation.

The New World has few rules, but a handful exist. For example, in California, if a grape is named on the label, that grape must make up at least 75 percent of that wine. In Oregon, it's a stricter 90 percent. In Australia, it's 85 percent. In the United States, if you state a vintage year, 95 percent of the wine must come from that vintage; in Chile, only 75 percent has to come from the stated year.

RULE BREAKERS

I warned you—there are always exceptions. One famous exception, a style of wine that brazenly broke out of strict Old World confines, is the aptly and unofficially nicknamed "Super Tuscan." Here's how it happened .

It turns out, World War II spread more than democracy; it spread Italian wine. Thirsty American soldiers who had been stationed in Italy became enamored with Chianti, the free-flowing Tuscan wine then packaged in the highly recognizable straw-covered carafes, and brought demand for the drink back home. Soon, Chianti—a slightly exotic but inexpensive and unpretentious spaghetti wine at the time—was in unprecedented demand.

Italians, being the enterprising sort, capitalized on their newfound celebrity by increasing production dramatically. For many producers, this meant adding copious amounts of neutral white grape juice (surprisingly, perfectly legal within the DOC wine law system) to their red wines to stretch the juice ever further. Throughout the 1950s and '60s, quantity rose while quality continued to plummet.

A handful of quality-conscious Chianti producers, increasingly frustrated with what they felt was an unjust, archaic, and restrictive system of wine laws, decided to simply opt out. They began to make the ultra-premium wines they wanted to make, with the grapes they wanted to use. Instead of using mostly the sangiovese grape and adding the mandatory requirements of other inferior grapes, they used 100 percent sangiovese or, even more shockingly, they mixed sangiovese with cabernet sauvignon or merlot, or both, or made wines with just cabernet. Instead of aging the new wines in traditionally huge oak casks, they used small, expensive French oak barrels, as they do in Bordeaux, to add refined structure and tannin to the wines. The result was big, serious wines that didn't fit in with the rest of Chianti. In fact, since they hadn't followed the rules, they couldn't even put the name *Chianti*

Did You Know? California has two very important schools for winemaking—University of California, Davis and California State University, Fresno. These schools are global leaders in viticulture and vinification. Even some Old World winemakers make the long voyage from Europe to California to learn more about the science of wine.

on their labels. These small-production, quality-driven wines were soon the most coveted and expensive in all of Italy. Nobly dubbed "Super Tuscans" by the press, they were also ironically demoted to Italy's lowest wine designation—vino di tavola, or table wine.

As status and demand for these rogue wines grew, the paradox became too much for the Italian government to take. If Italy's most-wanted wines didn't fit into the system, the system was being mocked. In the early 1990s, a new designation of Italian wine was created, specifically for the rule breakers: Indicazione Geografica Tipica, or IGT. Wines with this designation could state the place they came from on the label, but were held to none of the traditional winemaking laws of the area. Tuscany was the first area in Italy to apply for use of the IGT designation, but now many other regions also produce deviant wines.

I should note that the pendulum of the IGT revolution has since swung a bit. Although there is still plenty of cheap Chianti available today, the movement eventually spurred classic Chianti producers to become more thoughtful and quality-minded. It even encouraged the Italian government to amend some of the laws for making DOC wines—for instance, as of 1996, the longstanding tradition of adding white grapes has been banned in Chianti Classico. The Super Tuscan craze peaked in the early '90s and has waned considerably since then. The reason? Besides the normal ebb and flow of wine trends and a very plausible disenchantment with their three-figure price tags, the wine cognoscenti eventually began to question the Super Tuscan lack of "somewhereness." After a while, the latest and greatest wine from Tuscany started to taste like other non-distinctive New World wines—rich and ripe, with lots of oak . . . suddenly not so superlative.

A Few of the Original Super Tuscans

» Sassicaia by Tenuta San Guido
(cabernet sauvignon and cabernet franc)

» Vigorello by San Felice
(sangiovese, cabernet sauvignon, and merlot)

» Tignanello by Antinori
(sangiovese and cabernet sauvignon)

» Ornellaia by Tenuta dell'Ornellaia
(cabernet sauvignon, merlot, and cabernet franc)

» Masseto by Tenuta dell'Ornellaia
(merlot)

THE NAME GAME

One of the most confusing parts of learning about wine is figuring out what's in the bottle. This is especially challenging because the old and new systems label wine differently. To understand why the Old World generally names a wine after the place it comes from and the New World names the wine after the grapes that go into making it, let's meet Jacques and Jack.

Shortly after the earth cooled, in a little village in Burgundy, France, farmer **Jacques** grew chardonnay. He grew chardonnay because that's what his great-great-grandfather had discovered grew best on their sunny, southeast-facing vineyard in the town of Meursault. But Jacques wasn't the only one with a chardonnay love affair. Everyone in his town who made wine made chardonnay. In fact, chardonnay was the white grape grown in every village heading north for hundreds of kilometers. Putting chardonnay on his label wouldn't really tell his consumers—likely his neighbors, friends, relatives, and people in nearby towns—anything about what it tasted like. Putting the village name "Meursault" on the label, however, did. The wines from Meursault had a reputation for being opulent and sunny, with a delectable taste of roasted nuts. In this context, the appellation (or place-name) of Meursault (and farmer Jacques's vineyard name) meant something. Chardonnay did not.

Flash forward to the middle of the twentieth century. **Jack**, a successful California entrepreneur turned farmer, has risked everything for his dream of making wine. He's got an empty field and a thousand decisions to make. His potential customers are beginning to have access to hundreds of wines from all over the world, and all those choices can be overwhelming. On one hand, it will be hard for him to distinguish and market his no-name wines—no one's heard of Sonoma Valley, and even if they had, they wouldn't know what to expect from a bottle labeled as such. On the other hand, American consumers are eager to try wines, and increasingly frustrated with complicated foreign labels. New World wineries have made understanding wine even more confusing by stealing the names of famous Old World regions. (Cheap jug wines from California's Central Valley are labeled with names like *Burgundy*, *Chablis*, and *Chianti*—not only false advertising, but an insult to the European appellations.) The timing seemed right for nomenclature reform. Jack and some of his farmer friends had an idea: Why not name the wine after the grape that goes in it? For California wine, it would be more descriptive and easier to understand to put *chardonnay* on a bottle than to put the specific appellation on the label. The new model was a hit with consumers, and the labeling of wines by grape soon became a New World benchmark.

Today, in general, most Old World wine regions still boast appellation-only, or at least appellation-dominant, labels, though many of them are now allowed to also print the grapes used. Most New World wine regions name the bottle after the grape; the appellation is also located on the label, but it is much less prominent.

WINE LABEL ANATOMY

While we're on the subject of labels, here's a quick reference to deconstructing them.

OLD WORLD LABEL

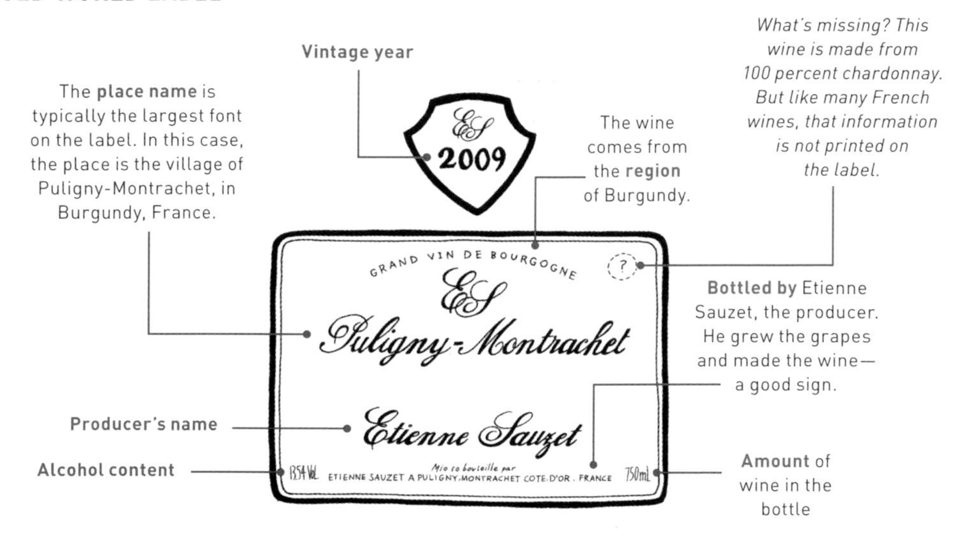

NEW WORLD LABEL

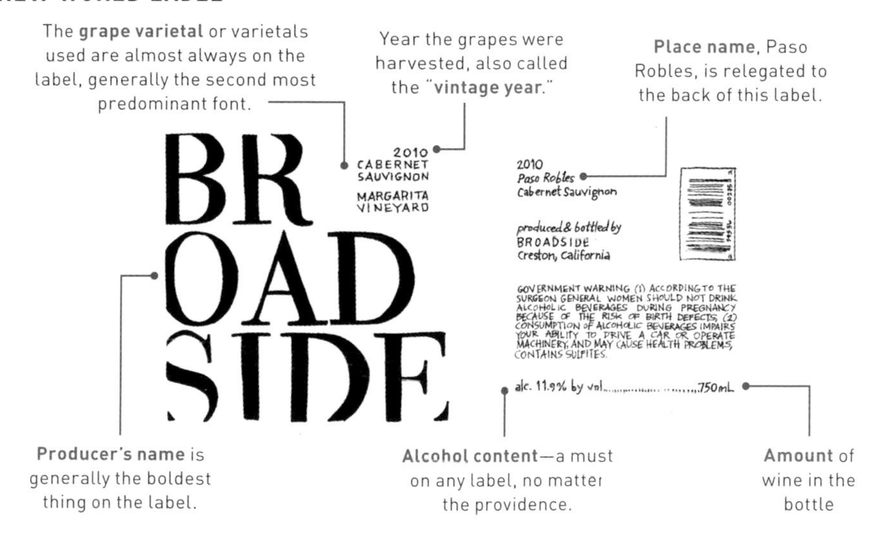

THE EXCEPTIONS

Ah yes, the exceptions section. There are some regions that don't follow the Old World/New World labeling conventions. For instance, traditional German labels usually display the grape name at least as prominently as the place-name. Similarly, the tiny region of Alsace, France, labels its wines by grape varietal.

Italy is more confusing. Many Italian wines are named for the appellation, some are named for the grape, and some state both the grape and the appellation. And in a couple of rare exceptions, an Italian wine bears a name that does not refer to either.

ANOTHER ANOMALY: BORDEAUX IS SLICK

We've established that Old World wine regions are often considered less than savvy when it comes to marketing their wines, but Bordeaux is an important and historic exception. For centuries, Bordeaux has sold *futures*. That is, it has been selling its best wines on spec, or *en primeur*. Those sharp chateau owners (traditionally wealthy bankers from Paris) devised a brilliant system whereby they happily collect payment on wines twelve to eighteen months before the wine is even put into the bottle. The system fuels demand, creates cash flow for the producers, and (hypothetically) guarantees that wines are sold at the lowest prices.

Did You Know? *d'* or *di* means "from" in Italian, so with any wine that is named (blank) di (blank), there is a good chance that the first word is the grape and the second one is the place.

It works like this: Each year, a few months after harvest, when the still-tough toddler wine is in barrel, international wine critics and buyers descend upon Bordeaux for a series of lavish galas, dinners, and preview tastings. After gauging the demand from buyers and press, the chateaus set their initial prices. The following spring, merchants begin taking the first orders—payment due in full from customers at the time of reservation. The Bordelais collect the money, sit on the wine, and begin shipping about two years later.

Theoretically, the idea makes sense. As a consumer, you get to reserve the wine you want (it is true, some in-demand wines are only sold as futures; they never see the inside of a wine shop) and you are locking it in at a supposed rock-bottom price. There are holes, however. The entire system is based on scarcity, but Bordeaux—even the most exclusive chateaus—make a ton of wine in comparison to vintners from equally acclaimed regions like Burgundy and Napa. With a few exceptions, it is likely you'll still be able to buy your favorite Bordeaux wines well after their official in-bottle release date.

People who regularly buy futures often talk about it as an investment. Buying today almost guarantees they can resell later at a higher price, or at least feel confident they got the best deal . . . right? Usually this is the case, but not always. Those speculative barrel tastings are tricky; tasters claim they can gather the essence of a wine and a vintage from very young juice, but often it tastes nothing like the finished wine. Typically, as of that first glance, the winemakers have yet to decide on the blend. Occasionally, if a wine or even a whole vintage is overhyped at the initial tastings, prices can actually fall over the years.

Is buying futures smart? You'll have to decide for yourself. Some people swear by the practice, but consider the cost of locking up your money for two years. And never consider the investment an absolute; though buying futures is no roulette, it still poses risk.

THE GREATEST DIVISION OF ALL

Now we're getting to the most applicable part of this chapter: New World and Old World wines taste different. In general, New World wines are big on body and fruit. They typically have high levels of alcohol and lower acidity. Flavors are bold and assertive. Old World wines, in contrast, are typically lighter in body and higher in acidity. They taste less like fruit and more like earth, which can manifest as aromas and flavors including granite, chalk, stones, flint, gravel, dust, dirt, mushrooms, wet horse, and manure. Getting thirsty?

Remember, this is a chapter of archetypes. There are exceptions. Some Old World winemakers, hoping to capitalize on the thirst of the substantial U.S. and British markets, are attempting to make fruitier, fuller-bodied wines. And many a winemaker in the New World will tell you that they are shooting for a more restrained "Old World style." The point is that even if there are exceptions, the people making them usually make reference to the respective Old or New Worlds.

You may already know which style you prefer. This simple conclusion is extremely helpful in the very beginning of your wine education. It slices all your choices in half. Walking into a wine store or a restaurant with a wine list as thick as a bible, and asserting that you prefer New or Old World wines gives you a major advantage. You've just defined your style.

An important caveat: While stating a preference for New or Old World is extremely valuable as a beginner, it can be detrimental to pigeonhole yourself forever. Your tastes will evolve. All that Old World earth might sound disgusting at first, but I promise I've seen many, many students who proclaim they will only ever love New World fruit bombs, but eventually become intrigued by the complexity and nuance of earthy Old World wines. Similarly, Old-World-only folks have been blown away once they open their palates to wines from Washington state, Argentina, New Zealand, and other newer regions. Define your style now, but later, when you're feeling more confident, don't be afraid to let it go.

Sacré bleu! This wine is obnoxious. Where is the dirt? All I smell is juicy fruit & I'm drunk after one glass.
CRIKEY, MATE! I'D LIKE SOME MORE WINE WITH MY WATER. I CAN'T SMELL A BLOOMIN' THING!

OLD WORLD/NEW WORLD CHEAT SHEET

	OLD WORLD	NEW WORLD
PLACE	Winemaking Europe and other areas in the Mediterranean basin with a long history of winemaking, namely **France**, **Italy**, **Germany**, **Spain**, **Hungary**, **Austria**, **Portugal**, **Greece**, **Romania**, and **Croatia**.	**Everywhere else.**
RULES	Tied to **tradition**, more rules and guidelines. Usually there's a strict government system in place to oversee growing grapes and making wine.	Close to no guidelines. A relative **free-for-all**. This freedom leads to creativity and innovations. Technologically advanced. First to experiment.
NAME	Wines generally (but not always) **named after the place** they come from (Bordeaux, Burgundy, Chianti, Rioja). This is a nod to the importance of the concept of terroir.	Wines generally **named after the grape** (cabernet sauvignon, merlot, sauvignon blanc, chardonnay).
STYLE	**More subtle aromas and flavors**, subdued colors. More refined, generally more earthy (expressive of terroir).	**More outgoing, intense.** Color is usually deep. Aromas more likely to "jump" out of the glass. Bombastic. Generally more fruit-forward.

“GOOD WINE IS A NECESSITY OF LIFE FOR ME.”

—Thomas Jefferson

Grapes to Know

Humans and grapes have grown up together. Archaeologists believe that grapes were one of the earliest wild fruits, sustaining primitive man alongside a steady diet of woolly mammoth. It is estimated that the cultivation of grapes for the purpose of making crude wine began around 6000 B.C., in Mesopotamia. From the Middle East, the grapevine spread to Greece and then Rome, where vast improvements in winemaking were made. The culture of wine flourished with the Roman Empire, swiftly securing wine's important position at the table and in the church. Suddenly, wine was deeply ingrained in the human experience, even considered vital to living a good, full life.

Today the grape is as significant as ever. Worldwide, there are about seventy-two million tons of grapes grown annually, making it the second most popular fruit, just behind oranges. Grapes are grown for eating, for drying into raisins, and also, thankfully, continue to be propagated for the pleasure of drinking. Of all the grape species on Earth, the most coveted for making fine wine is referred to as the European grapevine, or *Vitis vinifera*. Believe it or not, within that one species, there are almost ten thousand grape varieties known to man. The good news is that no one needs to memorize that daunting list, because only a few dozen have the ability to make decent wine. Of those precious few, there are even fewer that you'll see on a regular basis. Familiarizing yourself with the personality of these standouts will give you a solid foundation for learning about wine. Once you've identified some of your favorite grapes, you can try other grapes and wines that share similar characteristics.

This chapter profiles the nine most popular grape varieties—not only what the grape typically smells and tastes like, but where it's grown, why it's loved, and what's so special about it.

At the end of each grape profile, you'll find a list of similar grapes and wines you might also enjoy. I hope to make it fun and painless for you to experiment with new wines, while still staying within the core parameters of what you like. If you're a sauvignon blanc devotee, you like clean, fresh, citrusy wines with tangy acidity. You'll likely flip over albariño or grüner veltliner; these grapes have a lot in common with sauvignon blanc, but are a little more obscure and thus less likely to have caught your eye on a wine shop shelf or a restaurant wine list. When you're ready, use this section as a guide to help you break out of the rut of buying the same safe wine over and over.

SAUVIGNON BLANC

CHARDONNAY

RIESLING

PINOT NOIR

CABERNET SAUVIGNON

MERLOT

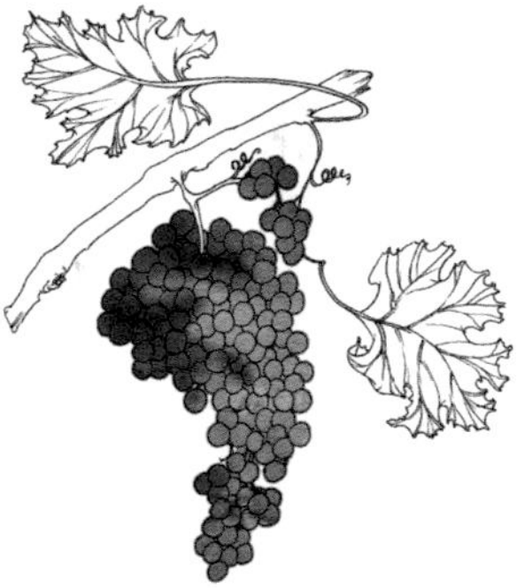

SANGIOVESE

ZINFANDEL

SYRAH

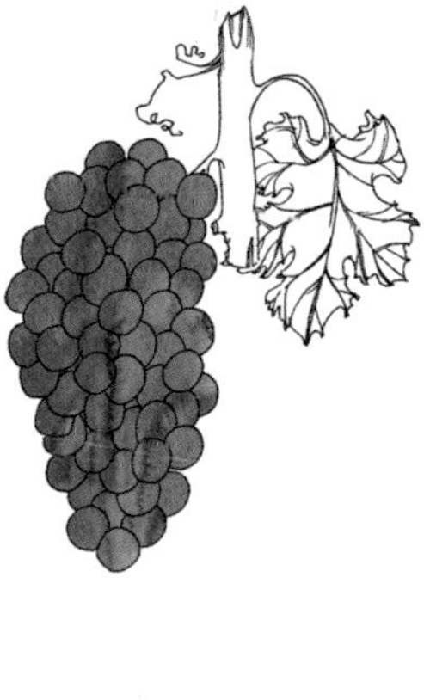

HAPPIEST HOMES FOR THE NINE MOST POPULAR GRAPES

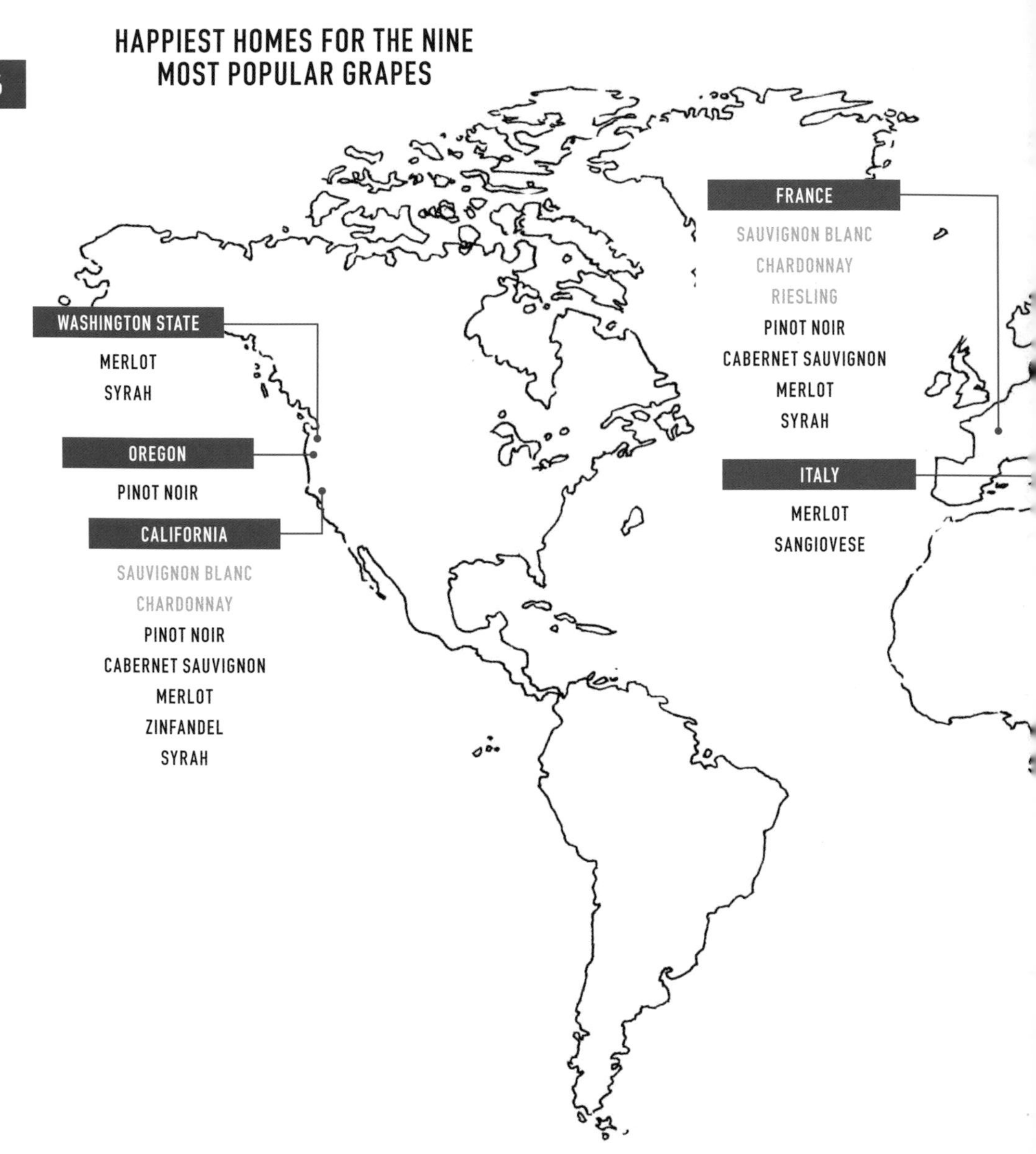

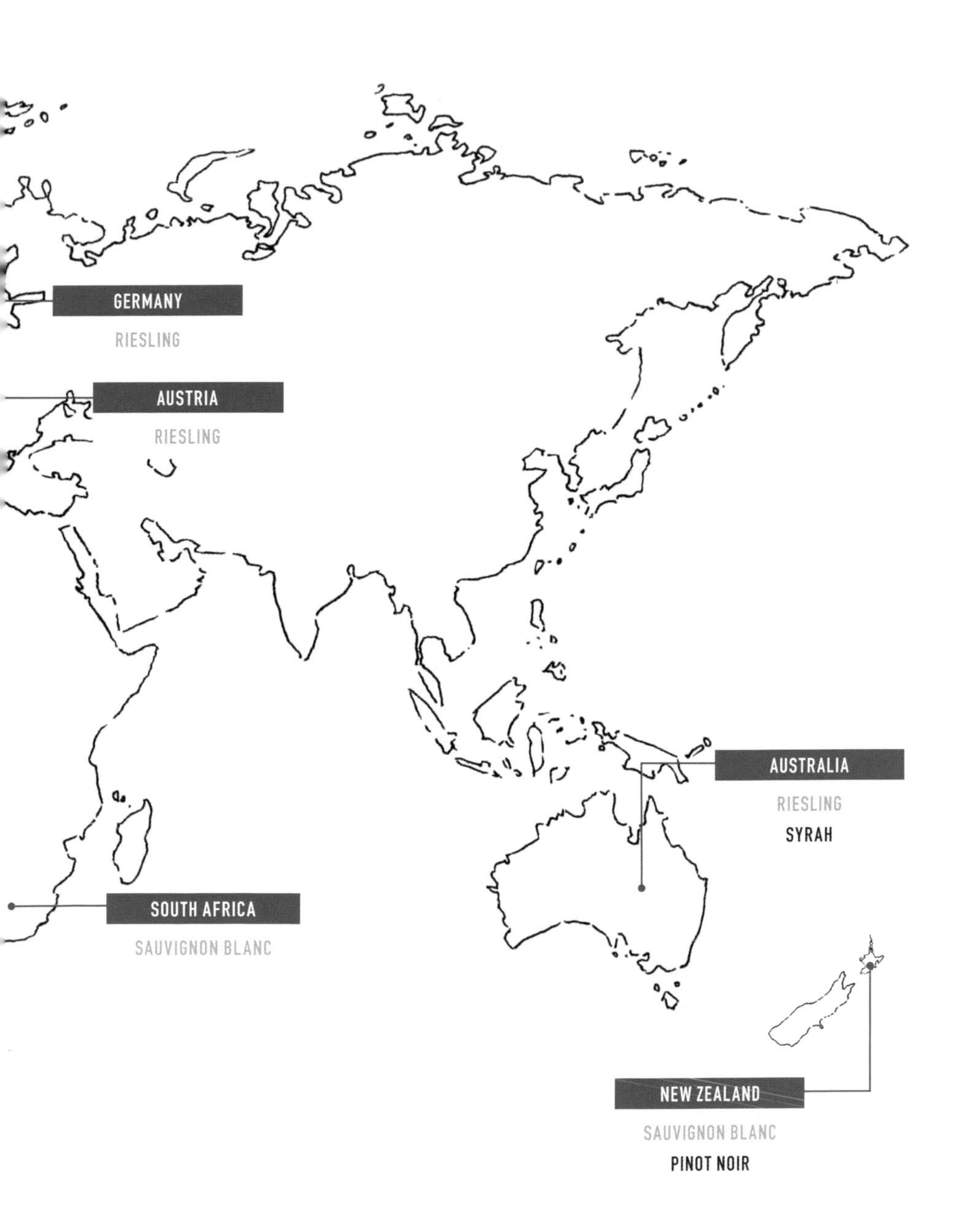
GERMANY
RIESLING
AUSTRIA
RIESLING
SOUTH AFRICA
SAUVIGNON BLANC
AUSTRALIA
RIESLING
SYRAH
NEW ZEALAND
SAUVIGNON BLANC
PINOT NOIR

SAUVIGNON BLANC
THE ACID QUEEN

/ SAW-vin-yawn BLOHNK/

Sauvignon blanc is aggressive. In fact, the French name *sauvignon blanc* translates to "savage white." Not only does this unruly grape grow wild in the vineyard, with loads of leaves bursting in every direction, but it's also forceful in the glass, confidently announcing itself with big, pungent aromatics. Then there's the grapefruit factor. If you can't stand it, I'd be inclined to steer you in a different direction for your whites. But if you're a fan of grapefruit—or at least the smell of it—chances are you're going to love sauvignon blanc; grapefruit is the single most identifiable character for this grape. Depending on where it grows, sauvignon blanc can also smell and taste like a variety of green herbs and veggies. Cool-climate versions smell like green peas, freshly cut grass, or asparagus, while warm-climate versions tend toward a more dried grass and herb smell—more like hay. Last, there's the grape's polarizing penchant for acidity. No matter where it's grown, well-made sauvignon blanc's high acidity will always make you pucker. Some might call the grape sour aand pronounce it too prickly to love. Others are seduced by the thirst-quenching taste and find sauvignon blanc to be the perfect companion to any food you'd squeeze a lemon on.

MOST NOTABLE VERSIONS

Loire Valley, France / luh-wah /

The Loire Valley is a thin, picturesque east-west strip of vineyards, medieval castles, troglodytes (people who live in caves!), and goat farms, stretching from the Atlantic Ocean inland. If sauvignon blanc had a birthplace, it would be here, in this white wine wonderland. In the Loire Valley, the grape is at its most sophisticated, most steely, and most connected with terroir. The valley's dramatically northern climate ensures a long, cool ripening season, which always leads to racy acidity in the finished wine. And the soil, a unique composition of chalk, gravel, and flint, generously contributes a beautiful "wet rocks," mineral taste to these sassy, classy wines. The best wines come from the villages of Sancerre, Pouilly Fumé, and Quincy, and they are all incredible with the fresh, tangy goat cheese that's made here.

Bordeaux, France / bor-DOE /

Not too far south of the Loire is another winegrowing region buttressed against the Atlantic: Bordeaux. Although Bordeaux is undeniably famous for red wines, white Bordeaux can be a stunning example of sauvignon blanc. Here the climate is decidedly warmer, especially with the moderating influence of the warm Atlantic Ocean. This warmth, combined with the Bordelais tradition of adding a healthy dollop of semillon (a grape with a rich, oily texture and a honeyed character) and barrel aging, make for a soft version of sauvignon blanc. Sure, that tart citrus character is still there, but it's wrapped in a cream puff. When you think of white Bordeaux, think silky, sexy, gentle, gravelly, grapefruity goodness.

New Zealand

It still blows my mind that a country so new to fine wine has made such a respected, showstopping entre. The New Zealand wine industry didn't get going until the 1990s. But in just a couple of short decades, it has created such a buzz and carved out such a defining niche that no world-class wine list would be complete without its claim to fame: sauvignon blanc. Sauvignon blanc from this cool-climate island country is the world's most aggressively aromatic and tart version of the grape. Stick your nose in the glass and you get a loud whiff of grapefruit, green peas, and asparagus screaming at you. If white Bordeaux is Vivaldi, New Zealand sauvignon blanc is Nine Inch Nails.

California

Taking its cue from Bordeaux, California's sauvignon blancs, hailing mostly from Napa, Sonoma, and Lake Counties, are creamy and soft. California's weather is even warmer and more temperate than Bordeaux, though, so there is less mineral tang and more ripe fruit. Aromas of fresh peaches, guava, passion fruit, and melon are often found in these rounder, richer versions of the grape. Here, the herbal quality comes out more like freshly cut grass or hay. And like Bordeaux, many of the more expensive versions spend a little time in oak barrels, adding to the creamy weight of the wine. Just like the stereotypical Californian, these wines are m-e-l-l-o-w.

South Africa

For many years, the phrase "South African wines" conjured up the image of funky, subpar vino, mostly meant for distillation into brandy. But with the fall of apartheid and a resurgence of quality-conscious producers, South Africa is churning out some beautiful, complex wines that you can't miss. In fact, as far as sauvignon blanc goes, this is one of my favorite regions. Widely available and relatively inexpensive, the South African version of the grape is like a cross between mineral-laden Sancerre and grapefruity New Zealand. The best examples are elegant without being austere, and still provide plenty of bright, citrusy fruit.

RECOMMENDATIONS

$

- Château Bonnet blanc Entre-Deux-Mers / *Bordeaux, France*
- Château Haut-Rian blanc / *Bordeaux, France*
- Joel Gott Wines sauvignon blanc / *California*
- Oyster Bay sauvignon blanc / *Marlborough, New Zealand*

$$

- Château Ducasse / *Bordeaux, France*
- Dog Point Vineyard sauvignon blanc / *Marlborough, New Zealand*
- Domaine Hippolyte Reverdy Sancerre / *Loire Valley, France*
- Honig Vineyard and Winery sauvignon blanc / *Napa Valley, California*
- Neil Ellis "Groenekloof" sauvignon blanc / *Stellenbosch, South Africa*
- Voss Vineyards sauvignon blanc / *Rutherford, Napa Valley, California*

$$$

- Cade Winery sauvignon blanc / *Napa Valley, California*
- Chalk Hill "Estate" sauvignon blanc / *Chalk Hill, Sonoma County, California*
- Château Carbonnieux blanc Pessac-Leognan / *Bordeaux, France*
- Domaine Vacheron Sancerre / *Loire Valley, France*
- Dragonette Cellars sauvignon blanc / *Happy Canyon, Santa Barbara County, California*
- Spring Mountain Vineyard "Estate" sauvignon blanc / *Spring Mountain District, Napa Valley, California*

OTHER GRAPES AND WINES YOU MIGHT LIKE

» albariño
» Chablis
» grüner veltliner
» Muscadet
» torrontés
» vernaccia di San Gimignano

CHARDONNAY
MISS POPULARITY

/ shar-doe-NAY /

Chardonnay is popular because it's easy. That is, compared with many other grapes, it's easy in the vineyard and easy to make into wine. It's also a chameleon, eagerly taking on the colors of a vineyard and of the winemaker who shepherds it from vine to bottle. I guess that's why chardonnay has such a broad spectrum of possible flavors. Sure, there are usually some apple and citrus flavors with any chardonnay, but beyond that, terroir shapes its taste.

Want a steely, lean, lemony version of chardonnay? Plant the grape in a super-chilly climate like Chablis, France, where it will be happy to retain tons of acidity and soak up all the minerals in the ground. How about a lush, tropical fruit style with a smooth, creamy mouthfeel? No problem, chardonnay can do that too. Vintners simply plant the vine in a warmer climate, and make sure to allow the wine some extra time to hang out in barrel with the dead yeast cells left over from fermentation. Chardonnay will enthusiastically absorb the yeasty flavor and creamy feel of these "lees" with no complaints. How about oak? This grape definitely doesn't need it to shine (as evidenced by the brilliant selection of unoaked chardonnays on the market) but if oak is desired, chardonnay is one of the most amiable white wine vehicles for oak flavor. It will take a swim in oak barrels and meet you on the other side smelling of toast and butterscotch. If there's one defining characteristic of this grape, it's that it's always different. That's why I grin when someone says they don't like chardonnay; I know that they just haven't found the right one yet.

MOST NOTABLE VERSIONS

Burgundy, France / BUR-gun-dee

Most wine geeks put Burgundy, France, on a pedestal. The mythical status of this region revolves around its two star grapes, pinot noir (red) and chardonnay (white). Both are believed to reach optimum potential in this very special spot. Despite its tiny production, this thin strip of coveted land boasts a lineup of legendary wines. Burgundian chardonnay is generally bright and minerally (think limestone and chalk). Specifically, wines from Chablis, in the northernmost end of Burgundy, are the world's most pure expression of the grape. They are ultra-lean, lemony, and chalky. The most acclaimed wines from the

Did You Know? Chardonnay is the second most widely planted white grape on the planet. The first is airén, a rather innocuous grape planted on one million acres in Spain. Most airén goes into the distillation of brandy.

southern half of Burgundy are still racy, but express riper apple flavor, and are sensually robed in the finest French oak, which gives the wine hints of butterscotch and toasted hazelnuts.

Champagne, France / sham-PAIN

Here's another teeny-tiny place with a huge reputation. Champagne is undeniably the world's most famous sparkling wine. By law, the wines must be made from a combination of one, two, or three of the approved grapes: chardonnay, pinot noir, or pinot meunier (a lower-quality country cousin of pinot noir; also red). Most Champagnes are blends of the three, with each grape contributing a little something special to the taste. In Champagne, chardonnay is the top performer, adding elegance and finesse. Some producers make a 100 percent chardonnay Champagne called *blanc de blancs* (white from whites). They are beautiful and long-lived, but can be very expensive.

California

Chardonnay is one of the grapes that put California on the world wine map. In 1978, at a highly publicized tasting contest later dubbed "The Judgment of Paris," the then-best California wines were tasted blind (or with their labels covered) against the most esteemed wines of France. In the chardonnay category, Chateau Montelena of Napa beat out all of France's most iconic chardonnays from Burgundy. The French judges were flabbergasted when their picks were revealed, and like it or not, they had to give credit to California for producing some incredible wine. (In the same tasting, Stag's Leap Wine Cellars S.L.V. cabernet sauvignon, also from Napa, beat out all of the top French cabernets. It was an astonishing victory!)

Today, California has about one hundred thousand acres planted to chardonnay, and is responsible for 25 percent of the worldwide production of the grape. You can buy hugely varying styles, in widely ranging price points, from all over the state. The most coveted versions come from the coolest climates, where chardonnay's ripe flavor, thanks to all that sunshine, is balanced with crisp acidity. Look for chardonnays made close to the coast. Sonoma Coast chardonnays are some of my favorites.

RECOMMENDATIONS

Chardonnay comes in a wide range of styles and flavors, but I've split my recommendations into two main categories. First, I recommend chardonnays that are clean and crisp (those with a more tart, refreshing taste and little to no oak). The second list includes chardonnays with more richness and body, and a creamier, more buttery taste (many of these also have oaky flavors).

Clean, crisp chardonnay

$

- A to Z chardonnay / *Oregon*
- Los Vascos chardonnay / *Colchagua Valley, Chile*
- Yalumba "Y Series" unwooded chardonnay / *South Australia, Australia*

$$

- Domaine Pierre Matrot Bourgogne blanc / *Burgundy, France*
- Maison William Fevre "Champs Royaux" / *Chablis, France*
- Olivier Leflaive "Les Sétilles" Bourgogne blanc / *Burgundy, France*
- Schug Carneros Estate Winery chardonnay / *Sonoma Coast, California*

$$$

- Chateau Montelena Winery chardonnay / *Napa Valley, California*
- Domaine Ballot-Millot & Fils "Narvaux" / *Meursault, Burgundy, France*
- Ramey Wine Cellars chardonnay / *Sonoma Coast, Sonoma County, California*

$$$$

- Domaine Étienne Sauzet Puligny-Montrachet / *Burgundy, France*
- Domaine Vincent Dauvissat "La Forest" / *Chablis, France*
- Far Niente Winery chardonnay / *Napa Valley, California*
- Maison Joseph Drouhin "Folatieres" / *Puligny-Montrachet, Burgundy, France*
- Pahlmeyer chardonnay / *Sonoma Coast, Sonoma County, California*

Full, rich, buttery chardonnay

$

- Chateau Ste. Michelle Winery chardonnay / *Columbia Valley, Washington state*
- Glen Carlou Wine Estate chardonnay / *Paarl, South Africa*
- Sebastiani Vineyards and Winery chardonnay / *Sonoma County, California*

$$

- Au Bon Climat Winery chardonnay / *Santa Barbara County, California*
- Bernardus Winery and Vineyard chardonnay / *Monterey County, California*
- Bodegas Catena Zapata chardonnay / *Mendoza, Argentina*
- Mount Eden Vineyards "Wolff vineyard" chardonnay / *Edna Valley, California*
- Viña Errázuriz "Wild Ferment" chardonnay / *Casablanca Valley, Chile*

$$$

- Gary Farrell Vineyards and Winery "Russian River Selection" chardonnay / *Russian River Valley, Sonoma County, California*
- Mer Soleil Vineyard "Barrel Fermented" chardonnay / *Central Coast, California*
- Neyers Vineyards chardonnay Carneros / *Napa Valley, California*

$$$$

- Kistler Vineyards "Les Noisetiers" chardonnay / *Sonoma Coast, Sonoma County, California*
- Newton Vineyard "Unfiltered" chardonnay / *Napa County, California*
- Shafer Vineyards "Red Shoulder Ranch" chardonnay / *Carneros, Napa Valley, California*

OTHER GRAPES AND WINES YOU MIGHT LIKE

If you like clean, crisp chardonnay:

» pinot blanc
» pinot gris/pinot grigio
» roussanne
» Sancerre

If you like more full, rich, oaky, and buttery versions of chardonnay:

» viognier
» semisweet Vouvray

RIESLING
THE NERD

/ REES-ling /

Nerds are always out of fashion. They are a little offbeat, a little reserved, generally misjudged, and underappreciated. Wine's indisputable nerd is riesling. Riesling is not like the others. First, it's usually naked and alone. I've yet to meet a riesling blended with any other grape or one that showed even a trace of oak; this grape shines when it's brazenly bare-skinned. This is because at its best it is so supremely talented at communicating terroir. There is no other grape that can as effortlessly and accurately taste like the place it was grown, yet still taste like itself. In this case, *itself* is a grape with pretty floral aroma, tangy acidity, a propensity for picking up mineral notes, and the potential to develop favorable petrol or rubber smells.

The most widespread misconception about riesling is that it's always sweet. Many Americans' impressions of the grape were established with the supercheap, sickeningly sweet jug wines from Germany that they guzzled in the 1970s and '80s. But basing riesling's reputation on those wines is like giving someone a McDonald's hamburger as their first and only reference to beef.

The truth is that riesling—even top-quality riesling—can indeed be very sweet. It can also be bone-dry. And to make things even more confusing, it can also land anywhere in between. The difference with higher-quality rieslings is that their sweetness comes from the natural ripeness of the grapes (as opposed to added sugar) and that it is expertly counterbalanced with an invigorating shock of acidity. This gives the best sweetish rieslings a yin-yang of sweet-and-sour—kind of like a glass of freshly squeezed lemonade. In addition to regular wines, riesling also makes some killer sparkling wines, as well as some of the most acclaimed dessert wines made.

MOST NOTABLE VERSIONS

Germany

Germany is riesling's mecca. No other country is as obsessed with the grape, or can offer such a breadth of variation. German labels are notoriously cryptic, but actually the most informative to the educated eye. In stereotypical fashion, Germans created an intricate (and very intimidating to pronounce) system of classifications for their national treasure, based on levels of ripeness. Your best bet when shopping for any riesling, especially from Germany, is to enlist the help of an expert who's familiar with the wine. He or she can help you understand the label and know what style of wine is in the bottle.

Alsace, France

Another place where the grape finds respect is the tiny wine region of Alsace, France. The Vosges Mountains to the west keep this stunningly beautiful place nice and dry. The northern location and an abundance of sunshine make for a long, steady growing season, producing mostly dry rieslings with slightly more body than their German neighbors.

Austria

When I think of the best Austrian rieslings, I think of refreshingly dry, stony, pure wines with lovely green and yellow fruit flavors. Typically, these have higher alcohol and more power than Germany's rieslings.

Australia

Australia's signature rieslings, most notably from the Eden and Clare Valleys, are ultradry and crisp, with a distinctive lime kick and an elegant mineral edge.

RECOMMENDATIONS

Dry

$

- **Frankland Estate "Rocky Gully" riesling** / *Great Southern, Australia*
- **Pacific Rim "dry" riesling** / *Columbia Valley, Washington state*
- **Peter Lehmann riesling** / *Eden Valley, Australia*
- **Robert Weil "Estate Dry" riesling** / *Rheingau, Germany*

$$

- **Graf Hardegg vom Schloss** / *Niederösterreich, Austria*
- **Kuentz-Bas riesling** / *Alsace, France*
- **Mesh riesling** / *Eden Valley, Australia*

$$$

- **Pewsey Vale Vineyard "The Contours" riesling** / *Eden Valley, South Australia*
- **Selbach-Oster "Zeltinger Schlossberg" spätlese riesling** / *Mosel-Saar-Ruwer, Germany*
- **Smith Madrone riesling** / *Napa Valley, California*

$$$$

- **Domaine Albert Boxler riesling "E" Sommerberg** / *Alsace, France*
- **Dönnhoff "Oberhäuser Brücke" spätlese riesling** / *Nahe, Germany*
- **Paulett Wines "Aged Release Polish Hill River" riesling** / *Clare Valley, Australia*

Off-Dry (Just a Hint of Sweetness)

$

- Dr. Loosen "Dr. L" riesling
  / Mosel-Saar-Ruwer, Germany
- Charles Smith "Kung Fu Girl" riesling
  / Columbia Valley, Washington state
- Hogue riesling
  / Columbia Valley, Washington state
- Willamette Valley Vineyards riesling
  / Willamette Valley, Oregon

$$

- Chateau Ste. Michelle Winery-Dr. Loosen "Eroica" riesling
  / Columbia Valley, Washington state
- Dr. Konstantin Frank Vinifera Wine Cellars "Semi-Dry" riesling
  / Finger Lakes, New York
- Long Shadows Vintners "Poet's Leap" riesling */ Columbia Valley, Washington state*

$$$

- Dr. Pauly-Bergweiler "Wehlener Sonnenuhr" spätlese riesling
  / Mosel-Saar-Ruwer, Germany
- J.J. Prum "Graacher Himmelreich" auslese riesling */ Mosel-Saar-Ruwer, Germany*
- Maximin Grünhäuser "Abtsberg" spätlese riesling */ Mosel-Saar-Ruwer, Germany*

$$$$

- Domaine Weinbach "Cuvée Saint Catherine" riesling */ Schlossberg, Alsace, France*

OTHER GRAPES AND WINES YOU MIGHT LIKE

If you like the dry style of riesling:

» arneis
» Gavi
» grüner veltliner
» Muscadet
» torrontés
» Vinho Verde

If you like off-dry or sweeter styles:

» gewürztraminer
» moscato d'Asti
» prosecco
» semisweet Vouvray

PINOT NOIR
THE SEDUCTRESS

/ PEE-no NWHAR /

Pinot noir gets under your skin like no other grape. First, pinot lures you in with distinctive, sensual aromatics. Pinot's perfume is both savory and earthy (like a wet forest floor) and incredibly feminine (like rose petals and raspberries). Pinot's smell can, in fact, be so intoxicating that superfans of the grape often spend a great deal of time just sniffing the wine before moving on to any actual drinking. In the mouth, pinot is equally entrancing, with a unique texture. Ultrathin skins mean very little tannin in the finished wine. The result is a light, smooth, luxuriously silky mouthfeel.

Maybe another part of pinot noir's allure is that it's maddeningly hard to get right. Often called high maintenance by grape growers and winemakers, it's difficult in both the vineyard and the winery. On the vine, those preciously thin skins make pinot highly susceptible to sunburn, disease, and pests. Unlike chardonnay or cabernet sauvignon—grapes that will happily take up residence in a variety of climates—pinot noir requires very specific, cool-climate conditions to grow well. Even when the environment is perfect and the growing season has been ideal, stellar pinot noir fruit is extremely fragile once harvested, and all throughout the winemaking process. So why go to all the trouble to grow this persnickety grape? Because when it's grown with the utmost care, in the optimum environment, with near perfect weather conditions, and treated with kid gloves throughout the winemaking process, pinot noir can make some of the sexiest, most intriguing, and most beautiful wines ever.

One unfortunate truth: You'll always pay more for pinot. Because pinot noir is such a challenge, the cost for quality is higher than for other varieties. You can find really good deals on bottlings of other grapes—cabernet sauvignon, merlot, malbec, zin—at around ten dollars. But for a decent bang-for-your-buck starter pinot noir that truly showcases the finesse and aroma that make this grape special, you have to spend more like twenty-five.

MOST NOTABLE VERSIONS

Burgundy, France / BUR-gun-dee

Not every pinot noir producer on the planet aspires to make pinot that tastes like it comes from Burgundy, France, but every one of them uses it as a reference point. Burgundian-style pinot noir is earthy and typically lean in comparison with other versions from around the globe. Flavors include cranberry, pomegranate, mineral, mushroom, and wet dirt. Long considered the birthplace and the soul of pinot noir, the best red Burgundies are iconic. It seems everyone wants a taste of this lauded juice, but production is minuscule. Thus, getting your hands on great bottles of Burgundy can be a very costly endeavor. It's also tricky to navigate Burgundy's vintages. The weather varies greatly from year to year, so even the same wine from the same producer can taste drastically different each vintage. Your best bet for buying Burgundy is to establish a relationship with a wine shop that is passionate about this region, and let them guide you. Be prepared to drop some serious cash for your diligent research.

California

California produces pinot noir that is much more outgoing than the Burgundian style. More sunshine means wines that are higher in alcohol, with the accent on ripe fruit instead of earth. California pinots are likely to taste like fresh raspberry, strawberry, or cherry. The best come from the coolest parts of the state: foggy, coastal areas with big temperature shifts from day to night, and dense cloud cover that protects the grapes from the intense sun. Try wines from Carneros, Russian River Valley, Mendocino, Sonoma Coast, Monterey, and coastal Santa Barbara.

Oregon

Oregon is often commended for striking the perfect balance between Burgundy and California. It's true, the wines have fruit-driven flavors like California, but they are also earthier and more restrained in comparison. One major advantage the grape has in Oregon is focus. The area is too damp and cool to grow much else; pinot is the local superstar. Weather is variable, so vintages may show quite a bit of difference in flavor. In a good year, though, Oregon pinots come out looking like a steal. They are more elegant than other American pinots, and they are priced at a fraction of their French counterparts.

New Zealand

New Zealand, with its cool, crisp climate, is turning out to be a superb location for pinot noir. In fact, Central Otago, the epicenter of pinot on the tiny South Island, is actually the southernmost winegrowing region (and one of the chilliest) in the world. Although New Zealand is relatively new to the pinot noir scene, I've had some incredibly promising examples.

RECOMMENDATIONS

$

- Cono Sur "Vision" pinot noir */ Chile*
- DeLoach "Heritage Reserve" pinot noir */ Russian River Valley, Sonoma County, California*
- Matua Valley pinot noir */ Marlborough, New Zealand*

$$

- Belle Glos Wines "Meiomi" pinot noir */ Sonoma Coast, Sonoma County, California*
- Cambria Estate Winery "Julia's Vineyard" pinot noir */ Santa Maria Valley, California*
- Saintsbury pinot noir */ Carneros, Napa Valley, California*
- Wallace Brook Cellars pinot noir */ Willamette Valley, Oregon*

$$$

- Bethel Heights Vineyard "Estate" pinot noir */ Eola-Amity Hills, Willamette Valley, Oregon*
- Domaine Joseph Drouhin "Clos des Mouches" */ Beaune, Burgundy, France*
- Failla pinot noir */ Sonoma Coast, Sonoma County, California*
- Hamilton Russell pinot noir */ Hemel-en-Aarde Valley, South Africa*
- La Follette Wines "Sangiacomo Vineyard" pinot noir */ Sonoma Coast, Sonoma County, California*
- Talley Estate pinot noir */ Arroyo Grande Valley, California*
- WillaKenzie Estate "Aliette" pinot noir */ Willamette Valley, Oregon*

$$$$

- Bergström Wines "Bergström Vineyard" pinot noir */ Willamette Valley, Oregon*
- Domaine Joseph Drouhin "Les Proces" */ Nuits-St.-Georges, Burgundy, France*
- Domaine Mongeard-Mugneret "Suchots" */ Vosne-Romanée, Burgundy, France*
- Hanzell Vineyards pinot noir */ Sonoma County, California*
- Shea Wine Cellars and Vineyard "Homer" pinot noir */ Willamette Valley, Oregon*
- ZD Wines reserve pinot noir */ Carneros, Napa Valley, California*

OTHER GRAPES AND WINES YOU MIGHT LIKE

» barbera
» Beaujolais
» grenache
» Valpolicella

ASSIGNMENT:

PINOT NOIR

Check out "Best of Pinot Noir," page 185, for a homework six-pack. These six wines are a great way to begin experimenting with the grape.

CABERNET SAUVIGNON
THE KING

/ cab-ur-NAY so-vin-YAWN /

Cabernet sauvignon is the undisputed king of grapes, its respect and adoration won during centuries of top performance in the vineyard, the winery, and the bottle. Cabernet's birthplace, and the place that launched it into celebrity, is Bordeaux, France, where the grape produces its most celebrated, most collected wines. But cabernet has never been content to rest on its French laurels. The grape has traveled well and is capable of making both good-value and premium-quality wine in most winegrowing regions.

Cabernet has been eagerly cultivated for many reasons. For one, it's a hearty, reliable crop. It has good disease and pest resistance, and thrives in a variety of climates and soils. Australia, South Africa, Chile, Argentina, Washington state, New Zealand, and Italy are all capable of producing beautiful cabernet, but Bordeaux and Napa are the grape's most important environs. Cabernet is also the most recognized grape in the world, which makes it easier to sell than lesser-known varieties. Familiarity, especially in the daunting domain of wine, is half the battle when it comes to marketing. Another part of cabernet's allure is that it endures. Not all cabernet is ageworthy, but many of the best bottles are built to persist, and improve, over decades; that in itself is the stuff wine legend is built on.

The most important factor in cabernet's rise to stardom, however, more important than anything else, is that people just like the way it tastes. To start with, tannin almost always has a commanding presence in wines made from cabernet sauvignon. The most iconic cabs are broad-shouldered, with a massive, powerful structure on which succulent fruit hangs. The fruit is usually the black kind—black currants, blackberries, black cherry—and is incrementally riper the more sunshine the grapes receive. Other common aromas and flavors include cocoa, cedar, leather, cigar box or tobacco, and mint. Most cabs also spend some time in oak barrels, which can add cedar and vanilla. There's a complexity to cabs that makes them interesting. Even simple versions typically have more going on than other wines at a similar price, and the best examples are downright intriguing, changing much over the course of years, or even just dinner.

The Other Cabernet: Cabernet Franc

There are two important cabernets: cabernet sauvignon and its less-loved little brother, cabernet franc. You don't often see cabernet franc bottled alone. (The Loire Valley in France is home to a few exceptions, most notably the minerally reds from the town of Chinon.) Typically, cabernet franc is blended with cabernet sauvignon and/or merlot to add tannin, acidity, or aroma (cabernet franc can smell like violets, green pepper, and coffee). When you hear people say "cab" or "cabernet" you can bet they are referring to the more famous, more highly acclaimed cabernet sauvignon.

MOST NOTABLE VERSIONS

Bordeaux / bor-DOE

The Gironde is the massive estuary at the conjunction of the Dordogne and Garonne rivers that leads straight through the heart of Bordeaux to the Atlantic Ocean. This body of water is special because it divides more than just geography; it is the defining line between the two main types of red wine made in this part of France. The left bank, or west side of the estuary, is considered the spiritual home of cabernet sauvignon. (Merlot dominates plantings on the right bank.) Left bank red wines are always rooted in cabernet sauvignon (typically 70 to 80 percent), but usually contain a large percentage of merlot, and can also include three other grapes: cabernet franc, petit verdot, and malbec. These are added to a much lesser extent, and sometimes not at all. You can find cabernet from Bordeaux for ten dollars, a thousand dollars, and everything in between. No matter the price point, though, it is typically staunch and earthy compared with cabernet sauvignon from other areas. Quintessential cabernet sauvignon from Bordeaux has more acidity, more tannin, and showcases more of the slightly underripe flavors of this grape: mint, tobacco leaf, and bell pepper.

BORDEAUX'S MOST MYTHICAL WINES

In 1855, Bordeaux needed a classification system for its best wines; they were to be on display that year at the Exposition of Paris. Wine brokers ranked the wines according to a chateau's reputation and the current trading price, which at that time was directly related to quality. Four Bordeaux estates were classified as "first-growth chateaus," or top-rated wineries. Although the list has gone relatively unchanged and unchallenged since its inception, one winery has been elevated from a second growth to a first growth. The top five estates, which fetch the highest prices in Bordeaux and enjoy royal-like status, are Château Mouton Rothschild, Château Lafite Rothschild, Château Margaux, Château Latour, and Château Haut-Brion.

Napa Valley

Excellent cabernet is grown all over the state of California, but no one does it like Napa. The tiny valley, for all its fame, only produces about 4 percent of California's total wine, the majority of it premium cabernet sauvignon. Napa cabernet, and American cabernet in general, is more round and supple than cab from Bordeaux. Higher alcohol and rich, rounded tannin is complemented by ripe black fruit, sometimes leaning toward jam and chocolate. Mountain fruit (wines made from fruit grown on, for example, Napa's Spring, Diamond, or Howell Mountains) can be more muscular and less fruity than fruit from the valley floor, where nutrients and water are abundant.

RECOMMENDATIONS

$

- Avalon Winery cabernet sauvignon / *Napa Valley, California*
- Columbia Crest "H3" cabernet sauvignon / *Horse Heaven Hills, Washington state*
- Lyeth Estate "L de Lyeth" cabernet sauvignon / *Sonoma County, California*

$$

- Château Aney Haut-Medoc / *Bordeaux, France*
- Château de Chantegrive Graves / *Bordeaux, France*
- Liberty School cabernet sauvignon / *Paso Robles, California*
- Santa Rita "Medella Real" cabernet sauvignon / *Maipo Valley, Chile*
- Simi Winery cabernet sauvignon / *Alexander Valley, Sonoma County, California*

$$$

- Château Haut-Beausejour Saint-Estèphe / *Bordeaux, France*
- Gundlach Bundschu Winery "Mountain Cuvee" / *Sonoma Valley, California*
- Hall Winery cabernet sauvignon / *Napa Valley, California*
- Heitz Cellar cabernet sauvignon / *Napa Valley, California*
- Oberon cabernet sauvignon / *Napa Valley, California*
- Rustenberg Wines "John X Merriman" / *Stellenbosch, South Africa*
- Vasse Felix cabernet sauvignon / *Margaret River, Australia*

$$$$

- Château Cos d'Estournel "Les Pagodes de Cos" Saint-Estèphe / *Bordeaux, France*
- Château Haut-Bailly Pessac-Léognan / *Bordeaux, France*
- Larkmead Vineyards cabernet sauvignon / *Napa Valley, California*
- Nickel & Nickel Winery "John C. Sullenger Vineyard" cabernet sauvignon / *Oakville, Napa Valley, California*
- Paradigm Winery cabernet sauvignon / *Oakville, Napa Valley, California*
- Spring Mountain Vineyard "Elivette" / *Spring Mountain District, Napa Valley, California*
- Stag's Leap Wine Cellars "S.L.V." / *Stags Leap District, Napa Valley, California*

OTHER GRAPES AND WINES YOU MIGHT LIKE

» Bandol
» Barbaresco and Barolo
» brunello di Montalcino
» cabernet franc
» carménère
» Cornas
» Portuguese dry red wines
» Priorat
» Ribera del Duero
» Taurasi

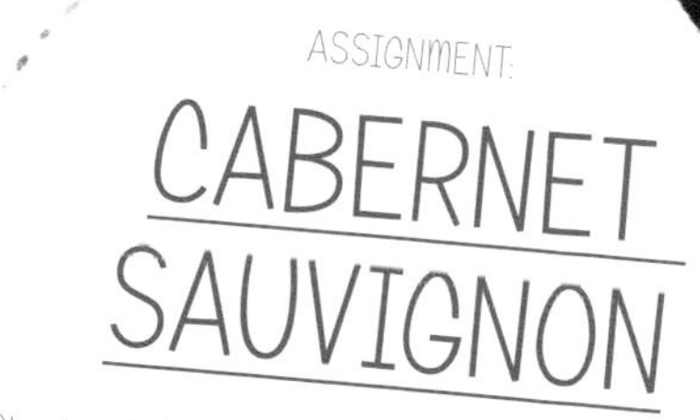

ASSIGNMENT:

CABERNET SAUVIGNON

Check out "Best of Cabernet Sauvignon," page 185, for a homework six-pack. These six wines are a great way to begin experimenting with the grape.

MERLOT
THE WALLFLOWER

/ mer-LOW /

In its best form, merlot can make delicious red wines; they can be plummy, with a deep, velvety texture, and aromas of blackberry, blueberry, violets, and sometimes smoke and mineral. It hasn't the tannic structure of cabernet sauvignon, nor the acidity, so it comes off as softer and easier to drink. The problem with merlot, and the reason why it has come under such scrutiny, is that it is rarely great. Often, the grape is lackadaisically made into easily drinkable but dull, flabby, inconsequential wine.

Pure single-varietal merlot wines are an anomaly. More often than not, merlot—even the best examples—needs some structural help, and usually finds it in the form of cabernet sauvignon and/or cabernet franc. When it is blended with one or more of the cabernets, merlot is often described as providing the "flesh" of the wine, while the cabernets give the wine its "bones."

MOST NOTABLE VERSIONS

Bordeaux / bor-DOE

The east side of Bordeaux's mighty Gironde estuary, the right bank, is a merlot sanctuary. Clay and limestone soils give birth to much mediocre merlot, but some is destined for excellence. Pomerol and Saint-Émilion are the two most prestigious regions. In good vintages, and from the best sites, merlot from here can achieve its highest potential. Wines like Château Pétrus (from Pomerol) can have captivating complexity and texture. Unfortunately, they usually come with an equally surreal price tag.

California

California's best merlots grow up next door to cabernet sauvignon in Napa. Much less merlot is grown in Napa, but what is grown is taken seriously and given similar, if not equal, treatment to cabernet. Most merlot from Napa and other parts of California is blended with some cabernet sauvignon, and will taste less earthy than French versions, showcasing ripe black fruits, juicy plums, higher alcohol, and a supple body.

Washington State

Like cabernet sauvignon and syrah, merlot has found a happy home in Washington state. As with the other grapes, Washington tends to capture the best of both worlds in merlot by combining the opulent fruitiness of the New World with more of an Old World–like structure. This is a region to watch if you are a merlot lover.

Did You Know? The name *merlot* comes from an old French word meaning "little blackbird." This title was probably given to the grape because its skins have a dark bluish black color.

Italy

Though certainly not considered a traditional Italian grape, merlot is producing some beautiful wines in Italy, from central Italy (Tuscany) and the very northeastern tip of the country (Friuli) as well as some breakout regions in the southern part of the country (Lazio) and (Campania).

RECOMMENDATIONS

$

- **Red Diamond Winery merlot** / *Washington state*
- **Snoqualmie Vineyards merlot** / *Columbia Valley, Washington state*

$$

- **Château Cap di Faugères Côtes de Castillon** / *Bordeaux, France*
- **Esprit de Pavie** / *Bordeaux, France*
- **L'Ecole No. 41 merlot** / *Columbia Valley, Washington state*
- **Swanson Vineyards and Winery merlot** / *Oakville, Napa Valley, California*

$$$

- **Barnett Vineyards merlot** / *Spring Mountain District, Napa Valley, California*
- **Blackbird Vineyards "Arise"** / *Napa Valley, California*
- **Falesco "Montiano"** / *Lazio, Italy*
- **Whitehall Lane Winery merlot** / *Napa Valley, California*

$$$$

- **Andrew Will Winery "Ciel du Cheval"** / *Yakima Valley, Washington state*
- **Avignonesi "Desiderio"** / *Cortona, Tuscany, Italy*
- **Château Bellevue** / *Saint-Émilion, Bordeaux, France*
- **Shafer Vineyards merlot** / *Napa Valley, California*

OTHER GRAPES AND WINES YOU MIGHT LIKE

» cabernet sauvignon
» carménère
» dolcetto
» Jumilla
» malbec

SANGIOVESE
THE ITALIAN ALL-STAR

/ san-gee-oh-VAZE-ee /

Wine is an inescapable part of Italian culture. It seems every nook and cranny of the country is planted with vines, and there are an astonishing two thousand-something documented native grape varieties growing there. Little bitty Italy is the world's second largest producer of wine, and the number-one consumer per capita. On average, Italians drink around seventy liters of wine each annually (about six times as much as Americans). But even with all this wine, there is one clear all-star: sangiovese.

Sangiovese is ancient. Its name literally translates to "blood of Jove," leading historians to suspect that it predates the Etruscans. Although Tuscany has long been considered its home, and is the region that produces the most regal examples of this grape, sangiovese has traveled to almost every corner of Italy. Today, more than 10 percent of Italy's vineyards are planted to the grape, and a huge range of flavors and quality exists.

What you'll always find in sangiovese, no matter where in Italy it's grown, is bright, tangy acidity and the flavors of dusty earth, saddle leather, and dried sour cherries.

Sangiovese and Its Many Monikers

Because sangiovese has made itself at home in vineyards all over Italy, it has inherited a litany of regionally specific nicknames, the most prominent being brunello, prugnolo gentile, morellino, nielluccio, sanvicetro, and sangioveto. The nicknames probably emerged because sangiovese has a tendency to mutate easily. That is, it adapts to its environment. This subtle morphing means that over time, sangiovese has taken on slightly different attributes (like thicker or thinner skins) depending on where it grows.

MOST NOTABLE VERSIONS

brunello di Montalcino / brew-NELL-oh dee mon-tall-CHEE-no

One of Italy's most esteemed wines, brunello di Montalcino is grown outside the charming Tuscan town of Montalcino and is always 100 percent sangiovese. *Brunello* literally means "little dark one"; the brunello clone of sangiovese is especially dark and rich. When this clone is planted in Montalcino's particularly warm, dry climate and the wine is subjected to the region's requirements for extended aging, it produces a powerful, stately version of sangiovese with more tannin, color, body, and richness than you'll find anywhere else. Brunello di Montalcino offers ripe fruit flavors, as well as complex aromas of chocolate and violets. It is expensive and can age well for several decades.

Some wine experts assert that great brunello does not even start to hit its stride until it's been in the bottle for at least ten years.

Rosso di Montalcino / ROW-so dee mon-tall-CHEE-no

If brunello di Montalcino sounds delicious, but you're on a budget, try Rosso di Montalcino, a younger, less prestigious wine made in a similar style. Like brunello, this wine is made from 100 percent sangiovese grapes and comes from the same town. The main difference is that Rosso di Montalcino wines are generally made from slightly less than exceptional grapes (the B team, if you will) and not aged nearly as long before release. These "baby brunellos," as they are affectionately called, are lighter, fresher, and do not have the aging ability that their big brothers do. But they're also usually about half the price.

Chianti / kee-AHN-tee

Chianti is no doubt Italy's most famous wine. In this region, sangiovese has no nickname—it is actually called sangiovese—and it makes up 80 to 100 percent of the blend. (Today's Chianti rules allow a handful of other indigenous grapes as well as cabernet sauvignon and merlot.) Although there is a very large range in quality, in general, most Chiantis are medium-bodied, with tangy acidity and dry tannin. Chianti Classico is a designation in which, by law, the grapes must come from the heart of the region. In good vintages, most producers make a *riserva*, or reserve, bottling. These are from the producer's best grapes, have a fuller body, and are aged longer before release.

morellino di Scansano / more-ah-LEE-no dee scahn-SAH-no

A dry, fragrant and youthful version of sangiovese can be found as morellino (the local nickname) di Scansano (from the town of Scansano). Many people think that the nickname morellino was derived from the Italian word *morello*, or "brown," a reference to the traditionally brown color of the Maremmano horses that also hail from this coastal Tuscan region. Alternatively, some think the name may have come from an association with the morello cherry, an almost inky-red cherry with tartness and acidity that is reminiscent of these wines. Typically, morellino di Scansano wines are good values.

Vino Nobile di Montepulciano / VEE-no NO-bee-lay dee mon-the-pull-chee-AH-no

The "Noble Wine" of Montepulciano is one of Italy's oldest documented wines. It was named "noble" because it was apparently a favorite of the noblemen of the seventeenth century. The sangiovese clone used for this wine is prugnolo gentile, and it usually makes up 80 to 100 percent of the blend. At its best, Vino Nobile is worthy of its name, and tastes like bright red fruit, plums, and toasty oak.

Did You Know? The *gallo nero* (black rooster) emblem you see adorning the neck of many Chianti Classico bottles is the symbol for the Consorzio del Vino Chianti Classico, an organization of producers formed to promote quality and awareness of the region. Theoretically, the mark should be an indication of supreme quality; in reality, it's not a guarantee.

RECOMMENDATIONS

$

- Badia a Coltibuono "Cetamura" Chianti */ Tuscany, Italy*
- Di Majo Norante sangiovese Terre degli Osci */ Molise, Italy*
- Erik Banti morellino di Scansano */ Tuscany, Italy*
- La Velona Rosso di Montalcino */ Tuscany, Italy*

$$

- Castellare Chianti Classico */ Tuscany, Italy*
- Castello di Abola Chianti Classico */ Tuscany, Italy*
- Frescobaldi "Nipozzano" riserva Chianti Rufina */ Tuscany, Italy*
- La Mozza I Perazzi morellino di Scansano */ Tuscany, Italy*
- Mocali Rosso di Montalcino */ Tuscany, Italy*

$$$

- Altesino Rosso di Montalcino */ Tuscany, Italy*
- Badia a Coltibuono riserva Chianti Classico */ Tuscany, Italy*
- Castello di Monsanto riserva Chianti Classico */ Tuscany, Italy*

$$$$

- Il Poggione riserva brunello di Montalcino */ Tuscany, Italy*
- Poggio Antico brunello di Montalcino */ Tuscany, Italy*
- Poliziano Vino Nobile di Montepulicano */ Tuscany, Italy*
- Ricasoli "Castello di Brolio" Chianti Classico */ Tuscany, Italy*

OTHER GRAPES AND WINES YOU MIGHT LIKE

» barbera
» dolcetto
» pinot noir
» red Rioja
» Valpolicella

ZINFANDEL
THE GOOD-TIME GRAPE

/ ZIN-fan-del /

Zinfandel is jolly. It is a grape that makes unapologetically full-throttle wines that are high in alcohol and rich with color, fruit, and life. Zinfandel is big and exuberant, and never too serious or stuffy. Even the most venerated versions of the grape would never be called graceful; rather, their charm is that they seem to surge with joyfulness and an indulgent hedonism. Along with warm spices like black pepper, clove, and sandalwood, the ripest fruit flavors—raisins, prunes, and blackberries bursting with juice—are what zinfandel is all about.

Zinfandel is less aristocratic than the other grapes in this chapter—it lacks a regal pedigree. In fact, up until very recently, it was considered California's bastard grape. Zinfandel was everywhere (it accounts for about 10 percent of the state's planted acres) but nobody knew where it had come from. Recent DNA studies have proved that it is genetically identical to Italy's primitivo grape and also a grape from Croatia, crljenak kaštelanski (tsurl-YEN-ak kash-tel-AHN-ski). Try saying that three times fast. So now it has a bit of ancestry, albeit obscure.

The antielitist grape comes with a bonus—its antielitist price. With a couple of outrageous exceptions (seriously, like two), most zinfandels are very reasonably priced, and even the best almost never top fifty dollars.

MOST NOTABLE VERSIONS

Not only is Zinfandel distinctly American but it is distinctly Californian, and finds its most happy habitats in the warmest corners of the state.

Sonoma County

The northern and most inland areas of Sonoma County are the ones known for producing exceptional zinfandel. Away from coastal fog, Dry Creek and Sonoma Valleys are the appellations most identified with the grape. In Sonoma's rural landscape, zinfandel grows extra brawny alongside apricot, peach, prune, and olive orchards.

Napa Valley

Napa is colossally partial to cabernet sauvignon, but you can find tiny pockets of zinfandel grown in most of its appellations. Zinfandel grown in Napa tends to be more expensive than Sonoma, and something about the Napa terroir brings out the grape's chocolaty character.

Paso Robles

Paso Robles is serious about zinfandel. The city has even been hosting an annual festival celebrating the grape for more than twenty years. Paso zin is intense, bold, and spicy.

Sierra Foothills

Due to vast elevation differences and growing conditions, a range of zinfandel styles are produced within this rugged appellation. Some are over-the-top fruit versions, while others are a bit more cabernet-like, with lots of tannin.

RECOMMENDATIONS

$

- **Bogle Vineyards "Old Vines" zinfandel** */ Sierra Foothills, California*
- **Cline Cellars "Ancient Vines" zinfandel** */ Sonoma County, California*
- **Lake Sonoma Winery zinfandel** */ Dry Creek Valley, Sonoma County, California*

$$

- **Murphy-Goode Winery "Liar's Dice" zinfandel** */ Sonoma County, California*
- **Quivira Vineyards and Winery zinfandel** */ Dry Creek Valley, Sonoma County, California*
- **Seghesio Family Vineyards zinfandel** */ Sonoma County, California*

$$$

- **Brown Estate zinfandel** */ Napa Valley, California*
- **Elyse Winery "Morisoli Vineyard" zinfandel** */ Rutherford, Napa Valley, California*
- **Grgich Hills Estate zinfandel** */ Napa Valley, California*
- **Hendry "Block 28" zinfandel** */ Napa Valley, California*
- **Ridge Vineyards zinfandel** */ Paso Robles, California*

OTHER GRAPES AND WINES YOU MIGHT LIKE

» Amarone
» Jumilla
» malbec
» nero d'Avola
» petite sirah
» primitivo
» syrah/shiraz
» Taurasi

SYRAH

THE DARK AND MYSTERIOUS ONE

/ sih-RAH /

Syrah is a grape capable of making complex, substantial, and sophisticated wines. At their best, the wines can be sinewy and powerful yet generously warm and round, with a rainbow of bold flavors: leather, black and blue fruit, smoke, tar, roasted meats, pepper, and spice. Syrah's origins are somewhat shrouded. Some believe the grape was brought to France from the region that is modern-day Iran as early as 600 B.C., while others remain adamant that it is native to France. Either way, the grape's heartland is inarguably France's Rhône Valley, and it is now also well established in Australia and North America. George Saintsbury, British scholar and wine critic, once remarked, "Syrah is the manliest wine I've ever drunk." I agree. Syrah is a burly, rugged sort of manly, and decidedly not for the faint of heart.

SYRAH = SHIRAZ Syrah and shiraz are exactly the same grape. When the French traveled to South Africa in the 1700s, syrah was one of the grapes they brought with them. In Africa, the grape was renamed "shiraz." Later, this same grape was taken from South Africa to Australia and the Aussies kept the shiraz name. Typically, it is called syrah in North America. Occasionally you may see a wine from California or Washington state that is labeled *shiraz*. Generally you can expect these to be made in an ultra-jammy Australian style.

SYRAH ≠ PETITE SIRAH For many years, people were confused about the exact relationship between syrah and petite sirah. Consumers had a tendency to get them mixed up, and for justifiable reason: Both grapes have the capacity to make massive, bold wines with lots of fruit and spice. Through extensive DNA research at the University of California, Davis, one of the most prestigious schools of viticulture, scientists discovered that the grape we call petite sirah, most often found in California and South America, is actually durif, an ancient French variety. Accounts of durif date back to around 1870 in the Rhône Valley of France, and show that this grape was a crossing (or cross-pollination) of syrah and another Rhône grape, peloursin. Petite sirah does not have the regality that syrah does, but it remains relatively important in both North and South America, where it produces fairly tannic, well-colored, sturdy wines. Petite sirah is often used to give a little oomph to less-than-oomphy zinfandel, cabernet sauvignon, and even pinot noir.

MOST NOTABLE VERSIONS

Northern Rhône Valley, France

In the menacingly steep hillsides of the Northern Rhône, where it would be too cold to grow this grape if not for the southeastern-facing slopes, syrah reaches its most dramatic potential. The wines from the appellations of Côte Rôtie (literally "roasted slope") and Hermitage are ageworthy wines that are usually made up of 100 percent syrah, although winemakers there sometimes add a tiny bit of white wine in the blend for added fragrance and complexity. Tastewise, syrah from the Rhône Valley has lots of tannin and a serious gamy, leathery grip. Cornas is a lesser known Rhône appellation, comprising 100 percent syrah, which is typically a great value; it has all the smoky, rough-hewn meat-like taste of Côte Rôtie and Hermitage—at about half the price.

Australia

Syrah is called *shiraz* here and pronounced "SHEEEE-raz," with a thick Australian accent. Many people associate Australia's version of the grape with the mass-produced, lackluster wines of huge corporations, but more and more small-production, hand-crafted wines are now being imported into the United States. The best accentuate the grape's warm blueberry jam, chocolate, and spice character.

California

Although syrah grows contentedly all over California, it is defining an especially compelling niche in the viticultural areas of the middle and southern Central Coast. In the late 1980s, a visionary group of winemakers calling themselves the Rhône Rangers set out to plant Rhône varietals (namely syrah, grenache, mourvèdre, and viognier) in this area. Paso Robles, Edna Valley, Arroyo Grande Valley, Santa Maria Valley, and Santa Ynez Valley are all Central Coast homes to syrah, a grape that is helping to call more attention to these appellations.

Washington State

Washington syrahs may be somewhat new, but recent vintages show immense promise. The best are intense, with a dark core of fruit and a lovely mineral component. They are undoubtedly American in taste, but somehow demonstrate more grace than many of their California cousins.

RECOMMENDATIONS FOR SYRAH AND SYRAH-BASED WINES

$

- Andrew Murray Vineyards "Tours les Jours" syrah */ Central Coast, California*
- d'Arenberg "Stump Jump" shiraz */ McLarenvale, Australia*
- Perrin et Fils reserve Côtes du Rhône */ Rhône Valley, France*
- Qupé syrah */ Central Coast, California*
- Saint Cosme Côtes du Rhône */ Rhône Valley, France*

$$

- Charles Smith Wines "Boom Boom" syrah */ Columbia Valley, Washington state*
- Jim Barry Wines "The Lodge Hill" shiraz */ Clare Valley, Australia*
- Thorne Clark Wines "Shotfire" shiraz */ Barossa Valley, South Australia*

$$$

- Jaffurs Wine Cellars syrah */ Santa Barbara County, California*
- Margerum Wine Company "M5" */ Santa Barbara County, California*
- Owen Rowe "Ex Umbris" syrah */ Columbia Valley, Washington state*

$$$$

- Alain Voge "Vieilles Vignes" */ Cornas, Rhône Valley, France*
- E. Guigal "Chateau D'Ampuis" */ Côte Rôtie, Rhône Valley, France*
- Tablas Creek Vineyard "Esprit de Beaucastel Rouge" */ Paso Robles, California*

OTHER GRAPES AND WINES YOU MIGHT LIKE

» petite sirah
» pinotage
» Priorat
» Ribera del Duero
» Taurasi
» zinfandel

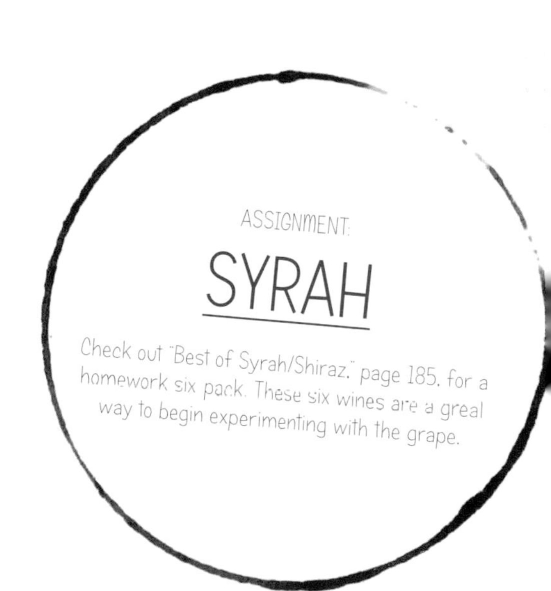

Take Care and Always Share

You've studied and shopped and, like a proud new parent, brought your new treasures home to settle in. The only thing left to do is to start cracking bottles and to begin integrating wine into your daily life. As you do, you'll certainly have questions. Where should special bottles be stored? How long can I age a wine? How long does a bottle stay good after I open it? What's the easiest way to open a bottle, and how do I get it open if I don't have a corkscrew? (Hint: where there's a will, there's a way.) How do I know how much wine to buy for a party? What are some creative ideas for wine gifts? This chapter is filled with practical, applicable everyday wine advice—stuff you can really use.

TAKE GOOD CARE OF YOUR BABIES

There are entire books dedicated to caring for wine, but the honest truth is, most of the time, it's not that important; nowadays, our wine is long gone before there's a chance that anything could happen to it. (Studies have shown that in the United States, the average time between the purchase of a bottle of wine and consumption of that bottle is around four hours!) If you buy a bottle and plan to drink it within hours or days, you don't have to worry too much about where and how you store it. Just remember not to let it get too hot and you'll be fine. However, if you've got a special bottle in your possession—one that you plan on keeping for a while—how you tend to it is crucial to how the wine will taste when you open it.

WHAT WINE NEEDS

Most important, wine needs a consistently cool temperature. Wine scientists have discovered that 55 degrees Fahrenheit is the ideal temperature for long-term storage (longer than a few months). Temperatures substantially warmer than that can lead to a premature demise, and temperatures a lot cooler can retard the wine's evolution. Wine also needs to hibernate in a cozy, dark, and still place. Heat, light, and vibration can all do damage. Last, humidity is important to consider when storing wines with corks. Over time, a dry cork gets porous and lets too much air leak in. Keep the inner end of a cork moist and supple by laying the bottle on its side. Keep the outer end moist by storing it in a location with at least 65 to 75 percent humidity.

LONG-TERM STORAGE

55°F

TEMPERATURE

65–75%

HUMIDITY

Obviously, underground wine cellars, basements, and wine refrigerators are all ideal for long-term wine storage. If you don't have access to a dark underground hole and don't want to spring for an expensive wine refrigerator, the next best option is to store your wines on their side at the bottom of an interior-walled closet. It's not glamorous, but it takes care of most of the requirements, and your wines will thank you by tasting delicious.

WHY NOT THE TRUSTY FRIDGE? Your fridge might seem like a good place to keep wine—after all, it's cold and dark in there, right? Although the fridge takes care of light and heat, its cold is too cold for long-term aging, and the lack of humidity that does wonders for your produce will likely dry out your corks. The fridge is fine for a week or so; if you're keeping a bottle longer than that, store it elsewhere.

HEAT DAMAGE

Cooked is slang for a bottle that's been damaged by heat, the most widespread and common form of wine abuse. It doesn't take long for heat to take its toll on wine, and the temperatures don't have to be extreme either. Sadly, in the time between when a wine is bottled and when it hits your lips, there are many opportunities for heat to harm it. Wine is vulnerable when it's still at the winery, on shipping containers traveling across the ocean, on delivery trucks, in distributor warehouses, at wine shops, in restaurants, and once it's home with you. Following is a list of what higher temperatures over an extended period of time, or repeated temperature variation, can do.

1. Higher temperatures can increase the wine's aging rate. It might sound desirable, but speedy wine aging is not a good thing. It simply means your wine is going to die faster, without the delectable side benefit of tertiary aromas and flavors that can only develop over a long period of slow, steady aging. Some things just take time.

2. Thermal expansion may cause the cork to push up from the bottle and wine to leak from the top. When opening a bottle of wine, if a track of wine is visible along the length of the cork or at the top of the cork, or the cork is partially pushed out of the bottle, it has most likely been heat damaged.

3. Heat-damaged wines often become prematurely oxidized, making them taste old and flat. As you now know, a tiny amount of oxygen exchange does occur with natural cork over an extended time period. Repeated temperature variation, however, can vary the pressure differential between the inside and outside of the bottle so much that it can actually pump air into the bottle, causing premature oxidation. Oxidized red wines may take on an orangey brick color; white wines a dark yellowish brown hue.

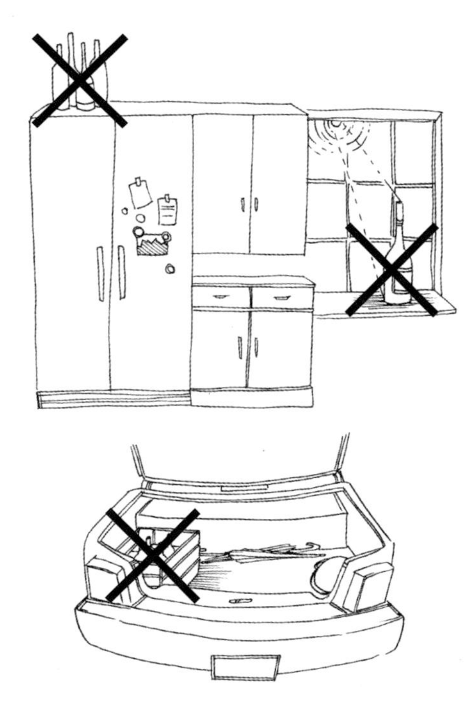

WINE'S LIFELINE

How long do you age wine? There's no short answer to this common question; following are just the most important factors to consider.

PRICE

If the wine costs less than twenty-five dollars or so, forget aging it altogether—just drink that baby. The number-one determinant of longevity is quality. You've got to start with good ingredients. As you already know, high price does not always mean high quality, but you should still count low-priced wines out; they are not meant for long-term cellaring.

This does not mean that all expensive wine has the capacity to taste good in ten or twenty years. The truth is, less and less wine is being made with the intention of aging. Winemakers know that consumers are impatient and want what they want *now*. So instead of designing wines for long-term cellaring, they are using a variety of winemaking techniques and farming practices to create wines that are ripe, lush, and friendly right out of the gate. The point is that more and more wines don't require any aging at all. They are meant to be consumed immediately.

STORAGE CONDITIONS

If you have been bad, and your special bottle of wine has been sitting somewhere I would disapprove of—on top of the fridge or radiator, on the kitchen windowsill, or in the trunk of your car—drink it now. I won't reprimand you. Fine wine neglect is punishment enough in itself, as you'll likely discover when you open the bottle. If you've been good, though, storing your fine wines properly, you can keep them longer. Optimally, time and the right conditions equal complexity and a seamless integration of flavors.

HOW YOU LIKE IT

Your taste buds rule, really. No matter what the experts say, how you like your wine (just like how you like your coffee or your kisses) is the ultimate indicator of your level of enjoyment. If you appreciate more subtlety and delicacy in your wines, wait a little longer to drink them. Time softens tannin, fades fruit, and introduces more earthy secondary flavors and aromas. If you like more everything in your wine—power, structure, grip, fruit—drink your wines when they are young.

GENERAL RULE FOR AGING FINE WINE

UP TO **10** YEARS FOR REDS

UP TO **5** YEARS FOR WHITES

POPPING PERFECTION

There is no magic date to open a bottle, but that's part of wine's allure. It's always changing and it keeps you guessing. The most qualified people to recommend a particular wine's peak date are the people who know it best: the winemakers who have a long history of tasting many vintages of the same wine. They can most accurately predict how a wine will change over time, based on their years of experience with and intimate relationship to that wine. (Almost all wineries have winemaker's tasting notes on their websites.) But even experts get surprised. I can't tell you how many times a wine or even a whole vintage of wines from a region has been hailed as "terrific" or "the best" only to fall flat over time. Conversely, a wine that may have scored poorly upon release can be tasted again years later and pleasantly surprise everyone. This is the reason collectors buy a case of the same wine and try a bottle every few years. It is fascinating to study how wine evolves.

Whatever you do, don't wait too long. It is much better to err on the side of caution and drink a wine a little early than to wait with bated breath in anticipation of perfection, only to open a crusty, crunchy, expensive bottle of vinegar.

Ageworthy Wines

The very best examples of the following wines are proven graceful agers.

Whites

- rieslings from Alsace, France, and Germany
- white Burgundy
- white Bordeaux
- vintage Champagne

Reds

- Barbaresco
- Barolo
- brunello di Montalcino
- California cabernet sauvignon
- Châteauneuf-du-Pape
- Côte Rôtie
- Hermitage
- red Burgundy
- red Bordeaux

Sweet Wines

- Madeira
- Sauternes
- vintage Port

“WINE IS
BOTTLED POETRY.”

—Robert Louis Stevenson

SERVING SECRETS

TEMPERATURE

Temperature plays a substantial role in how a wine tastes. Serving a wine too cold can rob it of flavor; serving it too hot magnifies alcohol. The old adage of "red wines at room temperature" is actually faulty. It seems the advice is a holdover from about three hundred years ago, before the advent of central air, when the room temperature in dank, drafty England was much cooler. Generally speaking, red wines taste best at 60 to 65 degrees. If you don't have a basement or wine fridge, I recommend popping your red wines in the fridge for twenty minutes or so before you drink them. A red wine served at today's room temperature is bound to taste mostly of alcohol. White wines should be served a little cooler, at 50 to 55 degrees, and sparkling wines even colder, at about 45 degrees. Don't worry about getting out a thermometer, though. Just try to remember the following.

sparkling wines: ice-cold

white wines, rosés, and dessert wines: fridge cold

red wines: slightly cool to the touch

WINE ORDER

If you're seriously evaluating a flight of wines, it is best to taste them in an order—generally, lighter wines first, heavier wines last. This will ensure that your tongue doesn't get coated with a big, hefty wine that desensitizes your taste buds and leaves them limp. If you've got a lineup that includes some special or older bottles, you might want to order the wines with the best or oldest bottles last. That being said, don't stress over this. Mixing wine order is fine, too, especially when the ultimate goal is happy bellies.

Did You Know? Some people prefer light red wines slightly chilled. As an experiment, try your next bottle of Beaujolais, pinot noir, barbera, or Chianti slightly chilled (put it in the fridge for at least twenty minutes before you imbibe), and see if you agree that the descriptors "refreshing" and "crisp" are not exclusive to white wines.

OPENING A BOTTLE OF WINE

1. Remove the foil cap. Use the blade on your corkscrew or a paring knife to cut the foil just below the glass lip. Alternatively, you can also just pull off the entire foil capsule with your hands.

2. Insert the wine opener (see "A Trusty Wine Opener," page 15) and gently extract the cork.

Note: If you've got a wine with a screw cap, skip steps 1 and 2 and simply twist the top for the *ahhh* . . . snap of freshness.

OPENING A BOTTLE OF SPARKLING WINE

1. Make sure it is well chilled. Too-warm wines will explode with froth when you pop the cork.

2. Remove the foil. Carefully untwist and loosen, but do not remove the wire cage. (It will help you keep your grip on the cork.) Make sure you keep your dominant thumb on the cork.

3. Keep a cloth napkin handy. While holding your thumb on the top of the cork—and pointing that cork away from anything or anyone—wrap the rest of your fingers on your dominant hand around the body of the cork and hold it in place with gentle pressure, as you twist the bottle with your other hand. You want the cork to emerge slowly and carefully. Contrary to popular belief, a loud pop is not desirable; the sign of a properly opened bottle is a gentle sigh. *Psssst*. I love that sound.

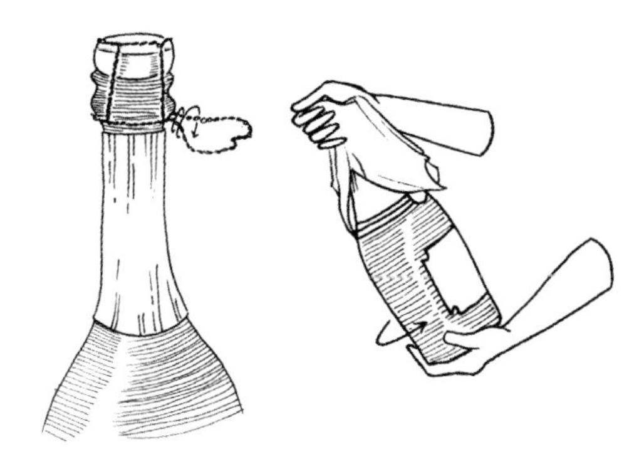

Did You Know? The average bottle of Champagne contains ninety pounds of pent-up pressure. That's why it is imperative that you not point the cork end at any person or fragile object while you're opening. You could do some major damage.

DECANTING

Oxygen can be wine's evil nemesis. But a little oxygen exposure when you first open a wine—especially a big, tannic wine—softens the wine's hard edges and makes it palate-friendly faster. Using a decanter to aerate, or let the wine breathe, is a larger-scale version of swirling wine in your glass.

It's a misbelief that simply opening a bottle and letting it sit on the counter is satisfactory to let a wine breathe. Only about a quarter-size surface area is exposed to oxygen when it sits in an open bottle. Instead, use a decanter or other wide-bottomed vessel you can easily pour out of again (a pitcher or vase will do) or pour small pours into wineglasses and start swirling.

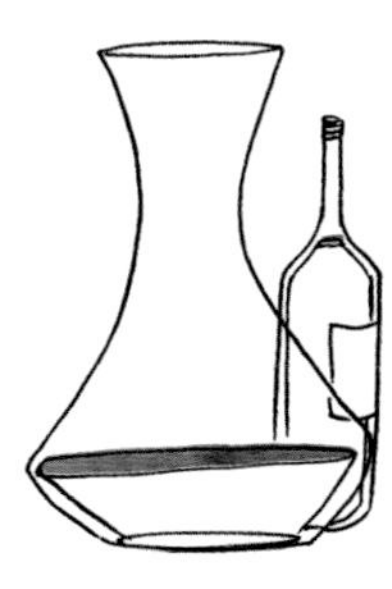

Decanting wine might seem ostentatious, a relic of a more formal time, but there are several instances when it really comes in handy.

1. An Unruly Young Red

Young red wines with brawny tannins can really benefit from a few minutes of aeration. Oxygen smooths out the rough edges of the wine, making it taste softer and more seamless when it hits your mouth. Usually about thirty minutes does the trick.

2. A Dirty Old Wine

Over the course of many years, some wines, especially those that are unfiltered, create sediment—dark floating flakes of precipitated tannin and pigment. Although consuming it is harmless, you probably don't want sediment in your glass because it tastes bitter and clouds up your wine. Grits are good; grit in your wine is not.

Separating wine from sediment is simple. Slowly, carefully, pour wine from the bottle into a decanter. Stop pouring when you start to see sediment, and toss those last few tablespoons of sediment-soaked wine out with the bottle.

3. Warming Up a Too-Cold Red

If a red wine seems a bit too chilly to drink, let it warm up in the decanter for a few minutes.

4. Foreplay

Like lighting candles and putting on just the right music, decanting can set the mood, and will typically invite veneration for a special bottle of vino.

POUR SIZE Remember, don't pour too much at once. A small serving (around 2 ounces) will do for tastings, and a half-glass pour (3 to 4 ounces) is perfect for dinners or events where people are sticking to one wine.

"WINE TO ME IS PASSION. IT'S FAMILY AND FRIENDS. IT'S WARMTH OF HEART AND GENEROSITY OF SPIRIT."

—Robert Mondavi

WINE 911

Beyond a bottle showing noticeable heat damage, oxidation, or emitting a downright rotten smell (see "Awful Aromas," page 70), there are a few other wine emergencies you will likely face at some point. Here's how to stay calm and carry on.

EMERGENCY ONE: NO CORKSCREW

Lusting over a bottle when you've got no corkscrew can induce panic. Fortunately, there are surprisingly effective alternatives to getting your bottle open.

Use Nature: Remove the foil cap and wrap the bottle in a towel, a jacket, or any other soft cloth. Gently but firmly begin to hit the bottom of the bottle against a large tree. Repeat this action until the cork almost pops out, then pull the whole thing out with your hands. Note: If you're performing this operation on sparkling wines, make sure you let the bottle rest (and the bubbles settle) somewhere cold for ten to fifteen minutes before pulling the cork out entirely. Otherwise, you could have a major explosion.

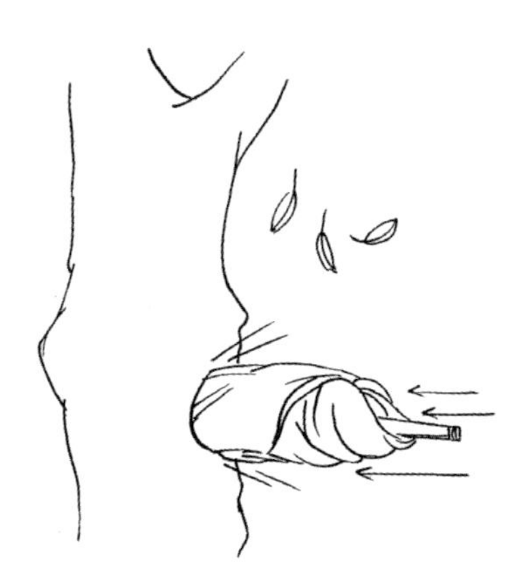

Get Your Toolbox: Insert a longish, wide-grained screw into the cork. When about half an inch of the screw is sticking out, pull the screw directly up with a pair of pliers or the claw of a hammer.

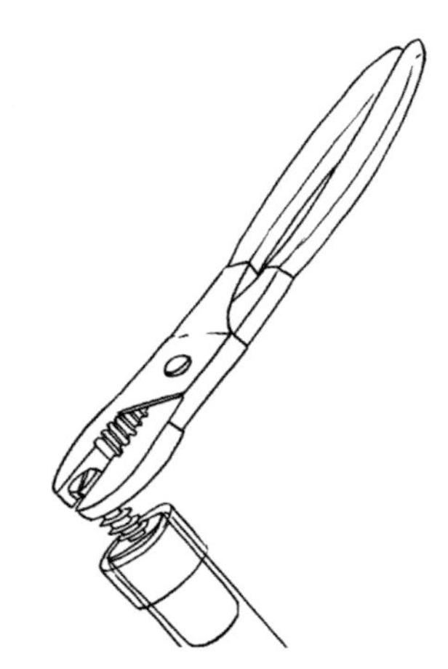

Go Fishing: Locate a wire coat hanger and bend the top to make a straight wire with a very small hook on the end. Gently insert this in between the bottle and the cork until the little hook rests below the bottom of the cork. Rotate the hanger until the hook pierces the cork. Pull up.

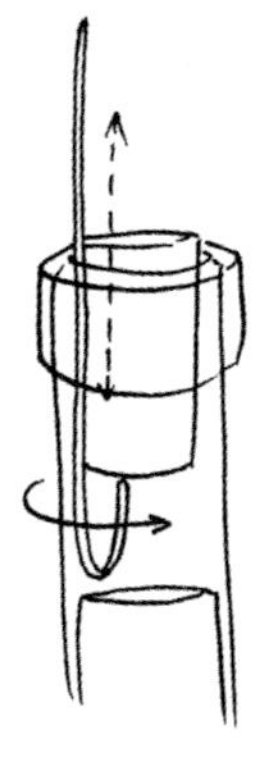

EMERGENCY TWO: A CORK BREAKS

When a cork breaks, it can be a real bummer. Here are your options.

(a) If the cork is broken, but part of it is still stuck in the neck of the bottle . . .

If you have an Ah-So (see page 16) available, now is the time to use it. Gently slip the prongs in between the cork and bottle and slowly pull up. If you don't have this handy tool, you can carefully keep working on the cork with the wine opener you have or you can push the remainder of the cork into the wine and skip ahead to the next problem.

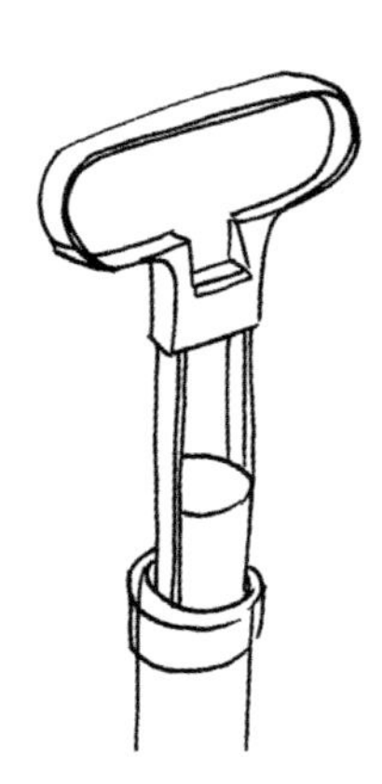

(b) If the cork fell apart and part of it is stuck in the wine . . .

Grab a mesh strainer (the finer the better) or a coffee filter. Slowly pour the wine through the strainer or filter into another container, catching the cork bits along the way. Don't worry about aesthetics; the container can be a pitcher, vase, large measuring bowl—any vessel that will allow you to pour the wine out again easily. (Because when all the cork drama is over, you're going to drink the wine.)

EMERGENCY THREE: STRANGE BITS IN YOUR BOTTLE OR GLASS

Looks like: Little bits of cork.
What it is: Little bits of cork.
What to do: See Emergency Two (b).

Looks like: Dark, solid, dried bits of wine that sink to the bottom or sides of the bottle or glass.
What it is: Sediment.
What to do: You can ignore (ingesting a bit of sediment will not hurt you) or separate the sediment from your wine by decanting (see page 132).

Looks like: Crystal-like formations on the bottom of the bottle or the underside of the cork. Most often found in white wines.
What it is: Potassium bitartrate crystals. These tasteless and harmless crystals (which are the same as cream of tartar) are

natural little bits of tartaric acid that separate from some white wines when they see a rapid, extreme drop in temperature. **What to do:** Ignore them. They will likely remain stuck to the cork or bottom of the bottle. The presence of potassium bitartrate crystals is not a fault. Drink on.

EMERGENCY FOUR: TEMPERATURE ISSUES

If you're about to serve a wine and suddenly find it's too hot, submerge the bottle in a bucket or sink filled with ice and water. In five (for reds), ten (for whites or rosés), or fifteen (for sparkling wines) minutes, you should be good to go.

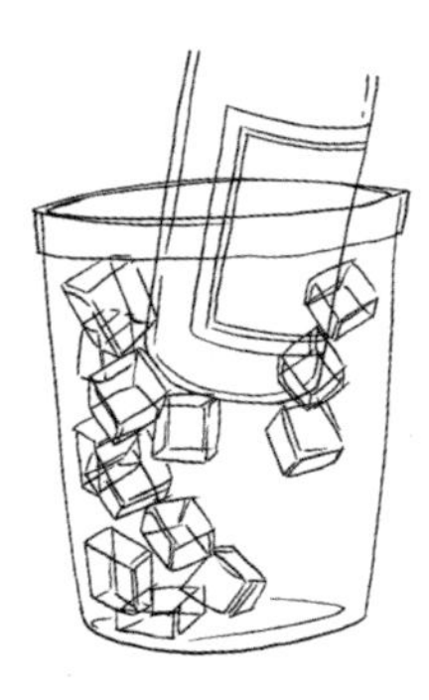

If you find your wine is too cold, use ambient temperature to your advantage. Either pour the wine into a decanter for ten minutes or pour small servings into wineglasses. If using glasses, let the wine sit alone for a few minutes or cup the glass in your hands, allowing the heat from your body to warm it.

EMERGENCY FIVE: RUNNING OUT

Running out of wine may be the worst kind of emergency there is, and one that's hard to fix without leaving the party. Your best bet is to take preliminary measures to ensure you always have enough on hand. Opposite is a handy guide to help you calculate how much wine you'll need.

HOW MUCH? A WINE BUYING GUIDE

Remember, don't pour too much at once. A small serving (around two ounces) will do for tastings, and a half-glass pour (three to four ounces) is perfect for dinners or events where people are sticking to one wine.

	LIGHTER DRINKERS	HEAVIER DRINKERS
WINE TASTING	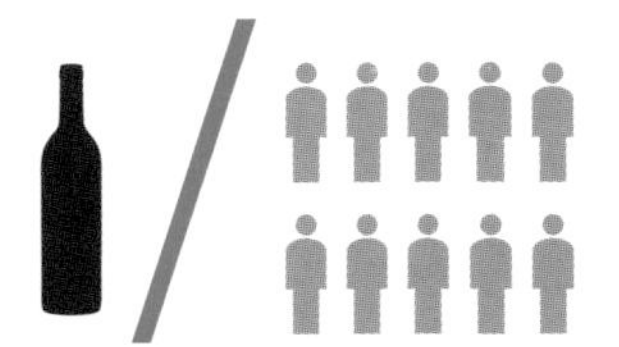 one bottle for every ten people	one bottle for every ten people, plus an extra bottle or two of each wine so people can go back to their favorites after the tasting is over
SIT-DOWN DINNER	 one bottle for every two people	 one bottle per person
COCKTAIL PARTY (1-2 HOURS)	 one bottle for every three people	 one bottle for every two people
COCKTAIL PARTY (3-4 HOURS)	 one bottle for every two people	one bottle per person

THE AFTER-PARTY ISN'T REALLY A PARTY AFTER ALL

How long does an open bottle of wine last? The simple answer is, however long it tastes good to you. The more complex answer is that wine starts breaking down as soon as you open the bottle and the wine is exposed to oxygen. The vibrancy and fruit will never again be as bright and shiny as when you first heard that pop (or crack if you've got a wine with a screw cap). After that, it's on a slippery slope to becoming vinegar. Delicate wines, like old wines or wines with bubbles, can be toast by the end of the night. Heartier wines—those with a lot of sugar, alcohol, acidity, or tannin to preserve them—can last a little longer. The true test is your taste buds. If a wine still tastes good to you on the third or fourth day, by all means, drink it. If it starts tasting droopy, chances are that its short life is over. The best prevention for premature demise is to drink the whole bottle on the night you open it. Go ahead; you now have my professional advice as an excuse.

KEEPING WINE ON LIFE SUPPORT

Here are a few tricks that will help you prolong a wine's life, once you open the bottle.

1. Keep it cool. Heat accelerates aging even after the bottle is open. Store unfinished whites and reds in the fridge.

2. Pump your unfinished wine bottle with an inert gas or a Vacu Vin, a handy mini pump that manually removes oxygen. A few shots of inert gas displace the oxygen in the bottle before you recork it. Both are available at most wine stores.

3. Save an empty half-bottle (375 ml) or two to have on hand. When you drink only half of a regular-size (750 ml) bottle, pour its remaining contents into the little bottle, stop it up, and store it in the fridge. You will leave only a tiny amount of the wine exposed to the dreaded evils of oxygen.

BRING OUT THE BIG GUNS

One memorable way to share wine is to open a large bottle. Big bottles are rare and interesting. They never fail to impress. The wine in them also ages more slowly, as there is a smaller amount exposed to oxygen, so you can sometimes find older vintages in large formats. Here's a quick reference to the most popular bottle sizes.

	VOLUME	BOTTLES	GLASSES
SPLIT	187 ml	¼	1.5
HALF	375 ml	½	3
BOTTLE	750 ml	1	6
MAGNUM	1.5 L	2	12
JEROBOAM	3 L	4	24
METHUSELAH	6 L	8	48
SALMANAZAR	9 L	12	72
BALTHAZAR	12 L	16	96
NEBUCHADNEZZAR	15 L	20	120

GREAT WINE GIFTS

Wine makes an awesome gift for beginners and connoisseurs alike. Putting a little thought and creativity into what you select will make it even more special. These are some of my favorite gifts for oenophiles.

A SINGLE, SPECIAL BOTTLE

Throughout this book, you'll find recommendations for wine I love; you can peruse these lists for inspiration. Another thought is to choose a bottle that is special to you and explain why with an enclosed note. Or you can look for a bottle with a specific vintage year to commemorate an event. For example, if a coworker is getting married in 2014, you can buy a bottle from that year with instructions that she should drink it on her tenth anniversary. For wines that people will be able to enjoy over the long term, look to the red or sweet wines of Bordeaux, France, or vintage Ports from Portugal.

A SUPERSIZED BOTTLE

Buy someone a large-format version of a favorite wine.

A FANCY WINE OPENER

A special opener is a great gift because the recipient will think of you every time they uncork a bottle.

A WINE AND CHEESE BASKET

Receiving a special bottle nested beside well-partnered cheeses is kind of like getting a party in a box (see "Cheese Pairing Guide: Thirty Top Cheeses and Their Perfect Wine Partners," page 148).

HIGH-QUALITY WINEGLASSES

You can go a lot of different directions with this gift. Two beautiful glasses are always a welcome gift—eight or ten is usually better.

A DESSERT WINE AND DARK CHOCOLATE

Combine a bottle of Banyuls or vintage Port with some artisan chocolate for a decadent present.

A DECANTER

A splurge for many, decanters make beautiful, useful wine gifts.

AN ATTRACTIVE WINE BUCKET AND A NICE BOTTLE OF SPARKLING WINE

A beautiful wine bucket is something you're less likely to buy yourself, but it can really come in handy when entertaining.

A WINE CLUB MEMBERSHIP

Wine club memberships can come in many shapes and forms. You could sign someone up for a wine club from a specific winery (sometimes the only way to get certain highly coveted bottles) or from a shop that aggregates great selections. Both wineries and shops usually offer a range of options based what you'd like to spend, and how often you're up for spending it (see "Join Wine Clubs," page 194).

Wine and Food

Wine and food are celebrated companions. For centuries, people have known that the only thing better than drinking great wine is eating while you are drinking great wine. Like any successful partnership, wine and food have the capacity to bring out the best in each other. Sure, they can be exceptional on their own, but every now and then, when the flavors of a wine come together in just the right way with the flavors and textures of a dish, it can feel like epicurean nirvana. Sometimes a flawless pairing is carefully planned, and sometimes it's an exquisite accident. Either way, once you've tasted for yourself that food and wine can in fact elevate each other, it's natural to want to repeat that kind of moment again and again.

GENERAL GUIDELINES FOR PAIRING

Wine experts can offer valuable insight and guidance when it comes to pairings. After all, it is their passion and profession; they can probably steer you in the right direction. (Make that a *good* direction.) There are no universal rights or wrongs when it comes to food and wine pairing. Even experts are subject to subjectivity. If you asked ten of the top sommeliers in the country to pick the perfect wine for a certain dish, chances are you'd get ten different, equally viable answers. Although everyone may have the same goal in mind when pairing—to create a synergy that is greater than each part alone—there are many ways to get there. Be open to suggestions from people who pair food and wine for a living, but ultimately, trust your intuition and make up your own mind once you've tasted a pairing. If you think it works, it does.

When there's not a wine guru around to lean on, don't stress over pairings. Many people mistakenly believe that they will ruin a meal if they make the wrong wine choice. The good news is that it's virtually impossible to wreck a good meal if you select a wine that you enjoy, regardless of what anyone else says. Remember, you are the boss of your tongue. Even if you make a less than harmonious choice (it happens all the time, even to the experts), what have you really lost? Think of pairing as an endless experiment—proceed knowing that there will always be surprises. And when you do find yourself tasting a transcendent coupling, revel in it. It will be over sooner than you'd like.

All that having been said, here are some basic tips that can help guide you toward better pairings.

KNOW WHAT YOU LIKE

If you're reading this, chances are you've had wine before. I'll even go a step further and bet that you've had wine that you liked and wine that you didn't like. You already have a starting point for creating pairings, and you can appreciate one of the most fundamental pairing principles: Personal preference trumps everything else. As a case in point, let's say you adore Champagne and loathe New Zealand sauvignon blanc. If given the opportunity to taste a stellar example of both wines paired with your crab cake, you're highly likely to deem the Champagne a better partner—even though they're both generally considered a match made in heaven for crab—simply because of your affinity for Champagne. I would never want to encourage you to limit experimenting with the unknown, but if you're shooting for a phenomenal pairing, consider what information you already have about who'll be experiencing it. Knowing what you (or they) enjoy is paramount to success in food and wine pairing.

MATCH INTENSITY

Matching intensity is the next most important part of the food and wine equation. If the balance between food and wine is off, one can overshadow the other into oblivion. If you serve a light and refreshing white wine, like pinot grigio, with pot roast, you'll hardly be able to taste the wine. You might as well drink water; because pot roast's deep, intense flavors will pummel the pinot grigio. On the other hand, serving the same wine with broiled grouper will give both the delicate wine and the delicate fish a chance to shine. Ultimately, you want the food and wine to be equally intense. Following are some examples of matching intensity.

INTENSE FOOD WITH INTENSE WINE

lamb and syrah

pasta with rich cream sauce and big, oaky chardonnay

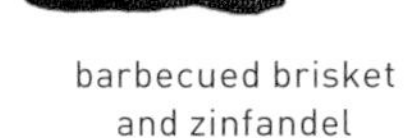

barbecued brisket and zinfandel

DELICATE FOOD WITH DELICATE WINE

broiled grouper and pinot grigio

caviar and Champagne

sushi and riesling

BUILD A BRIDGE

One surefire way to link food and wine is to find a common flavor. If you're starting with the food, pick out one main aroma or taste component you want to magnify and find a wine with a similar flavor. For example, a mushroom sauce on your chicken dish would likely pair well with pinot noir or Champagne; both can have an earthy, mushroomy flavor. Or you could start with the wine—say, a really fruity zinfandel—and pair it with a dish that has an echo of that fruit, like a meat dish that has a blueberry or blackberry sauce. This approach obviously works best if you already know what the wine tastes like, or have a very good idea of what it will taste like when you open it. Following are some examples of bridges.

FOOD	WINE
BACON 	Châteauneuf-du-Pape (this wine generally has a meaty aroma)
CILANTRO 	New Zealand sauvignon blanc (this wine has a green, herbal flavor)
NUTS 	Meursault (Meursault is known for a hazelnut taste)
LEMON 	Sancerre (Sancerre is very clean, tangy, tart, and citrusy)
CLOVES 	oaked chardonnay (oak in chardonnay can often smell like cloves)
CRANBERRY 	pinot noir (pinot noir typically has lean red fruit flavors)
MELON 	prosecco (prosecco is ripe and fruity, and usually smells like melon)

TIPTOE WITH TANNIN

Cabernet sauvignon and other thick-skinned grapes produce wine with bitter, dark fruit flavors and mouth-drying tannin. Wines with lots of tannin find their happiest match in foods with juicy protein and fat, such as a rare steak with good marbling. Like a gift to taste buds, the proteins and fat soften the tannin, making the wine taste smooth and fruity, and tannin cuts through fat and protein, refreshing your palate.

Loads of tannin can be really icky when paired with superspicy foods, sweet foods, oily foods, or salty foods, so avoid these.

STEAK SECRETS Steaks grilled with crushed black peppercorns sensitize your taste buds, making the wine taste even more fruity and robust.

REGIONALITY IS YOUR ULTIMATE DEFAULT

Finally, if you need pairing inspiration, look to the local cuisine of the wine region. This is much easier to do with European wine and food because they've grown up together, but it is possible in New World wine regions that have a gastronomic signature.

Regional Food and Wine Pairings

- **Tuscany, Italy:** pasta with tomato-based red sauce and Chianti
- **Burgundy, France:** beef and mushrooms with red Burgundy
- **Piedmont, Italy:** truffles and wild game with Barolo or Barbaresco
- **Loire Valley, France:** goat cheese and Sancerre

CHEESE MATTERS

Cheese and wine are natural companions, but a little planning can go a long way in making sure their interaction is delicious. Many of the general food and wine guidelines covered in this chapter (like matching intensity and regions) apply to cheese as well. There are just a couple more things to keep in mind as you plan your cheese-specific pairings.

CONSIDER AGE

Youthful cheeses, like a fresh goat cheese or ricotta, go best with a young, fresh wine, like sauvignon blanc. Similarly, aged cheeses, like Parmigiano-Reggiano, can stand up to a bigger, more intense wine, like brunello di Montalcino.

WHITE OVER RED

For years and years, people have been pairing big red wines with cheese. Sometimes it works. But in general, white wines—with their livelier acidity—better balance the fattiness of cheese. When in doubt, choose white over red.

THE BLUES

Blue cheeses, like Valdeón, Cabrales, Roquefort, and Stilton, are massively flavorful and rich. A first instinct is to pair them with big, tannic red wines. However, blue mold is notorious for completely stripping wines of any fruit. Dessert wines like Port, Sherry, and Madeira actually make much better partners. Their sweetness can stand up to the mold, and delectably counterbalance the salty flavors of the bluest blues.

Five Cheese-Pairing Platter Ideas

- **Champagne:** Brie, Morbier, Parmigiano-Reggiano
- **grüner veltliner:** Comté, fresh goat cheese, Tomme de Savoie
- **pinot noir:** Gruyère, Piave, Pont l'Évêque
- **Chianti:** Asiago, Pecorino Toscano, Taleggio
- **Malmsey Madeira** (see page 151): Gruyère, Stilton, Valdeón

---

CHEESE PAIRING GUIDE: TWENTY-NINE TOP CHEESES AND THEIR

Cheese/Country	Milk Type	Description	Perfect Wine Partners
ASIAGO *Italy*	cow	fruity and nutty	With young Asiago, try crisp Italian whites; with aged Asiago, try barbera, Chianti, or dolcetto.
BRIE *France*	cow	velvety soft, mush-room flavor	Champagne and chardonnays, especially earthy versions from Burgundy, are stellar pairings.
BRILLAT SAVARIN *France*	cow	fluffy texture; milky, sour cream smell	Champagne, white Burgundy, and chardonnays from the New World all work well.
CAMEMBERT *France*	cow	silky and creamy; mushroom aromas	Champagne, white Burgundy, and chardonnays from the New World all work well.
CANTAL *France*	cow	butter, milk, sour cream flavors	Rich whites, like chardonnay, or light and fruity reds like pinot noir or Beaujolais work best.
CHEDDAR *England and the United States*	cow	firm and creamy; fruity, nutty, caramel	Zinfandel, merlot, syrah, and cabernet sauvignon are all big wines that can handle cheddar's intensity.
COMTÉ *France*	cow	smooth but firm; sweet, salty, and tart	Comté is great with rich, spicy whites like gewürztraminer or Alsatian pinot gris. White Burgundy also works.
ÉPOISSES *France*	cow	mushroom and meat flavors	Rieslings, pinot gris (pinot grigio), and white and red Burgundies work best. Also try pinot noir or Beaujolais.
FETA *Greece*	sheep or mixed sheep-goat	salty and tangy; crumbly texture	Crisp Greek or Italian whites are magical pair-ings. Also try sauvignon blanc and dry rosés.
FONTINA D'AOSTA *Italy*	cow	firm, smooth; herba-ceous and nutty	White Burgundy and viognier work well for whites. Pinot noir is an excellent choice for red.
GORGONZOLA *Italy*	cow	pungent blue; creamy texture; spicy, salty taste	Fortified dessert wines, like Ports, Madeira, and sweeter styles of Sherry, work best.
GRUYÈRE *Switzerland*	cow	dense, firm, and smooth; hugely nutty and caramel-like with age	White Burgundy, chardonnay, and viognier are great whites to pair with Gruyère. For red, go for an earthy pinot noir. Dry and off-dry Sherry can also be phenomenal.
IDIAZÁBAL *Spain*	sheep	firm; tangy, buttery, and smoky	Earthy reds are best. Try Chianti or Rioja.
MAHÓN *Spain*	cow	semisoft; tangy and salty	With young Mahón, try fruity whites like albariño, torrontés, or pinot gris. Older Mahón is best with reds. Try Spanish reds like Jumilla, Rioja, or Ribera del Duero.
MANCHEGO *Spain*	sheep	firm, dry; salty and tangy; nuttiness grows with age	Spanish reds, like Rioja and Ribera del Duero, can be fabulous. Also many southern French reds, like Côtes du Rhône, work well.

PERFECT WINE PARTNERS

Cheese/Country	Milk Type	Description	Perfect Wine Partners
MIMOLETTE *France*	cow	firm and dry; salt, caramel, butterscotch	Buttery chardonnays are great.
MORBIER *France*	cow	creamy; mild mushroom and earth flavor	Champagne and other sparkling wines are terrific. Also try Alsatian pinot gris and white Burgundy.
MOZZARELLA DI BUFALA *Italy*	buffalo	creamy, sweet, milky	Italian whites are perfect. Also try dry rosés.
PARMIGIANO-REGGIANO *Italy*	cow	firm; crumbly; nutty, buttery, and meaty	Champagne and sparkling wines are incredible. Also try Barolo, Barbaresco, or brunello di Montalcino. Merlot and cabernet sauvignon can also work well.
PECORINO TOSCANO *Italy*	sheep	smooth; mild; sweet milk flavors	Crisp Italian whites are great partners. Chianti is a stellar red pairing.
PIAVE *Italy*	cow	firm; salty and sweet; caramel flavors as it ages	Rich whites are best; try chardonnay or viognier. Reds with fruit will also work. Try fruity pinot noir or zinfandel.
PONT L'ÉVÊQUE *France*	cow	creamy; pungent dirty sock smell, with a milder mushroom flavor	White Burgundy, chardonnay, and dry sparkling wines like Champagne work well. Pinot noir can also be an excellent partner.
RACLETTE *France and Switzerland*	cow	smooth and creamy; meaty, roasted nut flavor	Champagne and other dry sparkling wines, dry rieslings, and Alsatian pinot gris are terrific.
RONCAL *Spain*	sheep	firm, crumbly, sheepy aroma, salty and tangy	Spanish reds are a natural pairing. Try Jumilla, Rioja, or Ribera del Duero.
ROQUEFORT *France*	sheep	smooth but firm blue, with bold, spicy taste	Dessert wines can hold their own. Try Sauternes, Banyuls, or vintage Port.
STILTON *England*	cow	creamy blue; nutty, meaty, smoky, buttery flavor	Ports of all types are classic pairings. Also try Sherry and Madeira.
TALEGGIO *Italy*	cow	creamy, oozy texture; pungent smell of mushroom and meat; milder, buttery taste	Spicy whites like gewürztraminer, grüner veltliner, and Alsatian pinot gris are the best bets for whites. Reds can also work. Try Italian reds like Barolo, Barbaresco, barbera, and Chianti.
TOMME DE SAVOIE *France*	cow	semifirm; earthy, meaty aroma; a milder flavor	Young versions pair best with aromatic whites like riesling, gewürztraminer, and grüner veltliner. Aged versions are great with earthy pinot noir.
VALDEÓN *Spain*	sheep or mixed sheep-goat	creamy but crumbly; intensely salty, sharp, spicy blue	Fortified dessert wines like Port, Sherry, and Madeira work best.

“WINE MAKES A SYMPHONY OF A GOOD MEAL.”

—Fernande Garvin

DECADENT DEBAUCHERY: A MAP FOR YOUR SWEET TOOTH

I am all for hedonism, but you can have too much of a good thing, especially when it comes to sugar. "Dessert wines" come from all over the world and are made a variety of ways. The one thing they have in common is that they are all substantially sweet. The name, of course, lends one to think these wines are to be served with dessert. And while they certainly can be beautiful partners to sugary treats, I enjoy these wines most *as* dessert. Sweet wines are most brilliant when consumed on their own or with the contrasting flavor of salty cheese or nuts. If you are bent on serving double the dessert, just make sure the wine is always sweeter than the dish.

MY ALL-TIME FAVORITE DESSERT WINES

Madeira / mah-DEER-ah

This very special fortified wine comes from Portugal and goes through a unique heating process that renders it almost indestructible once you open it. Madeira can range from dry to very sweet. With dessert or as dessert, I recommend the sweetest style, called Malmsey. This rich wine can have sophisticated and complex flavors of brown sugar, toffee, roasted nuts, and orange peel. I like Malmsey Madeira alone, or with roasted almonds or a salty blue cheese.

Moscato d'Asti / mo-SCAH-toe dee AH-stee

Piedmont, Italy's moscato d'Asti is clean, fresh, floral, and citrusy. It is cheap and charming. Low alcohol, fewer bubbles, and a slightly sweet taste make it refreshing and irresistible. Try it paired with biscotti, sugar cookies, melon, prosciutto, apples, pears, and not-too-sweet fruit-based desserts.

Sauternes / saw-TERN

When most people think of Bordeaux, France, they first think of the famous dry red wines of the region. But Sauternes, and its value-driven cousin Barsac, are superlative dessert wines made from grapes infected with *Botrytis*. Thanks to vibrant acidity, the best age gracefully for decades and taste of opulent honey and dried apricots. Try Sauternes with blue cheese, peaches, apples, apricots, butter cake, nuts, foie gras, or sugar cookies.

NOBLE ROT There's nothing cute about a furry green grape covered in mold. But *Botrytis cinerea*, a mold lovingly referred to as "noble rot," is necessary to create some of the world's most revered sweet wine. Believe it or not, winemakers celebrate when they find this fungus in the vineyard. The rot is rare; only a few places provide the climactic conditions necessary for *Botrytis* to thrive. If the environment is just right, *Botrytis* slowly dehydrates grapes, leaving only highly concentrated sugars behind. When the moldy raisins are finally pressed, a beautiful wine emerges, with lush apricot, honey, and sweet tea opulence. The most famous and lauded examples of what the noble rot can achieve are found in the dessert wines of Sauternes (France), Beerenauslese and Trockenbeerenauslese (Germany), and Tokaji Aszú (Hungary).

Tokaji Aszú / toe-KY ah-ZOO

This rare, neglected wine was once a favorite of luminaries, including Pope Pius IV, Catherine the Great, Voltaire, Thomas Jefferson, Napoleon, and Queen Victoria. In fact, Louis XIV deemed Hungary's Tokaji "*vinum regum, rex vinoram*," the king of wines and wine of kings. Hungarians are so proud of their national treasure that it is even mentioned in the national anthem. Let me jump on the bandwagon and confirm: Tokaji Aszú is worthy of the hype. With lower alcohol (usually 10 to 11 percent) and bright, tangy acidity to balance the orange blossom, apricot, and delicate tea leaf flavors, this wine is in a category of its own. It is incredible chilled, alone or with aged Gouda, foie gras, or fruit-based desserts.

Bottle-Aged Port

One of the two main types of Port, bottle-aged Port retains its ruby red color because the majority of its aging is done in the bottle. Trademark flavors are red cherry and cocoa, so this is the type of Port to pair with chocolate. You can find simple, inexpensive versions, but the finest bottle-aged Ports are called vintage Ports. These come from a single, exceptional year, and they can be aged for decades. Because they age so well, fine vintage Ports make great gifts for momentous occasions like the birth of a child or a marriage. If you can find a vintage Port from the significant year, you'll likely have a beautiful wine to celebrate with in twenty or thirty years' time—if you can wait that long. Drink vintage Port with berries, cherries, chocolate, coffee- or espresso-flavored desserts, and blue cheeses.

Barrel-Aged Port

Unlike bottle-aged Ports, barrel-aged versions are aged in big oak casks and are intentionally exposed to small amounts of oxygen over time. This process turns them a deep, golden brown color, which is why these wines are also known as "tawny" Ports. There are very simple tawny Ports and much more rich, complex tawny Ports, which are expensive. Either way, barrel-aged Ports are ready to drink upon release and have amazing flavors of toffee, nuts, and caramel. Try them with baked apples, tarts, crisps, pies, nuts and nut-based desserts, cheddar cheese, caramel, and custards.

THE PORT STORY Up until the 1700s, the British drank mostly French wines. But escalating rivalry between the two countries led the British to drink more wines from Spain and Portugal. Back then, Portugal was known for its dry red table wines. Portuguese winemakers learned to add a small amount of grape spirits, or 150-proof clear brandy, to the wine to make it more stable during the long sea voyage to England. Things changed in 1820. That year, the grapes were ultra-ripe and the resulting wines turned out extra sweet. The vintage went over so well in England that Portuguese winemakers tried to re-create that taste. They started adding more grape spirits earlier, in order to arrest fermentation sooner, thus leaving more natural sugar in the wine. Gradually, over time, more and more grape spirits were added, and Port morphed into what it is now: a substantially fortified sweet wine.

Eiswein/Ice Wine / ICE-vine/ICE-wine

Austria, Germany, and Canada are serious about ice wine. They are all legally bound to make this mind-bogglingly sweet wine in the traditional way, which includes allowing grapes to hang on the vine long after the regular harvest. Eventually, winter sets in and they freeze, at which point they are picked by hand one frozen grape at a time, and are then gently pressed to produce teeny-tiny amounts of superconcentrated liquid sugar. Ice wines are so sweet that they taste best alone or when paired with salty foods. Try them with blue cheese, shortbread, and fruit or fruit-based desserts.

Banyuls / ban-YULES

This underappreciated dessert wine from southern France is fortified like Port and made mostly from grenache grapes. It is a perfect partner for dark chocolate, with its flavors of black plum, espresso, cherry, and chocolate. Drink it with chocolate, dried fruit, blue cheese, or tiramisu.

BUYING AND SERVING SWEET WINES

Most sweet wines taste best with a slight chill, which minimizes the alcohol flavor. Pop dessert wines in the fridge about thirty minutes before you plan to drink them.

Buying the right amount of dessert wine is a little tricky. Some dessert wines come in traditional 750-ml bottles, some in 375-ml half-bottles, and some in a 500-ml bottle. The general rule of thumb is that you'll need less than you think. Most dessert wines are so rich that people don't gulp them by the glassful like a dry table wine. Buy small, pour small, and you'll still be living large.

WINE + CHOCOLATE = FAKE FRIENDS

Wine + chocolate = heaven. Or at least, that's what you may have been told. As someone who has extensive experience with both, I feel it's my duty to reveal the unfortunate truth: Most chocolate and wine pairings are pretty awful. However, there *are* some killer combinations. Here's what you need to know when combining two of life's most exquisite palate pleasers.

CHOCOLATE RULES

Rules are one of my least favorite things in life, but sometimes they are necessary. Such is the case with wine and chocolate.

1. When choosing a wine to pair with chocolate, make sure the wine is very ripe and fruit-forward, leaning toward sweetness (or, in fact, sweet). The wine needs to be as sweet or sweeter than the chocolate, or the sugar in the chocolate will make the wine seem limp and acidic. Dessert wines are usually a safe bet, and for non-dessert wines, look to very sunny regions for the ripest fruit flavors; the warmest parts of California and Australia are good places to start.

2. In keeping with the previous rule, the less sweet the food (in this case, chocolate), the better chance the wine has of surviving the interaction. This is also a good general guideline for any dessert pairing, Look for high-quality chocolate with a cocoa count of 60 percent or higher.

Wines That Love Chocolate

- **Port:** Vintage Ports with their deep, dark cherry flavors are best.
- **Banyuls:** The chocolaty French cousin to Port, this dessert wine is lighter and silkier than Port.
- **zinfandel:** Not all table wines can stand up to chocolate, but the juiciest, ripest versions of zinfandel can.

OTHER TRICKY FOODS TO PAIR

ASPARAGUS AND ARTICHOKES

These two notoriously hard-to-pair veggies can make wine taste funky, but good pairings exist. Dry sparkling wines are a fitting option, as are light, high-acid, lemony white wines with an herbal edge—try sauvignon blanc, grüner veltliner, albariño, or Vinho Verde. One well-known tip for making artichokes a bit more wine-friendly is cooking them in water with lemon and salt. This helps mitigate the effects of cynarin, the culprit compound that clobbers wine.

SPICY FOODS

Spicy foods accentuate the alcohol and tannin in wine. If you served a big, tannic cabernet with something spicy, you'd multiply the heat and lose any chance of appreciating the wine. Instead, pair spicy food with ripe, fruity, low-alcohol wines. Off-dry riesling and gewürztraminer, with their touch of sweetness, are good bets as they tend to cool off your mouth in between bites. If you prefer red, try Beaujolais or a juicy New World pinot noir. Chilling your reds a bit before the meal will help make them even more refreshing in between bites of the spicy food.

FRUIT

Because fresh fruit is naturally sweet and also usually high in acidity, it can wreak havoc on wines, leaving them tasting sour and limp. I generally avoid pairing fruit with wines, but if you must, moscato d'Asti, prosecco, ice wine, and sweeter-style rieslings can do it with grace.

GREAT WINES FOR PAIRING

Some wines just seem a bit more eager to please when it comes to pairings. The following three are extremely versatile with a variety of foods; they make great choices when you have a table full of people all eating different things.

CHAMPAGNE

Most people don't think of food when they think of Champagne and other dry sparkling wines, but they can be some of the most flexible wines for pairing. Sparkling wines are superb with seafood, eggs, simple chicken dishes, veggies, fried and salty foods, and even spicy foods. Don't go pitting them against barbecue, steak, or other big, rich dishes, though; they aren't tough enough for that.

RIESLING

Riesling is the sommelier's darling for a couple of reasons: versatility and an innate ability to let the food shine. Rieslings can be bone-dry to very sweet, so knowing what you've got in the bottle is an important piece of information before pairing. Look for rieslings with just a touch of sweetness and the grape's signature tangy acidity, which pair gracefully with many dishes.

PINOT NOIR

Pinot noir is the go-to red for adaptability with food. Pinot has very little tannin and lower alcohol than many other reds, so it plays well with a wide variety of foods, from steaks to game to chicken to veggies and even fish.

WINES FOR COOKING

Steer clear of wines that say "for cooking" anywhere on the label. These are nasty wines with additives like salt and food coloring. You can find inexpensive but authentic alternatives that will actually enhance your food and that you won't mind sipping while you're doing all that cooking.

Cooking Wines You Can Also Drink While Cooking

- If the recipe calls for a **dry white**, try a California sauvignon blanc.
- If the recipe calls for a **dry red**, try a Côtes du Rhône, or a nero d'Avola or primitivo from Italy.
- If the recipe calls for **Sherry** or **Madeira**, use real Sherry or Madeira from Spain and Portugal, respectively. (The fake California cooking kind just doesn't cut it.) They might only be a couple of dollars more and will taste so much better.

Drink This, Eat That

Maybe you've got a special bottle you'd like to plan an elaborate meal around, or perhaps just last night's wine that you want to pair with tonight's takeout. Use this chapter as a resource when you're looking for food ideas to pair with wine. Not all wines and grapes are represented, but the most popular and classic ones are all here. Remember that just like in the rest of the book, for clarification purposes, grape names are lowercase and appellations (or place-names) are capitalized. White grapes and wines appear underlined in green, pinks in pink, and reds in red. If there is no coding, the wine can be either white or red. By no means should you limit yourself to the suggested pairings, but these can serve as a starting point, and will hopefully provide inspiration when needed.

aglianico

- beef (especially braised or grilled)
- earthy fall and winter soups and stews
- game
- mushrooms
- pizza (especially with meat)
- sausages

albariño

- ceviche
- lemon or lemon-based sauces
- salty food
- seafood
- shellfish

Amarone

- beef (especially braised)
- dark chocolate
- hard, aged cheeses
- mushrooms
- truffles

arneis

- asparagus and other green vegetables
- seafood

Bandol

- beef (especially braised or grilled)
- herbes de Provence (lavender, thyme, rosemary, sage)
- mushrooms
- olives

Banyuls

- chocolate
- strawberries

Barbaresco or Barolo

- beef (especially grilled or roasted)
- game birds
- lamb
- mushrooms
- truffles

barbera

- charcuterie
- pasta (especially with red sauces)
- pizza
- prosciutto
- tomatoes

barrel-aged Port

- banana-based desserts
- caramel
- custards
- nuts

Beaujolais

- charcuterie
- cherries
- chicken (especially roasted)
- ham
- pork
- salmon
- salty food
- spicy food
- turkey

Bordeaux (red)

- beef
- chicken
- game
- lamb
- meat loaf

Bordeaux (white)

- chicken (especially roasted)
- lemon or lemon-based sauces
- seafood

bottle-aged Port

- berries
- blue cheeses
- cherries
- chocolate (especially dark)
- coffee- or espresso-flavored desserts

brunello di Montalcino

- game (especially rabbit)
- mushrooms
- savory, earthy sauces
- truffles

Burgundy (red)

- bacon
- burgers (especially turkey or veggie)
- cherries
- chicken (especially roasted or in an earthy sauce)
- duck
- mushrooms
- salmon
- soft, ripe cheeses
- turkey
- truffles

Burgundy (white)

- chicken (especially fried or roasted)
- corn
- creamy sauces
- lemon or lemon-based sauces
- mushrooms
- seafood
- soft, rich cheeses
- turkey
- truffles

cabernet franc

- lamb
- meat loaf

cabernet sauvignon

- beef (especially grilled or roasted, or with an earthy sauce)
- black pepper
- burgers
- hard, aged cheeses
- lamb
- meat loaf

carménère

- beef (especially braised or roasted)
- chicken (especially dark meat)
- earthy sauces, soups, and stews

cava

- asparagus and other green veggies
- butter and buttery sauces
- caviar
- chicken (especially fried or roasted)
- creamy sauces
- corn
- eggs
- fried food
- lemon or lemon-based sauces
- mushrooms
- salty food
- seafood
- soft, rich cheeses
- spicy food

Chablis

- asparagus and other green veggies
- chicken (especially fried or roasted)
- lemon or lemon-based sauces
- seafood
- shellfish (especially oysters)

Champagne

- asparagus and other green veggies
- butter and buttery sauces
- caviar
- chicken (especially fried or roasted)
- corn
- creamy sauces
- eggs
- fried food
- lemon or lemon-based sauces
- mushrooms
- salty food
- seafood
- shellfish
- soft, rich cheeses
- spicy food
- truffles

chardonnay

- asparagus and other green veggies
- basil and other herbs
- butter and buttery sauces
- lemon or lemon-based sauces
- mushrooms
- mustard and mustard-based sauces
- pesto
- seafood
- shellfish

HEAVIER STYLE CHARDONNAY (RICH AND FULL, WITH A MORE BUTTERY AND OAKY FLAVOR)

- Alfredo and other creamy sauces
- butter and buttery sauces
- corn
- macaroni and cheese
- mushrooms
- pork (especially baked, grilled, or roasted)
- salmon
- soft, rich cheeses
- turkey

Châteauneuf-du-Pape

- beef (especially in an earthy sauce)
- herbes de Provence (lavender, thyme, rosemary, sage)
- mushrooms
- soups and stews with a rustic, earthy edge
- truffles

chenin blanc

- salty food
- spicy food

Chianti

- beans (especially soups and stews)
- beef (especially in a tomato sauce)
- game
- prosciutto
- tomato-based dishes
- veal

Chinon

- beef (especially grilled or roasted, or with an earthy sauce)
- chicken (especially roasted)
- lamb
- meat loaf

Cornas

- game
- lamb

Côte Rôtie

- game
- lamb
- mushrooms
- truffles

Côtes du Rhône

- chicken (especially roasted or in an earthy sauce)
- mushrooms
- truffles

Croze-Hermitage

- game
- lamb

dolcetto

- antipasti
- veal

falanghina

- salty food
- seafood (especially fried)

gamay

- charcuterie
- cherries
- chicken (especially roasted)
- ham
- pork (especially baked, grilled, or roasted)
- salmon
- salty food
- spicy food
- turkey

Gavi

- pesto
- seafood
- shellfish
- vegetables

gewürztraminer

- apples
- cabbage
- Chinese food
- ham
- Indian food
- pork
- sausages (especially grilled)
- spicy food
- Thai food
- turkey

Gigondas

- chicken (especially grilled)
- earthy soups and stews
- herbes de Provence (lavender, thyme, rosemary, and sage)
- vegetables (especially grilled)

grenache

- chicken (especially grilled)
- earthy soups, stews, and ragus
- herbes de Provence (lavender, thyme, rosemary, and sage)
- vegetables (especially grilled)

grüner veltliner

- asparagus and other green veggies
- salads
- seafood
- shellfish

Hermitage

- game
- lamb

ice wine

- fruit and fruit-based desserts

Jumilla

- beef (especially braised, grilled, or roasted)
- burgers
- game
- mushrooms
- soups and stews with an earthy edge
- vegetables (especially grilled)

Madeira

- banana-based desserts
- chocolate
- nuts (especially roasted and salted)

malbec

- beef (especially grilled)
- burgers
- meat loaf
- pizza (especially with meat)

merlot

- beef (especially grilled or roasted)
- beets
- burgers (beef, turkey, or veggie)
- duck
- meat loaf
- savory, earthy sauces
- veal

montepulciano d'Abruzzo

- pizza
- tomato-based dishes

morellino di Scansano

- fennel
- game
- mushrooms
- soups and stews with an earthy edge

moscato d'Asti

- fruit and fruit-based desserts

mourvèdre

- beef (especially braised)
- herbes de Provence (lavender, thyme, rosemary, and sage)
- game
- mushrooms
- soups and stews with an earthy edge

Muscadet

- anchovies
- oysters
- seafood
- shellfish

nebbiolo

- beef (especially grilled or roasted)
- game
- lamb
- mushrooms
- truffles

nero d'Avola

- beef
- olives
- pizza
- tomato-based sauces

Orvieto

- seafood
- shellfish
- vegetables (grilled or roasted)

petite sirah

- beef (especially braised or grilled)
- game
- pork (especially braised or grilled)

pinotage

- grilled or smoked meats
- mushrooms

pinot blanc

- chicken
- seafood
- turkey

pinot grigio/pinot gris

- melon
- pork (especially baked, grilled, or roasted)
- salads
- salmon
- seafood

pinot noir

- ahi tuna
- bacon
- burgers (especially turkey or veggie)
- cherries
- chicken (especially roasted or in an earthy sauce)
- duck
- ham
- mushrooms
- pork (especially baked, grilled, or roasted)
- salmon
- savory, earthy sauces
- soft, ripe cheeses
- strawberries
- truffles

Port (*see* barrel-aged Port or bottle-aged Port)

primitivo

- bacon
- beef (especially grilled)
- burgers (beef, turkey, and veggie)
- game
- mushrooms
- pizza
- sausages
- soups and stews with a meaty, smoky, or earthy flavor
- tomato-based dishes

Priorat

- beef (especially grilled or with an earthy sauce)
- soups and stews with a meaty, smoky, or earthy flavor
- vegetables (grilled)

prosecco

- biscotti and other cookies
- fruit

Ribera del Duero

- beef (especially braised or grilled)
- game
- grilled vegetables
- soups and stews with a hearty, earthy edge

riesling

DRY

- asparagus and other green veggies
- ceviche
- seafood
- shellfish

OFF-DRY

- apples
- beets
- cabbage
- Chinese food
- Indian food
- lemongrass
- pork
- spicy food
- Thai food

SWEET

- fruit or fruit-based desserts

Rioja (red)

- beef (especially braised)
- bell peppers
- duck
- meat loaf
- mushrooms
- olives
- paella
- sausages (especially chorizo)

rosé

- anchovies
- bell peppers
- charcuterie
- hot dogs
- olives
- paella
- prosciutto
- sausages
- spicy food

Rosso di Montalcino

- beans (especially soups and stews)
- beef (especially in a tomato sauce)
- mushrooms
- pizza
- prosciutto
- soups and stews with an earthy edge
- tomato-based dishes
- veal

roussanne

- chicken (especially grilled or roasted)
- seafood (especially grilled or roasted white fish)

Sancerre

- asparagus and other green veggies
- goat and other tangy cheeses
- lemon or lemon-based sauces
- salads
- seafood
- shellfish

sangiovese

- beans (especially soups and stews)
- beef (especially in a tomato sauce)
- game
- mushrooms
- pizza
- prosciutto
- sausages
- soups and stews with an earthy edge
- tomato-based dishes
- veal
- vegetables (especially grilled)

Sauternes

- foie gras
- salty cheeses

sauvignon blanc

- arugula
- asparagus and other green veggies
- basil and other herbs
- chicken (especially fried or roasted)
- Chinese food
- creamy sauces
- fried food
- lemongrass
- lemon or lemon-based sauces
- mustard and mustard-based sauces
- pesto
- salads
- seafood
- shellfish
- Thai food

semillon

- chicken (especially grilled or roasted)
- seafood

Sherry

DRY SHERRY

- fried food
- salty food

SWEET SHERRY

- apple- and pear-based desserts
- nuts and nut-based desserts
- salty cheeses

Soave

- basil and other herbs
- pesto
- seafood
- shellfish

Super Tuscan

- beans (especially white beans in soups and stews)
- beef (especially grilled or roasted)
- mushrooms
- polenta
- vegetables (especially bitter greens)

syrah/shiraz

- bacon
- barbecue
- beef (especially braised or grilled)
- black pepper
- burgers
- chili
- game
- lamb
- meat loaf

Taurasi

- beef (especially grilled)
- game
- lamb
- olives
- pizza
- sausages (especially grilled)

tempranillo

- beef (especially braised)
- bell peppers
- duck
- meat loaf
- mushrooms
- olives
- paella
- sausages (especially chorizo)

torrontés

- chicken (especially grilled or roasted)
- seafood
- shellfish
- spicy food

Valpolicella

- mushrooms
- pizza
- tomato-based dishes

vernaccia di San Gimignano

- seafood
- shellfish
- vegetables (simply grilled or roasted)

Vinho Verde

- salads
- seafood
- shellfish

viognier

- apricots
- butternut and other winter squash
- creamy sauces
- pork
- pumpkin
- sweet potatoes

Vouvray

DRY

- chicken
- seafood
- veal
- vegetables

OFF-DRY

- cheeses (especially strongly flavored, creamy cheeses)
- fruit

zinfandel

- bacon
- barbecue
- beef
- black pepper
- blue cheeses
- burgers (beef, turkey, and veggie)
- chili
- curry
- duck
- game
- hot dogs
- meat loaf
- mushrooms
- pizza
- sausages

Eat This, Drink That

Use this section as a resource for pairing when you're trying to make a match with particular flavors in food. If you've got a complex dish with lots of flavors, try to pick the most prominent one and look that up. Remember that just like in the rest of the book, for clarification purposes, when it comes to the wines, grape names are lowercase and place-names (appellations) are capitalized. White grapes and wines appear underlined in green, pinks in pink, and reds in red. If there is no coding, the wine can be either white or red. By no means are these the only wines that will work with each dish or flavor; I've chosen my favorites.

Alfredo sauce

- chardonnay (especially rich styles)

almonds (*see* nuts)

anchovies

- Muscadet
- rosé (dry, especially Spanish)
- sauvignon blanc
- Sherry (dry)

apples

- gewürztraminer
- riesling (off-dry)

apples in desserts

- ice wine
- riesling (off-dry to sweet)
- Sauternes
- Vouvray (sweet)

apricots

- riesling (off-dry to sweet)
- viognier

apricots in desserts

- ice wine
- Sauternes

artichokes

Note: cook artichokes in water with lemon and salt to make them more wine-friendly

- Champagne and other dry sparkling wines
- chardonnay (unoaked)
- grüner veltliner
- sauvignon blanc

arugula

- sauvignon blanc

asparagus

- Chablis
- chardonnay (crisp, clean, unoaked versions)
- grüner veltliner
- riesling (dry)
- sauvignon blanc

bacon

- pinot noir
- syrah/shiraz

bananas in desserts

- Madeira (sweet)
- tawny Port

barbecue

- syrah/shiraz
- zinfandel

beef

BRAISED

- Amarone
- brunello di Montalcino
- pinot noir
- syrah/shiraz
- zinfandel

ROASTED OR GRILLED

- Barbaresco
- Barolo
- brunello di Montalcino
- cabernet sauvignon
- merlot
- nebbiolo
- Priorat
- red Bordeaux
- Rioja
- syrah/shiraz
- zinfandel

WITH TOMATO SAUCE

- barbera
- brunello di Montalcino
- Chianti
- montepulciano d'Abruzzo
- nero d'Avola
- Rosso di Montalcino
- sangiovese
- Valpolicella
- Vino Nobile di Montepulciano

WITH A HEAVY, EARTHY SAUCE

- cabernet sauvignon
- Châteauneuf-du-Pape
- Priorat
- red Bordeaux
- Rioja
- syrah/shiraz
- zinfandel

beets

- merlot
- riesling (off-dry)

blueberry desserts

- ice wine
- riesling (sweet)

broccoli

- chardonnay
- sauvignon blanc

Brussels sprouts

- sauvignon blanc

burgers

BEEF

- cabernet sauvignon
- malbec
- merlot
- Portuguese reds (dry)
- Spanish reds
- syrah/shiraz
- zinfandel

TURKEY

- merlot
- pinot noir
- syrah/shiraz
- zinfandel

VEGGIE

- merlot
- pinot noir
- zinfandel

butter and butter sauces

- Champagne and other dry sparkling wines
- chardonnay

cabbage

- gewürztraminer
- riesling (dry)

calamari

- Champagne and other dry sparkling wines
- Italian whites
- grüner veltliner
- sauvignon blanc

catfish (*see* fish, delicately flavored)

caviar

- Champagne and other dry sparkling wines

ceviche

- albariño
- Sancerre
- sauvignon blanc
- Vinho Verde

charcuterie

- barbera
- Beaujolais
- Côtes du Rhône
- riesling (dry)
- rosé

cheese (*see also* Cheese Pairing Guide, page 148)

BLUE CHEESES

- Sauternes, Port, Madeira, and other dessert wines
- zinfandel

HARD, AGED, FLAVORFUL CHEESES

- Amarone
- Beaujolais
- pinot noir
- riesling (off-dry to sweeter styles)

SOFT, CREAMY CHEESES

- Chablis
- chardonnay
- chenin blanc
- pinot noir
- sauvignon blanc
- white Burgundy

cheeseburgers (*see* burgers)

cherries

- Beaujolais
- pinot noir

cherries in desserts

- Banyuls
- vintage Port

chicken

IN A CREAMY SAUCE

- Champagne and other dry sparkling wines
- chardonnay
- sauvignon blanc
- white Burgundy

IN A TOMATO SAUCE

- Chianti
- montepulciano d'Abruzzo
- Rosso di Montalcino
- sangiovese
- Valpolicella
- Vino Nobile di Montepulciano

EASTERN-INFLUENCED, BLACKENED, OR SPICY

- gewürztraminer
- riesling (off-dry)

FRIED

- albariño
- Champagne and other dry sparkling wines
- chardonnay (especially lean versions)
- Pouilly Fumé
- Sancerre
- sauvignon blanc

ROASTED

- Beaujolais
- chardonnay
- Côtes du Rhône
- gamay
- pinot noir
- red Burgundy
- Rioja
- white Burgundy

chili

- syrah/shiraz
- zinfandel

Chinese food

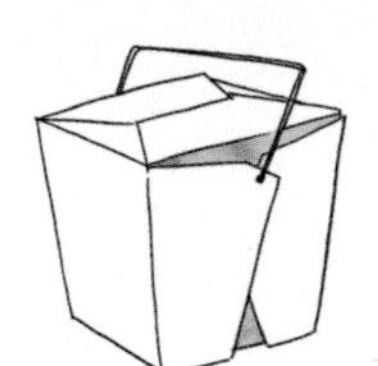

- Champagne and other dry sparkling wines
- gewürztraminer
- riesling (dry to off-dry)
- sauvignon blanc

chocolate

- Banyuls
- Madeira (sweet)
- vintage Port

clams

- Chablis
- Muscadet
- sauvignon blanc

corn

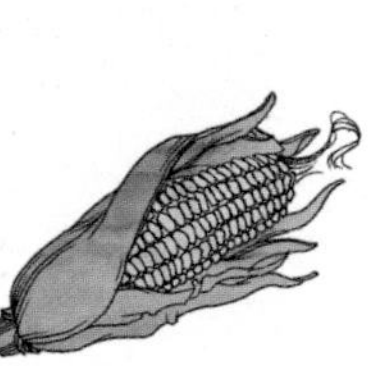

- Champagne and other dry sparkling wines
- chardonnay (especially rich, New World styles with oak)
- white Burgundy

crab

- Chablis
- Champagne and other dry sparkling wines
- chardonnay
- riesling (dry)
- white Burgundy

curry

- gewürztraminer
- riesling (off-dry)
- zinfandel

duck

- merlot
- pinot noir
- red Burgundy
- Rioja
- zinfandel

eggs

- Champagne and other dry sparkling wines

enchiladas

- Beaujolais
- sauvignon blanc

fajitas

- chardonnay
- sauvignon blanc
- zinfandel

figs/figs in desserts

- tawny Port
- zinfandel

fish (*see also* salmon)

DELICATELY FLAVORED (OR FISH IN A LEMON SAUCE)

- albariño
- Chablis
- Champagne and other dry sparkling wines
- chardonnay (but very light and crisp style)
- Italian whites
- Muscadet
- Pouilly Fumé
- sauvignon blanc
- Sancerre
- torrontés

RICHLY FLAVORED (OR FISH IN A RICHLY FLAVORED SAUCE)

- Champagne and other dry sparkling wines
- chardonnay
- white Burgundy

french fries

- Champagne and other dry sparkling wines
- white Burgundy

fried food

- Champagne and other dry sparkling wines
- sauvignon blanc
- Sherry (dry)
- white Burgundy

fruit

- ice wine
- moscato d'Asti
- riesling (sweet)

game

GAME BIRDS (SUCH AS GUINEA HEN, PHEASANT, QUAIL, SQUAB)

- pinot noir
- red Burgundy

GAME MEATS

- Barolo
- brunello di Montalcino
- Côte Rôtie
- Hermitage
- Rioja

grouper (*see* fish, delicately flavored)

halibut (*see* fish, delicately flavored)

ham

- Beaujolais
- gewürztraminer
- pinot noir

hamburgers (*see* burgers)

hot dogs

- pinot noir
- riesling (off-dry)

- rosé
- zinfandel

Indian food

- gewürztraminer
- riesling (off-dry)
- sauvignon blanc
- zinfandel

lamb

- Barbaresco
- Barolo
- Bordeaux
- cabernet franc
- cabernet sauvignon
- Cornas
- Côte Rôtie
- Hermitage or Croze-Hermitage
- nebbiolo
- syrah/shiraz

lasagne

- Barolo
- Barbaresco
- brunello di Montalcino
- Chianti
- montepulciano d'Abruzzo
- nebbiolo
- Rioja
- Rosso di Montalcino
- sangiovese
- tempranillo
- Valpolicella
- Vino Nobile di Montepulciano

lemon

- Chablis
- pinot grigio and other Italian whites
- Sancerre
- sauvignon blanc

lemongrass

- riesling (dry to off-dry)
- sauvignon blanc

lemon in desserts

- ice wine
- riesling (sweet)
- Sauternes

lobster

- Champagne
- chardonnay (especially white Burgundy)
- semisweet Vouvray

macaroni and cheese

- chardonnay
- pinot noir

mahimahi (*see* fish, delicately flavored)

mangoes

- chardonnay
- riesling (off-dry to sweet)

marinara sauce

- Barbaresco
- Barolo
- brunello di Montalcino
- Chianti
- montepulciano d'Abruzzo
- nebbiolo
- Rioja
- Rosso di Montalcino
- sangiovese
- tempranillo
- Valpolicella
- Vino Nobile di Montepulciano

meat loaf

- cabernet franc
- cabernet sauvignon
- Côtes du Rhône
- malbec
- merlot
- red Bordeaux
- Rioja
- syrah/shiraz
- zinfandel

melon

- moscato d'Asti
- pinot grigio/pinot gris
- prosecco

Mexican food

- malbec
- merlot
- riesling (off-dry)
- sauvignon blanc
- zinfandel

mushrooms

- Champagne and other dry sparkling wines
- chardonnay
- pinot noir
- red Bordeaux
- red burgundy
- Rioja
- white burgundy
- zinfandel

mussels

- Muscadet
- sauvignon blanc

mustard and mustard-based sauces

- chardonnay (unoaked)
- sauvignon blanc
- zinfandel

nuts

- barrel-aged Port
- Madeira
- Sherry (all styles dry to sweet)

olives

BLACK

- Bandol
- Rioja
- Southern Italian reds (especially nero d'Avola and Taurasi)

GREEN

- sauvignon blanc
- Sherry (dry)

oysters

- Chablis
- Champagne
- sauvignon blanc (especially Sancerre)

paella

- Rioja
- rosé
- Sherry (dry)
- Spanish reds
- tempranillo

pasta carbonara

- chardonnay
- pinot noir

peaches

- demi-sec Champagne (slightly sweet)
- ice wine
- moscato d'Asti
- prosecco
- riesling (sweet)
- Sauternes

pears

- riesling (off-dry to sweet)
- Sauternes

peas

- chardonnay
- grüner veltliner
- sauvignon blanc

pecans (*see* nuts)

pepper (black)

- cabernet sauvignon
- syrah/shiraz
- zinfandel

peppers (bell)

- rosé
- sauvignon blanc
- viognier

pesto

- chardonnay (unoaked)
- Italian whites
- sauvignon blanc

pizza

- Italian reds
- malbec
- zinfandel

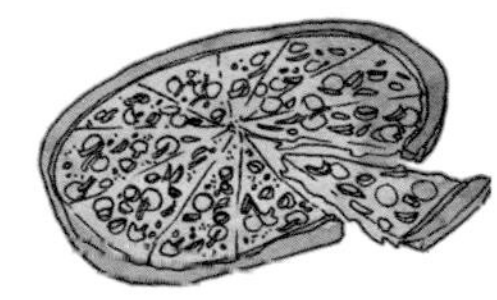

polenta

- chardonnay (especially creamy, buttery styles)
- merlot
- pinot noir

popcorn

- Champagne and other dry sparkling wine
- chardonnay (especially creamy, buttery styles)

potato chips

- Champagne and other dry sparkling wines

pork

BAKED, ROASTED, OR GRILLED

- Beaujolais
- chardonnay
- gamay
- pinot grigio/pinot gris
- pinot noir
- sauvignon blanc

BARBECUE

- syrah/shiraz
- zinfandel

EASTERN-INFLUENCED, CHINESE, INDIAN, ETC. AND ESPECIALLY SPICY

- gewürztraminer
- riesling (off-dry)

prosciutto

- barbera
- Chianti
- dolcetto
- pinot grigio/pinot gris
- rosé Champagne
- Valpolicella

pumpkin

- barrel-aged Port
- viognier

rabbit

- Barbaresco
- Barolo
- Chianti
- Côte Rôtie
- pinot noir
- red Bordeaux
- syrah/shiraz
- zinfandel

raspberries

- riesling (off-dry to sweet)
- rosé Champagne

ribs

- malbec
- syrah/shiraz
- zinfandel

risotto

- Barbaresco
- barbera
- chardonnay (especially creamy, buttery styles)
- pinot noir
- white Burgundy

salad (green)

- Chablis
- grüner veltliner
- sauvignon blanc

salmon

- Beaujolais
- chardonnay
- pinot grigio/pinot gris
- pinot noir
- red Burgundy
- rosé

sausage

- Beaujolais
- Côtes du Rhône
- merlot
- riesling (dry or off-dry)
- syrah/shiraz
- zinfandel

scallops

- Chablis
- Champagne and other dry sparkling wines
- chardonnay
- riesling (dry or off-dry)
- sauvignon blanc
- white Burgundy

sea bass (*see* fish, delicately flavored)

shrimp

SCAMPI

- pinot grigio/pinot gris
- sauvignon blanc

WITH A SPICY SAUCE

- gewürztraminer
- riesling (off-dry)

sole (*see* fish, delicately flavored)

soy sauce

- gewürztraminer
- pinot noir (especially fruity style from California)
- riesling (dry or off-dry)

spaghetti and meatballs

- Barbaresco
- Barolo
- brunello di Montalcino
- Chianti
- montepulciano d'Abruzzo
- nebbiolo
- Rioja
- Rosso di Montalcino
- sangiovese
- tempranillo
- Valpolicella
- Vino Nobile di Montepulciano

spinach

- chardonnay (unoaked)
- Italian whites
- sauvignon blanc

strawberries

- Banyuls
- demi-sec Champagne
- moscato d'Asti
- pinot noir
- rosé Champagne

steak (*see* beef)

sushi

Note: avoid wines with oak; stick with pure, clean, high-acid wines

- Champagne and other dry sparkling wines
- riesling (dry)
- sauvignon blanc

sweet potatoes

- chardonnay
- gewürztraminer
- viognier

swordfish (*see* fish, delicately flavored)

Thai food

- gewürztraminer
- riesling (off-dry)
- sauvignon blanc
- syrah/shiraz

tomatoes

- Barbaresco
- Barolo
- brunello di Montalcino
- Chianti
- montepulciano d'Abruzzo
- nebbiolo
- Rioja
- Rosso di Montalcino
- sangiovese
- sauvignon blanc
- tempranillo
- Valpolicella
- Vino Nobile di Montepulciano

trout (*see* fish, delicately flavored)

truffles

- Barbaresco
- Barolo
- Champagne
- Côtes du Rhône
- pinot noir
- red Burgundy
- white Burgundy

tuna (*see* fish, richly flavored)

turkey (roasted)

- Beaujolais
- chardonnay
- gamay
- gewürztraminer
- pinot noir
- red Burgundy
- sauvignon blanc
- white Burgundy

vanilla

- Champagne and other dry sparkling wines
- moscato d'Asti
- riesling (sweet)

veal

IN AN ACIDIC SAUCE, LIKE LEMON OR TOMATO

- Barbaresco
- Barolo
- brunello di Montalcino
- Chianti
- nebbiolo
- Rioja
- sangiovese
- tempranillo

IN A SAVORY SAUCE, LIKE MUSHROOM

- Barbaresco
- Barolo
- red Bordeaux
- brunello di Montalcino
- cabernet franc
- cabernet sauvignon
- Côtes du Rhône
- merlot
- nebbiolo
- pinot noir

venison

- Barbaresco
- Barolo
- red Bordeaux
- syrah/shiraz
- zinfandel

What Next?

Hopefully, you're now feeling a little smarter when it comes to wine. You can talk some talk and you're ready to put all this newfound know-how into action. What now, you ask?

TASTE LOTS OF WINE.

Like I've said before, nothing—no book, no person, no website—can replace the value of tasting lots and lots of wine. Building your library of tasting experiences is the single most important part of your education, and this chapter contains instructions on the best ways to do just that. The following is my take on the best stuff to read, drink, and do next. This chapter offers guidance on attending wine tastings and events, visiting wineries, starting a wine tasting group, and hosting wine parties, plus diligent research via homework six-packs and additional reading to keep you thirsty.

GO TO TASTINGS AND WINE EVENTS

Whenever you have the chance to compare and contrast multiple bottles at the same time, you stand to learn more than if you were just focused on one bottle. Wine tastings and events are great ways to gain exposure to many wines in one sitting, without having to foot the bill for all of the bottles yourself. Search for wine tastings in your area at LocalWineEvents.com.

START A WINE TASTING GROUP

Another fun educational endeavor is to start a tasting group among friends (or better yet, make new friends by starting a wine tasting group). If you take the time to organize it, you'll be surprised at how many people pop out of the woodwork, eager to join you. In fact, you'll probably have to turn some folks down, so it doesn't get out of control. Wine has social pull, I'm telling you. Here's how to do it.

1. Decide how big your group will be. Up to ten people can comfortably taste a single bottle (each gets about a two-ounce pour and you have a bit of extra wine for user error). Six to ten people is perfect for a wine tasting group—enough for some good banter and energy, but not so many that it turns into a rager.

2. Meet regularly. Once a month is a good starting point.

3. Assign themes. You can use homework six-packs (see page 183) as a guide to exploring different regions and grapes, or you can come up with your own. The idea is to taste a group of wines that have something in common (be they all from New Zealand or all made from the riesling grape). That way, you train your brain to find associations. If you taste like this on a regular basis, you'll be blown away by how fast you learn. Six bottles is the magic number—it's enough wine to educate and entertain, but not so much that it's overwhelming. Many retailers also give discounts when you buy six bottles at a time.

4. Share the cost. One of the best things about a tasting group is that you don't have to pay for all the wine! There are a lot of ways to split the bill; the easiest is to rotate the shopping each month. When one person is held accountable, it's less complicated, and it ensures you get the right combination of wines. You'll want to decide on a target dollar amount (for example, two hundred dollars per six-pack). This will deter anyone from being too miserly or going totally overboard with spending. If you're going to use the homework six-packs, I'd advise you to take the list into a good wine retailer, let them know how much you want to spend, and ask them to help you find the best examples of those types of wines.

5. Establish the feel ahead of time. Some tasting groups operate very formally, with library-like silence while tasting and taking notes. Others just set the wine out as a centerpiece for conversation. I'd shoot for something in between. Taking some notes before you share encourages people to form their own opinions—without being swayed by more vocal members of the group. If your group decides to take notes, it should be part of the host's duty to have pens and paper ready.

6. Concealing and revealing the wines adds to the fun. Trying putting all the bottles in paper bags to add a blind-tasting element to the evening. It's also exciting to reveal prices *after* everyone has given their take on the wines. This can be especially entertaining if you throw in at least one low-priced wine and one expensive wine. I love seeing people go gaga over a bottle and then learning it costs only six dollars.

HOMEWORK SIX-PACKS

Homework has never been this fun. The following six-packs serve as a basis for exploring a grape or region, or for contrasting certain wines. If you can't find a particular wine on the list, ask for help. Knowledgeable wine shop staff can help you find an appropriate substitute. When tasting, try to compare what you experience in the different bottles—and go back and re-taste as much as you like. It might seem like a party in a box, but this is one of the best ways to train your brain on wine.

NAPA VS. BORDEAUX

» Napa sauvignon blanc
» white Bordeaux
» Napa merlot
» merlot-based right-bank red Bordeaux
» Napa cabernet sauvignon
» cabernet sauvignon–based left-bank red Bordeaux

SONOMA VS. BURGUNDY

» unoaked chardonnay from Sonoma
» Chablis
» oaked chardonnay from Sonoma
» white Burgundy from Meursault
» Sonoma pinot noir
» red Burgundy from Gevrey-Chambertin or Nuits-Saint-Georges

CALIFORNIA PINOT NOIR

» Russian River Valley pinot noir
» Sonoma Coast pinot noir
» Carneros pinot noir
» Santa Barbara County pinot noir
» Monterey or Carmel Valley pinot noir
» Mendocino County pinot noir

BEST OF NAPA SAMPLER

» Carneros pinot noir
» Carneros sparkling wine
» Carneros chardonnay
» cabernet sauvignon from a mountain appellation (Howell Mountain, Diamond Mountain District, Spring Mountain District, or Mt. Veeder)
» cabernet sauvignon from a valley floor appellation (Oakville, Oak Knoll District, Rutherford, or Yountville)
» Stags Leap District cabernet sauvignon

PACIFIC NORTHWEST SAMPLER

- Oregon pinot gris
- Willamette Valley pinot noir
- Oregon pinot noir from a more specific appellation in the Willamette Valley (Chehalem Mountains, Dundee Hills, Eola-Amity Hills, or Ribbon Ridge)
- Washington state merlot
- Washington state cabernet sauvignon
- Washington state syrah

GERMAN SAMPLER

- dry kabinett riesling
- off-dry spätlese riesling
- off-dry auslese riesling
- spätburgunder (German pinot noir)
- sekt (German sparkling wine)
- German dessert wine (beerenauslese or trockenbeerenauslese)

AUSTRALIAN SAMPLER

- Margaret River cabernet sauvignon or cabernet blend
- Barossa Valley shiraz
- Clare Valley or Eden Valley dry riesling
- Coonawarra cabernet sauvignon
- Padthaway chardonnay or sauvignon blanc
- Australian dessert wine or "stickie"

NEW ZEALAND SAMPLER

- Marlborough sauvignon blanc
- Marlborough pinot noir
- Marlborough chardonnay
- Central Otago pinot noir
- cabernet sauvignon–based wine from Hawke's Bay
- syrah-based wine from Hawke's Bay

NORTHERN ITALY

- Barolo or Barbaresco
- Amarone
- barbera
- dolcetto
- prosecco
- moscato d'Asti

CENTRAL AND SOUTHERN ITALY

- Chianti Riserva
- brunello di Montalcino
- Super Tuscan
- montepulciano d'Abruzzo
- nero d'Avola or primitivo
- Soave or Orvieto

FRENCH WHITES SAMPLER

- Champagne
- white Bordeaux
- Sancerre
- Chablis
- white Burgundy from Pouilly-Fuissé or Viré-Clessé
- white Burgundy from Puligny-Montrachet, Chassagne-Montrachet, or Meursault

FRENCH REDS SAMPLER

- cabernet sauvignon–based red Bordeaux
- merlot-based red Bordeaux
- red Burgundy
- Côtes du Rhône
- Côte Rôtie or Hermitage
- Châteauneuf-du-Pape

SPANISH SAMPLER

- albariño
- cava
- Priorat
- Rioja
- Ribera del Duero
- oloroso Sherry or a Spanish rosé

SPARKLING WINE SAMPLER

- NV or vintage Champagne
- rosé Champagne
- prosecco
- California sparkling wine
- cava
- sekt (German sparkling wine) or sparkling shiraz

ROSÉ SAMPLER

- French rosé from Bandol, France
- French rosé from the Rhône Valley, France (Côtes du Rhône, Tavel, or Lirac)
- French rosé from the Loire Valley, France
- rosé sparkling wine from Champagne, France or California
- Spanish rosé
- California rosé

BEST OF PINOT NOIR

- Oregon pinot noir
- California pinot noir
- German spätburgunder
- New Zealand pinot noir
- red Burgundy
- South African pinot noir

BEST OF CABERNET SAUVIGNON

- Napa cabernet sauvignon
- Sonoma cabernet sauvignon
- South African cabernet sauvignon
- cabernet sauvignon–based left-bank red Bordeaux
- Argentinean or Chilean cabernet sauvignon
- Washington state cabernet sauvignon

BEST OF SAUVIGNON BLANC

- Sonoma or Napa sauvignon blanc
- Sancerre
- white Bordeaux
- New Zealand sauvignon blanc
- South African sauvignon blanc
- Sauternes

BEST OF SYRAH/SHIRAZ

- California syrah
- Barossa Valley shiraz
- Australian shiraz from McClaren Vale, Coonawarra, Langhorne Creek, Kangaroo Island, Padthaway, or Wrattonbully
- Côte Rôtie or Hermitage
- Côtes du Rhône
- Washington state syrah

THROW A WINE PARTY

Less commitment than forming a tasting group, a wine tasting party is another terrific excuse to simultaneously imbibe and educate. Here are three ideas for fun wine-focused fetes, sans the snobbery.

WINE PARTY IDEA NO. 1: MATCH MY MAMA'S MEAT LOAF WINE CHALLENGE

The Idea

A pairing party with a challenge: Which of your guests can best match a wine of their choice with a delectable meat loaf recipe? Everyone votes but only one lucky guest will go home with the prize.

Meat loaf haters, suspend your general skepticism; this recipe is so good, and different, that it inspired a wine tasting party. Just try it. Truth be told, it isn't *my* mama's recipe. Ota, the creator of the recipes, is my husband's father's mother's mother. Each generation has tweaked the formula a bit, and the result isn't so much a loaf as a gourmet batch of personal-sized meat muffins. Yum.

Party Planning

Send six to eight guests an invitation to the Match My Mama's Meat Loaf Wine Challenge. Let them know you'll be featuring a distinguished recipe, and you'd like them to bring two (yes, two) bottles of a wine they want to submit in the pairing contest. You can explain to them that one of the bottles is for the actual contest; the additional bottles of wine will be given as the grand prize to whoever brings the winning bottle.

At the party, make sure you place each contest bottle in a numbered paper bag, so there's no bias in the voting. After everyone has had a chance to try each wine, take a vote on which bottle paired best with the meat loaf. Reveal the winner, and let him go home with his hefty prize (and hopefully some leftovers!).

Ota's Monster Meat Loaf Muffins

Optional side dishes for this are cheesy scalloped potatoes, gourmet mac and cheese, garlic smashed potatoes, corn on the cob, and garlicky green beans.

Note: Use jumbo muffin tins, not regular cupcake-size muffin tins.

MAKES 12 MONSTER MUFFINS

- **2 medium yellow onions, diced**
- **1 egg**
- **¾ cup ketchup**
- **⅓ cup yellow mustard**
- **1 tablespoon fresh lemon juice**
- **3 tablespoons Worcestershire sauce**
- **2 tablespoons capers**
- **½ cup sweet pickle relish**
- **3 tablespoons light brown sugar**
- **1 tablespoon Tabasco**
- **1 pound ground beef chuck (80 percent fat)**
- **1 pound ground pork**
- **1 pound ground veal**
- **2 tablespoons kosher salt**
- **2 tablespoons coarsely ground pepper**
- **3 cups panko bread crumbs, plus more as needed**
- **Bourbon Ketchup (recipe follows)**

Preheat the oven to 400°F.

Place the onions, egg, ketchup, mustard, lemon juice, Worcestershire, capers, relish, brown sugar, and Tabasco in a blender and blend, but do not puree.

Add the beef, pork, and veal to a large mixing bowl and mix with your hands until combined. Add the salt and pepper and mix until blended.

Transfer the contents of the blender to the bowl, and combine with the meat (still using your hands). Add the bread crumbs and mix until combined. You may add more bread crumbs to adjust the consistency if needed. The mixture should be wetter than a typical hamburger patty.

With your hands, form the meat loaf mixture into baseball-size balls and place in ungreased muffin tins.

Bake for 40 minutes. Remove the muffin tins from the oven. Turn off the oven and turn on the broiler. Meanwhile, baste the tops of the meat loaf muffins generously with bourbon ketchup.

Broil for 5 minutes or until the ketchup has caramelized. Serve hot.

Bourbon Ketchup

MAKES ABOUT 3 CUPS

- **3 cups ketchup**
- **½ cup bourbon**
- **½ cup light brown sugar**
- **2 tablespoons Tabasco**

Combine the ketchup, bourbon, brown sugar, and Tabasco in a small saucepan and cook over medium heat until the consistency reduces to that of regular ketchup, 8 to 10 minutes. If you are feeling extra adventurous, try flambéing the ketchup: Wait to add the bourbon until the other ingredients are hot. Add the bourbon, and then ignite it with a long match or lighter flame to burn the alcohol off. This adds another interesting flavor and makes you look like a pro in the kitchen.

WINE PARTY IDEA NO. 2: PIZZA PARTY

The Idea

This party is a laid-back regional pairing experiment focused on the wines of Southern Italy and the country's iconic culinary staple—pizza.

I love the combination of beer and pizza, but there are plenty of delicious wines that work too. Some of the best options come from the same place pizza does—Southern Italy. The wines of Abruzzo, Apulia, Basilicata, Campania, Calabria, and Sicily were once considered plonk, but there has recently been a resurgence in quality from these regions. More and more scrumptious wines with personality are emerging from Southern Italy, and the even better news is that you don't have to spend a fortune to try them.

Party Planning

This is a casual party you could easily throw together for five to fifty people. You'll need to buy one bottle of each wine listed here for every ten people. Pour a taste of each at a time and mix and match with a variety of high-quality, handcrafted pizzas. For extra fun, you can have everyone vote on their favorite combination of wine and pie.

Montepulciano d'Abruzzo

I adore the combination of rustic earthiness and big fruit in these wines. They are unapologetically characterful and usually extreme values. They are made from the montepulciano grape and are from Abruzzo, near the heel on the "boot" of Italy.

Nero d'Avola

The hot, dry island of Sicily is often Italy's most productive wine region, turning out scores of bulk red, white, and sweet wine. Nero d'Avola, full of personality, is one of the island's best wines for the money.

Taurasi

The aglianico grape is the base for this wine, which is probably the most well known and respected of all the Southern Italian reds. It is a deeply colored, almost black wine. It almost tastes black, too, with flavors of tar, bitter chocolate, leather, and sun-scorched fruit.

Negroamaro

Rugged but juicy, *negroamaro*, the grape name, literally means "black bitter" in Italian. These chewy, dense, and tannic wines come alive with rich foods like sausage pizza.

Primitivo

Because of its Italian stamp of rustic earthiness, you may not at first recognize it, but primitivo is actually the same grape as California's zinfandel. The telltale über-ripe fruit should be your best clue.

WINE PARTY IDEA NO. 3: SOUTH IN YOUR MOUTH

The Idea

A night of surprising pairings: extravagant wines with simple, down-home cooking.

In my life, I've been lucky enough to call a handful of beautiful and eccentric places home: South Florida, Dallas, San Francisco, Sonoma, Nashville, and Chicago. Every place has its own slant on the epicurean world, but if there's one thing I've learned from my adventure in the South, it's that even though the food might not look all that sophisticated, Southerners take it very seriously.

The juxtaposition of this party is what makes it so fun: humble, classic Southern cooking paired with highbrow wine. You might not normally think of white Burgundy or Champagne when you think of fried chicken, but trust me . . . it is amazing. Hopefully, you and your guests will walk away realizing that sometimes the most unexpected pairings are the most thrilling! Yeehaw.

Party Planning

Invite six to ten guests to the party. Buy one bottle of each of the following wines listed. Pour a taste (about two ounces, or a third of a glass) of each wine with the suggested food pairing.

Pairing One

Champagne (the real French stuff) paired with french fries, tater tots, plain kettle chip potato chips, hush puppies, fried chicken, or catfish.

Why it works: Champagne, dry and tart, acts like a squeeze of lemon juice on any of the above fried foods—the effervescence brightens flavors and provides a refreshing juxtaposition to the fat and salt.

Pairing Two

White Burgundy (try a wine from Meursault, Pouilly-Fuissé, or Viré-Clessé) paired with fried chicken, macaroni and cheese, or corn on the cob.

Why it works: White Burgundy is 100 percent chardonnay, and chardonnay from any of these southern villages tastes especially sun-kissed. The ripe, slightly nutty, and buttery flavors of the wine complement the richness of the suggested pairings, but their tangy acidity cuts through the fat, providing a refreshing contrast.

Pairing Three

California Zinfandel paired with pulled pork sandwiches and coleslaw relish, hamburgers, or barbecue baby back ribs.

Why it works: Juicy and full-bodied, high-alcohol zinfandels have flavors of blackberry jam, raisins, prunes, and pepper. The wine's big, bold, fruit-driven presence stands up to larger-than-life flavors like barbecue.

Pairing Four

South African pinotage paired with hot dogs, corn dogs, Lit'l Smokies, ham, or pigs in a blanket.

Why it works: Pinotage is wild. South Africans created their signature grape by crossbreeding two varieties—pinot noir and cinsault—in an effort to make a more resilient and hearty wine that still had the grace and aromatics of pinot noir. The result, although popular there, doesn't taste much like the goal. Instead, most pinotage is an odd mix of spicy, smoky flavors and a loud, unapologetic aroma of raw meat, sometimes also combined with bananas and other tropical fruit. It's carnal, which makes it a perfect partner to meaty, smoky Southern foods.

VISIT WINERIES

Like field trips for your tongue, visiting wineries can be an incredible way to learn. Getting an intimate, firsthand perspective on how a winery operates is invaluable, and usually pretty romantic. (If you've never walked a row of vines with a winemaker, or taken in the yeasty perfume of a room of fermenting wine, you are in for a real treat!) I always learn something when I visit a new winery; I'm certain you will too.

One fun wine bonus we haven't even touched on yet—all of the best wine regions just happen to be in the most beautiful corners of the earth, with great weather for most of the year. (Clever little grapes.) Wine-focused travel is the way to go, so start your bucket list now. Here's my best advice (and some other great resources) for planning your trip. For even more detail and specific recommended itineraries to select wine regions, visit my website, melaniewagnerwine.com.

SIX TIPS FOR VISITING WINERIES

1. Do Some Research

Learning a bit about a region before you dive in will help you make the most of your trip. Print a map, investigate interesting places, and create a plan before you get there. Here are some of the best regionally specific websites with loads of info on wine tourism.

- **Australia:** Tourism Australia *australia.com*
- **Austria:** Austrian National Tourist Office *austria.info*
- **Bordeaux, France:** Bordeaux Office of Tourism *bordeaux-tourisme.com*
- **Burgundy, France:** Burgundy Regional Tourism Council *burgundy-tourism.com*
- **Champagne, France:** The Comité Interprofessionnel du Vin de Champagne *champagne.fr*
- **Germany:** Wines of Germany *germanwineusa.org*
- **Greece:** National Inter-Professional Organization of Vine and Wine of Greece *newwinesofgreece.com*
- **Italy:** Movimento Turismo del Vino *movimentoturismovino.it*
- **Mendocino, California:** Mendocino County Wine & Winegrapes *mendowine.com*
- **Napa, California:** Napa Valley Vintners *napavintners.com*
- **New York State:** Finger Lakes Tourism Alliance *fingerlakes.org*
- **New Zealand:** New Zealand Wine *nzwine.com*
- **Oregon:** Oregon Wine Board *oregonwine.org*
- **Paso Robles, California:** Paso Robles Wine Country Alliance *pasowine.com*
- **Portugal:** Portuguese Trade Bureau *visitportugal.com*
- **Santa Barbara County, California:** Santa Barbara County Vintners' Association *sbcountywines.com*
- **Santa Cruz Mountains, California:** Santa Cruz Mountains Winegrowers *scmwa.com*
- **Sonoma, California:** Sonoma Valley Visitor's Bureau *sonomavalley.com*
- **South Africa:** South African Tourism Bureau *southafrica.net*
- **Spain:** Trade Commission of Spain *spain.info*
- **Washington State:** Washington Wine Commission *washingtonwine.org*

2. Make Reservations (But Not Too Many)

Sure, every winery and wine region has its own feel, but, collectively, people who make wine are an extremely hospitable sort. Like a bunch of old Italian grandmas, they take care of you, and you can tell they enjoy doing it. You'll find some wineries are open to the public, which means you can drop in unannounced, and some are open by reservation only. In either case, making reservations tells a winery that you've made them a priority, and they always appreciate that. Even given their proclivity to roll out the red carpet, you can set yourself up for the warmest welcome possible by letting them know you're coming.

That having been said, don't set such a tight schedule of reservations for yourself that you can't enjoy each visit. Oftentimes, you'll find tours can last a little longer than planned, and if you're having a great time, you may want to linger; wine country is no place for rushing around. You also want to leave space in your schedule for a little adventure. Maybe you spot a great antique shop or an ice-cream parlor or a few wineries that aren't on the map (oh, they're there). Leave plenty of time in between appointments for exploring. I think three reservations in one day is doable and sets a nice pace. Additionally, the vibe will be less Disney-ish if you can avoid weekends, and if you look for wineries a little off the beaten path. Steer clear of wineries that advertise on billboards.

THE DIFFERENCE BETWEEN A TASTING AND A TOUR A tasting is a simple affair: show up, taste wine, pay, and exit. Tastings occur in the tasting room (generally identifiable as the room that looks like a bar); you may also be invited to taste outdoors if the weather is nice.

A tour is a longer (usually about an hour), more involved, behind-the-scenes look at the process of winemaking at a particular winery. Some tours cost money; others are free. A tour is led by someone from the winery (an employee at larger wineries, sometimes the winemaker or owner at very small ones). Depending on the size of the winery and your group, you may be alone or you may be accompanied by other visitors. In addition to learning about the different phases of winemaking, you usually get a detailed history of the winery and insight into particular wines and vintages. Once you hit a few tours, you'll notice similarities (if you've seen one stainless-steel tank, you've seen them all), but if you have the time, you'll always pick up something new with each visit. Happily, tours end with a tasting. I recommend a mix of tours and tastings for any wine trip.

3. Get an Early Start

"Early" is a loose term when it comes to wine tourism. Most wineries open for tours and tastings around ten or eleven a.m. Getting your day started when theirs does ensures a few things:

(a) You'll cover more ground.

(b) You'll up your shot at VIP status. A winery is much more likely to open special bottles at the beginning of the day, when they know more people will be coming through to taste. Showing up ten minutes before they close will only guarantee you the dregs.

(c) You'll have time to fit in a lunch break, especially important as it relates to the next bit of advice . . .

4. Don't Get Wasted

The combination is intoxicating: crunchy gravel underfoot, gorgeous rolling vine-yards as far as the eye can see, kind people, fresh air, warm sunshine, colorful flora and fauna everywhere (wine country dogs are the *best*!), and the magnetic allure of the farmer-chic lifestyle. Add a fountain or two and free-flowing wine to the picture and you've got yourself a recipe for getting really, really tipsy. Make sure you drink lots of water, take breaks, and eat often. Assign a designated driver for the day, hire a car, or transport yourself with a bike to avoid any potential combination of drinking and driving. Remember that it's OK to spit every now and then, too (See "Spit or Swallow?" page 73). No one will be insulted if you don't finish every wine, or any wine for that matter.

5. Be Prepared to Spend a Little Money

In the olden days, visiting wineries was free. Now, most charge a fee for tasting and/or tours. In the United States, that charge usually ranges from five to fifteen dollars, but many wineries allow you to apply it directly to the purchase of wine. Which leads me to my next thought . . . While you're there, buy wine! Wine makes a great souvenir. Every time you open a bottle you can relive your fabulous trip. (It also makes a nice consolation prize for anyone who didn't make it to wine country with you.)

6. Be Prepared to Take Your Purchase on the Road

And don't forget, if you're buying wine and taking it with you—as opposed to having the winery ship it to you later—make sure you don't leave it in a hot car. When I'm planning a warm-weather wine pilgrimage, I bring along a cooler and ice to store my booty.

Did You Know? Some wineries have very small production wines that they sell only at the winery. These are usually passion projects for the winemaker and can be good values.

JOIN WINE CLUBS

Wine clubs put shopping on autopilot with a trusted source. (Plus it's a treat to come home to a surprise box of wine.) Most wineries have a wine club, as do certain wine merchants and organizations. With many of them, you can decide on the price point you are comfortable with, and choose how often you'd like shipments.

MY FAVORITE WINE CLUBS

Kermit Lynch Wine Merchant: This iconic Berkeley, California, importer ships hand-selected wines from France and Italy for a once-a month shipment. His two- or four-bottle options make a terrific gift for the European wine lover. Kermitlynch.com

Acme Fine Wines: If you are into finding out about California's hottest undiscovered gems before anyone else, look no further than this incredible Napa-centric shop. The staff has their finger on the pulse of what's next in Napa, and there are a variety of options for club membership. Acmefinewines.com

***Food & Wine* magazine:** There are several options for pricing and frequency with this top wine club. An added bonus: the wines come with recipe pairings. Fwwineclub.com

READ ON!

In addition to all the tasting you'll be doing, it's informative—and fun—to keep reading about wine. Whether it's an industry magazine, a blog, or one of the following fascinating wine books, you're certain to pick up some new piece of knowledge every time you dive into the prose of these respected sources.

MY FAVORITE WINE MAGAZINES

» *Decanter* *decanter.com*

» *Food & Wine* *foodandwine.com*

» *Wine & Spirits* *wineandspiritsmagazine.com*

» *Wine Spectator* *winespectator.com*

BLOGS

» *Diner's Journal*, Eric Asimov, *New York Times*, *dinersjournal.blogs.nytimes.com/author/eric-asimov*

» *Purple Pages*, Jancis Robinson *jancisrobinson.com*

» *Vinography*, Alder Yarrow *vinography.com*

» *Melanie Wagner Wine,* Melanie Wagner *melaniewagnerwine.com*

BOOKS

For Detailed Information and Reference

» *Grapes and Wines*, Oz Clarke

» *The New France*, Andrew Jefford

» *The Oxford Companion to Wine*, Jancis Robinson

» *Secrets of the Sommeliers*, Rajat Parr and Jordan Mackay

» *What to Drink with What You Eat*, Andrew Dornenburg and Karen Page

» *The Wine Bible*, Karen MacNeil

For Less Reference, More Romance

» *Adventures on the Wine Route*, Kermit Lynch

» *Educating Peter*, Lettie Teague

» *House of Mondavi*, Julia Flynn Siler

» *Reading Between the Wines*, Terry Theise

» *Vineyards in the Sky*, Eleanor Ray with Barbara Marinacci

» *The Widow Clicquot*, Tilar J. Mazzeo

WINE SCHOOLS, CLASSES, AND EDUCATIONAL WEBSITES

» American Institute of Wine and Food *aiwf.org*

» Court of Master Sommeliers *mastersommeliers.org*

» Culinary Institute of America *ciaprochef.com/winestudies*

» Free the Grapes (information regarding U.S. wine shipping laws) *freethegrapes.com*

» Institute of Masters of Wine *mastersofwine.org*

» International Wine Center *internationalwinecenter.com*

» Society of Wine Educators *societyofwineeducators.org*

» Wine and Spirits Education Trust *wsetglobal.com*

» The Wine Institute *wineinstitute.org*

"DRINK WINE, AND YOU WILL SLEEP WELL. SLEEP, AND YOU WILL NOT SIN. AVOID SIN, AND YOU WILL BE SAVED. ERGO, DRINK WINE AND BE SAVED."

—Medieval German saying

TWENTY-FIVE RELIABLE GROCERY STORE BRANDS

- Alamos Winery / *Argentina*
- Beaulieu Vineyard / *California*
- Bogle Vineyards / *California*
- Chateau Ste. Michelle Winery / *Washington state*
- Cline Cellars / *California*
- Columbia Crest Winery / *Washington state*
- Edna Valley Vineyard / *California*
- E. Guigal / *France*
- Fairview / *South Africa*
- George Duboeuf / *France*
- Hess Collection / *California*
- Jaume Serra Cristalino Winery / *Spain*
- Kenwood Vineyards / *California*
- La Crema Winery / *California*
- La Vieille Ferme / *France*
- Marqués de Cáceres / *Spain*
- Oxford Landing Estates / *Australia*
- Paringa Vineyards / *Australia*
- Robert Mondavi Wines / *California*
- Santa Rita / *Chile*
- Segura Viudas Heredad / *Spain*
- St. Supéry Vineyards and Winery / *California*
- Villa Maria Estate / *New Zealand*
- Yalumba / *Australia*
- Zardetto / *Italy*

TWENTY-FIVE WINES ON A DIME

Let me introduce you to some of the best wines you've never heard of . . . all $15 or under.

WHITES

- Boutari moschofilero / *Mantinia, Greece*
- Burgans albariño / *Rias Baixas, Spain*
- Château Haut Rian blanc / *Bordeaux, France*
- Domaine Pichot le Peu de la Moriette Vouvray / *Loire Valley, France*
- Crios de Susana Balbo torrontés / *Argentina*
- Hugues Beaulieu Picpoul de Pinet / *Languedoc, France*
- Kris pinot grigio / *Veneto, Italy*
- Martin Codax albariño / *Rias Baixas, Spain*
- Naia verdejo / *Rueda, Spain*
- Nora albariño / *Rias Baixas, Spain*
- Telmo Rodríguez Basa / *Rueda, Spain*

REDS

- Allegrini Valpolicella / *Veneto, Italy*
- BenMarco malbec / *Mendoza, Argentina*
- Boekenhoutskloof "The Wolftrap" / *South Africa*
- Borsao Tres Picos garnacha / *Spain*
- Cantele primitivo / *Salento, Italy*
- Casa Castillo monastrell / *Jumilla, Spain*
- Castell del Remei Gotim Bru / *Costers del Segre, Spain*
- Colosi Rosso nero d'Avola / *Sicily, Italy*
- Doña Paula "Los Cardos" cabernet sauvignon / *Mendoza, Argentina*
- Duboeuf Morgon Beaujolais / *France*
- Juan Gil monastrell / *Jumilla, Spain*
- Perrin Côtes du Rhône / *France*
- Protocolo tinto / *La Mancha, Spain*
- Valle Reale Vigneto Vigne Nuove montepulciano d'Abruzzo / *Italy*

ONLINE WINE RETAILERS

I've amply voiced my opinion about the benefits of forming a relationship with a local wine retail shop. I do understand, however, that there are times when online shopping is more appropriate or convenient. For those times, here are some of the best online wine shops in the country.

- Bounty Hunter *bountyhunterwine.com*
- K & L Wine Merchants *klwines.com*
- Kermit Lynch *kermitlynch.com*
- North Berkeley *northberkeleyimports.com*
- Northwest Wine *northwest-wine.com*
- The Rare Wine Company *rarewineco.com*
- Twenty Twenty Wine Merchants *2020wines.com*
- Vinfolio *vinfolio.com*
- Wine.com *wine.com*
- Zachy's *zachys.com*

Glossary of Wines

aglianico / ahg-lee-AH-ni-ko / **grape** / $-$$$

HAPPIEST HOME: southern Italy

DEFINING AROMAS/FLAVORS: smoke, leather, mineral, black fruit, dark chocolate, coffee

Aglianico makes some of the most interesting and complex red wines of southern Italy, namely in the appellations of Taurasi and aglianico del Vulture. Generally bold and dry, they are substantially tannic, and are sophisticated for the money.

albariño / al-bah-REEN-yo / **grape** / $-$$

HAPPIEST HOME: Galicia, Spain

DEFINING AROMAS/FLAVORS: flowers, peaches, citrus

The albariño grape makes Spain's best white wines. Albariños have a unique combination of crisp acidity and a lightly creamy mouthfeel, and are worth seeking out as they are generally terrific values. Most Spanish wine is labeled with the place-name, but wines made from albariño are named after the grape.

Amarone / am-ah-RO-nee / **type of wine** / $$$-$$$$

LOCATION: Veneto, Italy

GRAPES: corvina, rondinella, molinara, and negrara

DEFINING AROMAS/FLAVORS: dark chocolate, jammy black fruits, fig, raisin, earth

Amarone is a very special wine, made only in the Valpolicella appellation of northern Italy, near Venice. Amarone is made with the same grapes as regular Valpolicella reds, but after an extended harvest, extra-ripe grapes are allowed to dry for three or four months, further concentrating their sugar before pressing. This unique process is called *recioto*. The resulting wines have a rich, lush texture and high alcohol. Flavors are bold, concentrated, and chocolate-like.

arneis / ahr-NAYZ / **grape** / $$-$$$

HAPPIEST HOME: Piedmont, Italy

DEFINING AROMAS/FLAVORS: pear, almond, apricot

Arneis means "little rascal" in Italian. The grape is difficult to grow, and thus not found often outside of its home in northern Italy. It creates dry, refreshing, elegant wines.

Bandol / ban-DOLL / **appellation** / $$-$$$

LOCATION: Provence, France

GRAPES: mostly mourvèdre, with a handful of other varieties permitted, namely cinsault and grenache

DEFINING AROMAS/FLAVORS: leather, earth, spice, cinnamon

Considered by many as one of the finest appellations in the southernmost part of France, Bandol is best known for its deliciously dry rosés. The region also produces beautiful red wines of depth, power, and character. Like the sun-drenched landscape, the flavors of Bandol wines can be rugged and wild.

Banyuls / ban-YULES / **appellation** / $$-$$$

LOCATION: Languedoc-Roussillon, France

GRAPES: predominantly grenache

DEFINING AROMAS/FLAVORS: coffee, chocolate, nuts, tea

A sweet fortified wine, Banyuls is lighter and easier to drink than many dessert wines. Its intriguing flavors make it perfect to drink solo, though it is also a good partner for chocolate. For more detail on Banyuls, see page 153.

Barbaresco / bar-bah-RESK-oh / **appellation** / $$$–$$$$

LOCATION: Piedmont, Italy

GRAPE: nebbiolo

DEFINING AROMAS/FLAVORS: tar, rose petals, earth, chocolate, fig, violets, licorice

Barbaresco and Barolo are the queen and king (respectively) of Piedmontese red wines. Both appellations make wine exclusively from the elusive nebbiolo grape, and the resulting wines have similar flavors. Both are aristocratic, tannic wines that are built to last for many years. Barbaresco is considered the more feminine tasting of the two—with a slightly more elegant texture that's not quite as formidable as the more masculine Barolo. Barolo also has longer aging requirements before it can be released.

barbera / bar-BEAR-ah / **grape** / $–$$

HAPPIEST HOME: Piedmont, Italy

DEFINING AROMAS/FLAVORS: blackberry, black cherry, plum

Barbera makes incredibly juicy, fresh, and food-friendly wines, thanks to the grape's naturally high acidity. The best examples of barbera are grown in the Piedmont region of northern Italy, in the towns of Alba and Asti, where you'll find them appropriately dubbed barbera d'Alba and barbera d'Asti.

Barolo / bah-RO-lo / **appellation** / $$$–$$$$

LOCATION: Piedmont, Italy

GRAPE: nebbiolo

DEFINING AROMAS/FLAVORS: tar, rose petals, earth, chocolate, fig, violets, licorice

Barolo is the undeniable king of Northern Italian red wines. Hugely tannic and intoxicatingly aromatic (usually only after many years of bottle aging), these wines are considered some of the most special and interesting in the world. Some producers are now trying to make Barolo that has more upfront fruit flavor and less tannin, so that consumers don't have to wait twenty years to experience what the wine is all about. But the best Barolos (just like their sister wine, Barbaresco) need time to reach their full potential.

Beaujolais / bo-jho-LAY / **appellation** / $–$$

LOCATION: France

GRAPE: gamay

DEFINING AROMAS/FLAVORS: strawberry, raspberry, cherry, rose petal, earth

The large Beaujolais appellation lies just south of Burgundy, but is a world apart from its more esteemed northern neighbor. Most Beaujolais is simple, inexpensive, fruity wine meant to be consumed very young (especially in the case of Beaujolais nouveau—a special category of wine released just weeks after harvest). However, the singular grape of this region (gamay), given the right terroir and quality-minded viticulture and vinification, can produce some beautiful wines with a complex aromatic profile that are a bargain for the price. For more details on Beaujolais and an in-depth explanation of the difference between cru Beaujolais and Beaujolais nouveau, see page 59.

Bordeaux: red / bor-DOE / **appellation** / $-$$$$

LOCATION: France

GRAPES: cabernet sauvignon, merlot, cabernet franc, petit verdot, malbec

DEFINING AROMAS/FLAVORS: plum, currant, black fruit, mint, eucalyptus, green pepper, tobacco, cedar, coffee, vanilla, mineral, spice

Although the word *Bordeaux* may conjure up images of some of the world's most highly prized red wines, many good values can be found here too. Bordeaux makes a lot of wine—in fact, it's the largest fine-wine region in the world. Most red wines are made with either a substantial amount of cabernet sauvignon plus the addition of some merlot and/or cabernet franc, or a substantial amount of merlot, plus the addition of some cabernet sauvignon and/or cabernet franc. For more details on cabernet sauvignon–based Bordeaux, see page 112, and for more information on merlot–based Bordeaux wines, see page 114.

Bordeaux: white / bor-DOE / **appellation** / $-$$$

LOCATION: France

GRAPES: sauvignon blanc, semillon, and sometimes a small amount of muscadelle

DEFINING AROMAS/FLAVORS: grapefruit, lemon, hay, honey, mineral

Most white Bordeaux is a delicious blend of crisp sauvignon blanc and creamy semillon. There are good, lemony-flavored values to be had with the simplest wines of the appellation, and also extremely elegant, mineral-driven versions that cost quite a bit more. For more details on white Bordeaux, see page 98.

brunello di Montalcino / brew-NELL-oh dee mon-tall-CHEE-no / **grape** and **appellation** / $$$-$$$$

LOCATION: Tuscany, Italy

GRAPE: brunello (a sangiovese clone)

DEFINING AROMAS/FLAVORS: dark cherry, earth, violets, chocolate

Brunello, the nickname for the especially dark, rich sangiovese clone that grows in the town of Montepulciano, creates one of the most respected and lasting red wines in Italy. Big, powerful, and tannic, they age very well in bottle. For more details on brunello di Montalcino, see page 116.

Burgundy: red / BUR-gun-dee / **appellation** / $$-$$$$

LOCATION: France

GRAPE: pinot noir

DEFINING AROMAS/FLAVORS: raspberry, cherry, earth, mushroom, game, rose, peony, violet, ginger, licorice

Expect to pay a lot to experience the Burgundy that legends are made of. The red wines from this tiny strip of land come in many quality levels, but it is only at the very top echelon that one can perhaps begin to see for oneself what all the hype is about. Intriguing aromatics, sensual texture, and captivating complexity all seduce in this region's best red wines, made exclusively from pinot noir. For more details on pinot noir from Burgundy, see page 108.

Burgundy: white / BUR-gun-dee / **appellation** / $$-$$$$

LOCATION: France

GRAPE: chardonnay

DEFINING AROMAS/FLAVORS: lemon, apple, peach, vanilla, hazelnut, mineral, white flowers, toast, butter, butterscotch, caramel

Burgundy might be small in size, but it has earned a colossal reputation, for both red and white wines. Burgundy has a complex system of nesting appellations, ranging from the all-encompassing Bourgogne Blanc (meaning the grapes can come from anywhere in Burgundy) to subregions like Chablis and the Côte d'Or, which get more and more specific. Eventually, Burgundy even classifies wines down to particular vineyards (like Montrachet—a single vineyard site considered to produce the best white wine in all of France, perhaps in all of the world). All whites are made exclusively from chardonnay and, when they are good, are considered the pinnacle of what the grape can achieve. The best are lush but with a racy streak of acidity that keeps them elegant. Graceful, profound, and complex, they are made in minute quantities, and fetch extremely high prices. For more details on chardonnay from Burgundy, see page 101.

---

cabernet franc / cab-ur-NAY FRONK / **grape** / $$-$$$$

HAPPIEST HOMES: Loire Valley, France; Bordeaux, France

DEFINING AROMAS/FLAVORS: raspberry, tobacco, green pepper, coffee, violets

Rarely bottled on its own outside of the Loire Valley in France, this grape is more famously blended with cabernet sauvignon and/or merlot (it is said to contribute finesse and perfume). The best Loire Valley appellations to look for include Chinon, Anjou, and Saumur, where in addition to red wine, cabernet franc is the main component of some delicious rosé.

---

cabernet sauvignon / cab-ur-NAY so-vin-YAWN / **grape** / $-$$$$

HAPPIEST HOMES: Bordeaux, France; Napa, California

DEFINING AROMAS/FLAVORS: black currant, blackberry, cedar, mint, pencil lead, leather, eucalyptus

Cabernet sauvignon, the world's most popular and esteemed red grape, makes wines of vastly varying quality levels and styles and is successfully cultivated in many winemaking regions around the globe. Thick-skinned berries create wines with lots of color and tannin. It is often found blended with merlot and/or cabernet franc (both thought to help soften cabernet sauvignon's potentially hard edges). The best examples age very well in bottle. For more details on cabernet sauvignon, see page 111.

---

carménère / car-men-YARE / **grape** / $-$$

HAPPIEST HOME: Chile

DEFINING AROMAS/FLAVORS: cherry, smoke, earth, chocolate

Originally from Bordeaux, France, but relatively obscure there today, carménère is now found all over Chile, where it can make easy-drinking wines of good value.

---

cava / KAH-vah / **type of wine** / $-$$

LOCATION: Spain

GRAPES: parellada, macabeo, xarel-lo, chardonnay

DEFINING AROMAS/FLAVORS: lemon, green apple, toast, earth

Cava can come from all over Spain, but most of it is made in the Penedès region, near Barcelona. One of the world's best wine bargains, Spain's sparkling wine is generally simple, straightforward, and super-tasty for the price. For more details on cava, see page 40.

Chablis / sha-BLEE / **appellation** / $$-$$$

LOCATION: Burgundy, France

GRAPE: chardonnay

DEFINING AROMAS/FLAVORS: lemon, chalk, gunflint

Chablis, the very northernmost tip of Burgundy, produces lean, lithe versions of chardonnay. These wines have a bold shock of acidity and a signature mineral component. For more details on Chablis, see page 101.

Champagne / sham-PAIN / **appellation** / $$$-$$$$

LOCATION: northern France

GRAPES: chardonnay, pinot noir, pinot meunier

DEFINING AROMAS/FLAVORS: lemon, apple, toast, yeast, chalk, vanilla, nuts, mushroom

Champagne is the world's most famous sparkling wine. It is made from chardonnay, pinot noir, or pinot meunier (or most likely, a blend of the three). Growing grapes and making the wine destined to become Champagne is extremely labor-intensive, and as a result, most Champagne is expensive. Both white and rosé versions are made, and although most Champagne is very dry, there are sweeter versions. For more details on Champagne, see page 38.

chardonnay / shar-doe-NAY / **grape** / $-$$$$

HAPPIEST HOMES: Champagne, France; Burgundy, France; Chablis, France; California

DEFINING AROMAS/FLAVORS: citrus, vanilla, apple, butter

Chardonnay is undeniably the world's most popular white grape. It grows well around the world and creates a wide range of styles—Chardonnay can be light and tangy or rich and creamy, it can taste like lemon and minerals or lush tropical fruit and oak, and it can cost five dollars or five hundred. For more details on chardonnay, see page 101.

Châteauneuf-du-Pape / sha-toe-NOOF doo POP / **appellation** / $$$-$$$$

LOCATION: southern Rhône Valley, France

GRAPES: grenache, syrah, mourvèdre, cinsault, muscardin, counoise, vaccarèse, terret noir, clairette, bourboulenc, roussanne, picpoul, picardan

DEFINING AROMAS/FLAVORS: red fruit, spice, herbes de Provence, bacon, earth, game, meat, tar, leather

Famously, there are actually thirteen grape varieties permitted in the prestigious southern Rhône Valley appellation of Châteauneuf-du-Pape. However, most producers use only a few, and some make wines exclusively from the major grape of the region, grenache. The wines are dense and serious, with big, gamy, earthy flavors that are heavenly with rustic Provençal food. Although rare, there are also some incredibly complex white wines from Châteauneuf-du-Pape, made from a blend of roussanne and marsanne.

chenin blanc / SHEN-in BLOHNK / **grape** / $-$$$

HAPPIEST HOME: Loire Valley, France

DEFINING AROMAS/FLAVORS: pear, quince, melon, apricot, honey

Chenin blanc makes simple, fresh white wines in many parts of California and all over South Africa (where it is known as *steen*). But the grape can achieve spectacular brilliance in the Loire Valley appellations of Savennières, Vouvray, and Saumur, where it is made into still wines that range from bone-dry to very sweet; it is even used to make some stellar sparkling wines.

Chianti / kee-AHN-tee / **appellation** / $$–$$$$

LOCATION: Tuscany, Italy

GRAPES: primarily sangiovese, with the potential addition of canaiolo, cabernet sauvignon, merlot, trebbiano, and malvasia

DEFINING AROMAS/FLAVORS: dried cherry, dusty earth, tobacco, cedar, smoke, leather, iron, orange peel

Chianti is Italy's most popular wine, and the good news is that quality continues to improve in this ancient region. There are inexpensive, super-simple versions available, but Chianti starts getting a lot more interesting and aromatic in the versions that cost around fifty dollars. For more details on Chianti, see page 117.

Chinon / shee-NON / **appellation** / $$–$$$

LOCATION: Loire Valley, France

GRAPE: cabernet franc

DEFINING AROMAS/FLAVORS: raspberry, violet, cassis, granite, iron

The appellation of Chinon (and its lesser known sister appellations of Bourgueil and Saint-Nicolas-de-Bourgueil) produces light, fragrant red wines made exclusively from the cabernet franc grape.

Cornas / core-NAS / **appellation** / $$–$$$

LOCATION: northern Rhône Valley, France

GRAPE: syrah

DEFINING AROMAS/FLAVORS: burnt fruit, earth, spice, leather, pepper

Cornas is a massively tannic, bold red wine made exclusively from syrah. The appellation is not as prestigious as its famous neighbors Côte Rôtie and Hermitage, but Cornas bottlings are considerably less expensive and generally considered a terrific value if you're looking for staunch, interesting French syrah.

cortese / core-TAY-say / **grape** / $$–$$$

HAPPIEST HOME: Piedmont, Italy

DEFINING AROMAS/FLAVORS: pear, lime

Cortese makes clean, elegant wines, most notably from around the town of Gavi in Piedmont, Italy, with a wine called cortese di Gavi.

Côte Rôtie / COAT ro-TEE / **appellation** / $$$–$$$$

LOCATION: northern Rhône Valley, France

GRAPES: syrah, plus a small amount of viognier

DEFINING AROMAS/FLAVORS: meat, pepper, black fruit, smoke, mineral, bacon

Côte Rôtie is a tiny but eminent appellation producing some of the best examples of syrah on the planet. Here, the syrah grapevine clings to menacingly steep granite hillsides—the resulting wines showcase syrah's animalistic, meaty side, but are minerally and elegant at the same time. Vintners are allowed to add a very small amount of viognier (a white grape) to the blend, which can heighten aromatics.

Côtes du Rhône / COAT doo ROAN / **appellation** / $–$$

LOCATION: southern Rhône Valley, France

GRAPES: grenache, syrah, mourvèdre, cinsault, carignan

DEFINING AROMAS/FLAVORS: juicy red and black fruit, spice, earth

There are red, white, and rosé wines made in this massive southern Rhône appellation, but the reds are the real stars. Côtes du Rhône reds provide great value for those looking to find affordable, easygoing, food-friendly wines with character.

Croze-Hermitage / KROZ AIR-me-taj / **appellation** / $$–$$$

LOCATION: northern Rhône Valley, France

GRAPES: syrah, with roussanne and marsanne

DEFINING AROMAS/FLAVORS: leather, meat, black cherry, earth

This appellation surrounds its more esteemed big brother, Hermitage. Though the wines are not as special, good values can be had.

dolcetto / doll-CHET-oh / **grape** / $–$$

HAPPIEST HOME: Piedmont, Italy

DEFINING AROMAS/FLAVORS: black cherry, licorice, prune

Curiously, the "little sweet one" typically finishes with a distinctively bitter almond taste. The best dolcetto is grown around the Piedmont towns of Alba and Asti, where it makes wines called dolcetto d'Alba and dolcetto d'Asti. Low acidity limits the life span of wines made from this grape—most are meant to be imbibed within a year or two of harvest.

falanghina / fal-ahn-GEE-nah / **grape** / $$

HAPPIEST HOME: Campania, Italy

DEFINING AROMAS/FLAVORS: apple, citrus, mineral

Crisply acidic, but full-bodied, sometimes with an almost oily texture, wines made from falanghina have a lot of personality for the price. Look for falanghina grown in the appellation of Sannio, in the Campania region of southern Italy.

Gavi / GAH-vee / **appellation** / $$–$$$

LOCATION: Piedmont, Italy

GRAPE: cortese

DEFINING AROMAS/FLAVORS: lemon, green apple, white flowers, honeydew melon

Gavi's high acid and light body make for a dry, vibrant, and elegant wine that is delicious with seafood. Some consider it one of Italy's best white wines.

gewürztraminer / gah-VERT-strah-mee-ner / **grape** / $$–$$$

HAPPIEST HOMES: Alsace, France; Germany; Austria

DEFINING AROMAS/FLAVORS: rose petals, lychee, honeysuckle, peach

Gewürztraminer creates wines that are intensely and distinctively aromatic and also extremely full-bodied. It is taken most seriously in Alsace, France.

Gigondas / JHEE-gone-das / **appellation** / $$–$$$

LOCATION: southern Rhône Valley, France

GRAPES: primarily grenache, with lesser amounts of syrah and mourvèdre

DEFINING AROMAS/FLAVORS: earth, leather, berries, spice

Gigondas can be charming in a rustic, honest way. Bright berry flavors meld beautifully with earth and spice to create wines that are interesting, especially for their typically modest prices.

grenache / gren-OSH / **grape** / $-$$$$

HAPPIEST HOMES: southern France; Spain; Australia

DEFINING AROMAS/FLAVORS: red fruit, candied fruit, white pepper

Because grenache (called *garnacha* in Spain) tends to lack color, acid, and tannin, it is often blended with other grapes—principally syrah. The grape achieves its greatest potential in the wines of the southern Rhône Valley, specifically Châteauneuf-du-Pape, where it is one of thirteen permitted varieties, but typically comprises 80 to 100 percent of the wine. Grenache is also one of the two principal grapes in Spain's red Rioja wines, and makes fabulous rosés all over Spain and southern France. In addition, grenache is the main grape in many dessert wines, most notably Banyuls.

grüner veltliner / GROO-ner velt-LEE-ner / **grape** / $-$$

HAPPIEST HOME: Austria

DEFINING AROMAS/FLAVORS: exotic tropical fruit, white pepper

Naturally high acidity creates crisp, tangy wines that are typically complex for the price. Grüner, as it is affectionately abbreviated, is the signature grape of Austria, accounting for almost half of the country's vineyard plantings.

Hermitage / AIR-me-taj / **appellation** / $-$$$

LOCATION: northern Rhône Valley, France

GRAPES: predominantly syrah, possibly with small amounts of roussanne and marsanne

DEFINING AROMAS/FLAVORS: leather, meat, smoke, bacon, blackberry, black cherry, earth, granite

Hermitage and its neighboring appellation Côte Rôtie are considered the two most prestigious red wines of the northern Rhône Valley. Both are powerful, complex wines, with a meaty syrah core, but Hermitage is considered the more rugged and manly of the two. Most Hermitage is relatively expensive; Croze-Hermitage (a larger appellation surrounding the small hill of Hermitage) from a reliable producer can be a good alternative.

ice wine / **type of wine** / $$-$$$$

LOCATION: Austria, Germany, Canada

GRAPES: riesling, vidal blanc, and cabernet franc are the most popular

Ice wine (*eiswein* in Germany and *icewine* in Canada) is a dessert wine made from grapes that have been left to freeze on the vine long after harvest. The water in the grapes freezes, but not the sugars or acids. When pressed, the juice is hauntingly sweet and concentrated. Only a few places have the right climactic conditions to make ice wine (Austria, Germany, and Canada have the most luck), and when the grapes are pressed, minute quantities of juice come out. Thus, ice wine is typically very expensive.

Jumilla / hoo-MEE-lah / **appellation** / $-$$

LOCATION: Spain

GRAPES: mostly mourvèdre

DEFINING AROMAS/FLAVORS: blackberry, black cherry, plum, spice, mineral

Jumilla reds are full bodied, with jam-like flavors of black fruits and plums and a slight mineral edge. Good examples can be real values, providing a lot of character for the money.

Madeira / mah-DEER-ah / **appellation** / $$–$$$$

LOCATION: Madeira, Portugal

GRAPES: bual, malmsey, sercial, verdelho, tinta negra mole

DEFINING AROMAS/FLAVORS: toffee, caramel, burnt sugar, roasted nuts, orange peel

Like Port, Madeira is a fortified wine, although the styles of Madeira range from bracingly dry to very sweet. All have a toffee- and caramel-like flavor and naturally high acidity that keeps them refreshing regardless of the sugar levels. They are essentially indestructible once opened, since they've already been oxidized through their labor-intensive aging process. For more details on Madeira, see page 151.

malbec / mal-BECK / **grape** / $–$$$

HAPPIEST HOMES: Argentina; Cahors, France

DEFINING AROMAS/FLAVORS: plum, raisin, violets

Technically, malbec is one of the five grapes permitted in red Bordeaux. However, it has never been an important grape there and is rarely seen in modern blends. Instead, it has found a new home in Argentina, where it has become the predominant red varietal and is taken more seriously than it ever was in Bordeaux. The grape provides deep color, substantial tannin, and a juicy fruit flavor. Many are good values.

merlot / mer-LOW / **grape** / $–$$$$

HAPPIEST HOMES: Bordeaux, France; Napa, California; Washington state

DEFINING AROMAS/FLAVORS: berries, plum

Merlot is one of the five permitted grape varieties in red Bordeaux and is the most widely planted grape in that region. Although the grape is extremely popular all over the world, it makes wines of the highest quality in the Bordeaux regions of Saint-Émilion and Pomerol. As in those appellations, merlot from other parts of the world is often blended with the more structured and tannic cabernet sauvignon (and/or cabernet franc). Inexpensive merlot is rarely exceptional. For more details on merlot, see page 114.

montepulciano d'Abruzzo / mon-teh-pull-chee-AH-no dee ah-BROOT-zo / **grape** and **appellation** / $–$$

LOCATION: Abruzzo, Italy

GRAPES: montepulciano, sangiovese

DEFINING AROMAS/FLAVORS: blackberries, spice, pepper

The montepulciano grape, grown in the Abruzzo region of southern Italy, creates dry, full-bodied wines full of spice and tannin.

morellino di Scansano / more-ah-LEE-no dee scahn-SAH-no / **grape** and **appellation** / $–$$

LOCATION: Tuscany, Italy

GRAPE: morellino (a sangiovese clone)

DEFINING AROMAS/FLAVORS: bright cherry, earth

The town of Scansano makes some beautifully bright, youthful, tart cherry versions of the sangiovese grape (nicknamed morellino in this region). Many are good values. For more details on morellino di Scansano, see page 117.

moscato d'Asti / moe-SCAH-toe dee AH-stee / **grape** and **appellation** / $$

LOCATION: Piedmont, Italy

GRAPE: moscato (muscat)

DEFINING AROMAS/FLAVORS: peach, melon, white flowers

The deliciously fruity and floral grape moscato makes sparkling wines all over the town of Asti. Much of it is destined to become semi-sweet bulk wine labeled simply *Asti* and commonly known as *Asti Spumante*. However, some moscato has a higher calling. Wines labeled *moscato d'Asti* are considered the more refined sister of Asti. These wines are also semisweet and intoxicatingly floral and fruity, but have less pressure (fewer bubbles), less alcohol, and are more delicate and elegant.

mourvèdre / more-VED-rah / **grape** / $-$$$$

HAPPIEST HOMES: southern France, Spain, Australia

DEFINING AROMAS/FLAVORS: jammy black fruit, prune, earth

Mouvèdre likes it hot; the grape needs intense heat to ripen properly. Rarely bottled alone, it provides body and deep, jam-like fruit flavors to blends made with other grapes (most often grenache and syrah). You can find it in many wines of southern France, most important, Châteauneuf-du-Pape, Côtes du Rhône, and Bandol. (In Bandol, mourvèdre accounts for at least 50 percent of the blends in both red and rosé wines.) In Spain, it is known as monastrell and is found all over the country but makes its best wines in the region of Jumilla.

Muscadet / MOOSE-kah-day / **appellation** / $$

LOCATION: Loire Valley, France

GRAPE: melon de Bourgogne

DEFINING AROMAS/FLAVORS: lemon, salt, mineral

Considered by many as the quintessential oyster wine, Muscadet has a light body, crisp acidity, and is generally bone-dry and delicate.

nebbiolo / neb-ee-OH-low / **grape** / $$$-$$$$

HAPPIEST HOME: Piedmont, Italy

DEFINING AROMAS/FLAVORS: tar, rose petal, wild herbs, truffles

Rarely found outside of the Piedmont region of northern Italy (because it is so difficult to grow), nebbiolo is the lone variety used to produce two of Italy's most distinguished wines—Barolo and Barbaresco—from neighboring villages. Powerfully tannic, most nebbiolo needs plenty of time in the bottle to soften. (It is often recommended that you wait twenty years or more before popping the cork on some of the best Barolos and Barbarescos.) After years of aging, these wines can be some of the most interesting and aromatically complex wines in the world—with distinctive aromas of rose petals and tar.

negroamaro / nehg-ro-ah-MAH-ro / **grape** / $-$$

HAPPIEST HOME: Puglia, Italy

DEFINING AROMAS/FLAVORS: black fruit, dried herbs, earth, leather

Negro ("black") and *amaro* ("bitter") combine to create the aptly named grape, which tends to have a rustic, bitter quality to its black fruit flavor and is often found blended with other Italian varieties. It is grown all over southern Italy, but most noted in wines from the appellation of Salice Salentino in the Apulia region (the heel of the boot). The best wines are good values and can be outstanding partners to equally humble Mediterranean foods.

nero d'Avola / NEH-ro dee AH-vo-lah / **grape** / $-$$

HAPPIEST HOME: Sicily, Italy

DEFINING AROMAS/FLAVORS: blackberry jam, earth, pepper

The grape nero d'Avola was named after the town of Avola, on the island of Sicily, where it grows best. Also known as *calabrese*, this grape produces full-bodied, rustically charming, and inexpensive red wines.

petite sirah / peh-TEET sih-RAH / **grape** / $$-$$$

HAPPIEST HOME: California

DEFINING AROMAS/FLAVORS: blackberry, plum, blueberry

Petite sirah produces a tannic, intensely inky colored wine. It can make serious wines on its own but is not hugely popular. The grape is often blended with zinfandel, adding structure and complexity to zin's tendency toward over-ripe flabbiness. See page 121 for details on how petite sirah and syrah are related.

petit verdot / peh-TEET vair-DOE / **grape** / $-$$$

HAPPIEST HOMES: Bordeaux, France; California; Australia

DEFINING AROMAS/FLAVORS: black fruit, leather, tar, molasses

Hardly ever found as a stand-alone varietal, petit verdot is principally used (very judiciously I might add) as a blending grape; it adds tannin, color, and a dark, rustic element to more refined grapes.

pinotage / PEE-no-TAJ / **grape** / $-$$

HAPPIEST HOME: South Africa

DEFINING AROMAS/FLAVORS: meat, smoke, red fruit

Pinotage is a crossing (or cross-pollination) of cinsault and pinot noir. It was created by a professor in 1925 in South Africa, who was attempting to create a new variety that would potentially capture the best attributes from both parent grapes—he wanted cinsault's heat tolerance and productivity and pinot noir's more refined taste, aroma, and texture. The resulting grape has had mixed reviews for nearly a century. Occasionally it makes serious, complex wines, but many times wines made from the grape turn out funky—with overly animal odors or strange smells of paint or banana.

pinot blanc / PEE-no BLOHNK / **grape** / $$-$$$

HAPPIEST HOME: Germany, Austria, northern Italy

DEFINING AROMAS/FLAVORS: apple, almond

Known as *weissburgunder* in Germany and Austria and *pinot bianco* in Italy, this grape produces fairly neutral white wines with low aromatics and high acidity.

pinot grigio / PEE-no GREE-jo / **grape** / $-$$

HAPPIEST HOME: northern Italy; Alsace, France; Oregon

DEFINING AROMAS/FLAVORS: apple, pear, lemon, wildflowers

Although Italy churns out a great deal of lackluster pinot grigio, some quality-minded producers make crisp, beautiful wines, especially from the Friuli region. Alsace, France, treats the grape most seriously; there, the white wines made with pinot gris (the French name for the same grape) achieve more richness and body. Oregon also makes some delicious wines from this grape, in the French style.

pinot gris / PEE-no GREE

See pinot grigio.

pinot meunier / PEE-no moon-YAY / **grape** / $-$$$

HAPPIEST HOME: Champagne, France

DEFINING AROMAS/FLAVORS: red fruits

Rarely seen as a stand-alone varietal, pinot meunier is famous as one of the three permitted grape varieties in Champagne, France. (Chardonnay and pinot noir are the other two.) Pinot meunier is said to add fruitiness and body to the blend. It is the least regal of the three grapes, but the easiest to grow—and curiously, although many Champagne producers like to brag about how little pinot meunier is in their blend, it remains the number-one planted varietal in the region.

pinot noir / PEE-no NWHAR / **grape** / $$-$$$$

HAPPIEST HOMES: Burgundy, France; Champagne, France; Oregon; California; New Zealand; Germany

DEFINING AROMAS/FLAVORS: raspberry, cherry, earth, mushroom, rose petal

Pinot noir is one finicky (and costly) grape to grow, but that doesn't diminish its popularity the world over. Pinot noir's allure lies in its captivating aromatics and smooth, silky texture. Pinot, as it is often abbreviated, is a thin-skinned grape, and thus it creates wines that are typically low in tannin and softer in color than many other red wines. The grape's spiritual home is Burgundy, France, and it alone is the grape responsible for the highly esteemed and coveted red wines of the region. It is one of the three grapes permitted in Champagne, but is rarely blended with other grapes outside of that region. For more details on pinot noir, see page 108.

Port / **appellation** / $-$$$$

LOCATION: Duoro Valley, Portugal

GRAPES: tinta barroca, tinta cão, tinta roriz (tempranillo), touriga francesa, touriga nacional

DEFINING AROMAS/FLAVORS: cherry, chocolate, raisin, plums, pepper (bottle-aged Port); toffee, caramel, nuts, brown sugar (barrel-aged Port)

Port is a sweet fortified wine made exclusively in the Duoro Valley of Portugal. More than one hundred grape varieties are allowed in the production of Port, but typically only the five above are used for making fine wine. There are two main types of Port—bottle-aged Port, which is red, with flavors of chocolate and cherries, and barrel-aged Port, which is aged in large barrels and exposed to oxygen throughout the winemaking process, thus taking on a brown color and flavors of toffee and nuts. Both are made in a wide range of styles and quality levels. The most famous type of Port is vintage Port, a type of bottle-aged Port that is only made in stellar years, from the very finest Port grapes. Vintage Port is capable of aging for decades. For more information on both vintage and barrel-aged Port, see page 152.

Pouilly Fumé / pwee foo-MAY / **appellation** / $$-$$$

LOCATION: Loire Valley, France

GRAPE: sauvignon blanc

DEFINING AROMAS/FLAVORS: grapefruit, lemon, flint, mineral

The Pouilly Fumé appellation, neighbor to Sancerre, lies at the very eastern tip of the Loire Valley in France. The dry, elegant wines are similar in flavor to Sancerre, with high acidity and a soulful mineral character.

primitivo / prih-mih-TEE-voe / **grape** / $-$$

HAPPIEST HOME: southern Italy

DEFINING AROMAS/FLAVORS: Jam-like black and red fruit, clove, spice

DNA tests have confirmed that southern Italy's primitivo grape is indeed the genetic twin to zinfandel, a grape many thought was indigenous to California. While Italy's version is slightly more coarse and rustic, primitivo has all the ripe, jammy fruit flavors and spice of the best zinfandels, and usually offers very good value for the money.

Priorat / PREE-oh-rot / **appellation** / $$-$$$$

LOCATION: Spain

GRAPES: most notably grenache, with carignan, cabernet sauvignon, merlot, and syrah

DEFINING AROMAS/FLAVORS: black fruit, tar, mineral

Priorat is a tiny area known for producing very high-quality wines of power and intensity. Special slate soils on steep hillsides and an inhospitable climate make for vines that struggle, and in return create wines that showcase bold flavor and a deep, dark mineral core.

prosecco / pro-SECK-oh / **type of wine** / $-$$

LOCATION: northern Italy

GRAPE: glera (formerly known as prosecco)

DEFINING AROMAS/FLAVORS: peaches, melon, apricot, honeysuckle

Fresh, fruity, and delightfully affordable, prosecco is a terrific alternative to other more expensive sparkling wines—but be careful not to expect too much. These wines are meant to be simple and easy to drink; they don't claim the depth and seriousness of their French cousins.

Ribera del Duero / ree-BEAR-ah del DWAIR-oh / **appellation** / $$$-$$$$

LOCATION: Spain

GRAPES: tinto fino (tempranillo)

DEFINING AROMAS/FLAVORS: chocolate, plum, blackberry, licorice, leather

Tempranillo grown in this unforgiving continental climate in the middle of Spain has evolved to create more powerful, structured wines than it does in Rioja. Generally tannin is abundant, but in the best wines, they come off as velvety and ripe. Ribera del Duero wines are considered some of the best in Spain.

riesling / REES-ling / **grape** / $-$$$$

HAPPIEST HOMES: Germany; Alsace, France; Austria; Australia; Washington state

DEFINING AROMAS/FLAVORS: apple, peach, pear, lime, rose petal, gunflint, diesel, steel

Powerfully and uniquely aromatic (no other grape smells like flowers *and* gasoline), riesling can make show-stopping white wines. Naturally high in acidity, the best versions are capable of aging for decades. Riesling loves cold weather and thrives in Germany, Austria, and the Alsace region of France. Washington state is producing wines of good value from the grape, and Australia makes some stellar examples as well. For more details on riesling, see page 105.

Rioja / ree-OH-ha / **appellation** / $$–$$$$

LOCATION: Spain

GRAPES: predominantly tempranillo and grenache

DEFINING AROMAS/FLAVORS: leather, dusty earth, mushroom, berries, oak, vanilla

Spain's most famous appellation, Rioja makes red, white, and rosé wines. The best reds are elegant and earthy, and aged longer than any other Spanish wines before release.

Rosso di Montalcino / ROW-so dee mon-tall-CHEE-no / **appellation** / $$–$$$

LOCATION: Tuscany, Italy

GRAPE: sangiovese

DEFINING AROMAS/FLAVORS: dark cherry, plum, chocolate, earth

Rosso di Montalcino is considered the little sister of brunello di Montalcino. Rosso wines are typically made with younger grapes from less desirable vineyards, the yields are not as restricted, and winemaking and aging are not as strictly regulated. That said, Rosso di Montalcino can be a great value for someone looking for the flavor of brunello di Montalcino without the price tag. In poor vintages especially, they can be quite good, since some brunello producers forgo making brunello altogether and put those grapes into a Rosso di Montalcino wine those years. For more details on Rosso di Montalcino, see page 117.

roussanne / rue-SAHN / **grape** / $$–$$$

HAPPIEST HOME: Rhône Valley, France

DEFINING AROMAS/FLAVORS: wildflowers, herbs, tea

Rarely bottled solo, roussanne is a French grape prized for its very high acidity and aromatics. It is considered the perfect blending partner to another white grape of the Rhône, marsanne, which can be flabby and lifeless without the addition of roussanne's vivacity. Find it in the white Rhône wines of Saint-Joseph, Hermitage, and Croze-Hermitage, as well as white Châteauneuf-du-Pape.

Saint-Émilion / saint eh-MEEL-ee-on / **appellation** / $$–$$$$

LOCATION: Bordeaux, France

GRAPES: predominantly merlot, usually with the addition of cabernet sauvignon, and/or cabernet franc

DEFINING AROMAS/FLAVORS: plum, black fruit, vanilla, earth

Saint-Émilion is considered one of the best places to grow merlot. There are wines of all prices and quality levels made here, and the best showcase the excellence this grape can achieve, when it is taken seriously and given the right environment.

Sancerre / sahn-SAIR / **appellation** / $$–$$$

LOCATION: Loire Valley, France

GRAPE: sauvignon blanc

DEFINING AROMAS/FLAVORS: grapefruit, gooseberries, chalk, wet rocks

Bone-dry and minerally, Sancerre is one of the most sophisticated versions of sauvignon blanc. These wines are extremely elegant and refined, and rarely cost more than forty dollars, even for the best bottles.

sangiovese / san-gee-oh-VAZE-ee / **grape** / $–$$$$

HAPPIEST HOME: Tuscany, Italy

DEFINING AROMAS/FLAVORS: dried cherry, herbs, dusty earth

Sangiovese is the quintessential Italian grape. It is grown all over the country and makes wines in a wide variety of prices and styles. The best examples come from the Tuscan appellations of Chianti, brunello di Montalcino, Rosso di Montalcino, Vino Nobile di Montepulciano, and morellino di Scansano. There are also excellent, more flashy, and fruit-forward versions of sangiovese grown in Tuscany that don't fit into traditional wine-making regimes (see Rule Breakers, page 84). For more details on sangiovese, see page 116.

Sauternes / saw-TERN / **appellation** / $$–$$$$

LOCATION: Bordeaux, France

GRAPES: sauvignon blanc, semillon

DEFINING AROMAS/FLAVORS: honey, tea, apricot

Opulent and long-lived, the best dessert wines from the Bordeaux appellation of Sauternes taste like liquid sunshine. These special wines are created only in years when *Botrytis cinerea*, "the noble rot" (see page 151), successfully attacks and dehydrates ripe grape bunches. For more details on Sauternes, see page 151.

sauvignon blanc / so-vin-YAWN BLOHNK / **grape** / $–$$$

HAPPIEST HOMES: Loire Valley, France; Bordeaux, France; New Zealand; South Africa; California

DEFINING AROMAS/FLAVORS: grapefruit, fresh cut grass, asparagus, green beans, peas, herbs (basil, oregano), hay, tropical fruit

Sauvignon blanc's aggressively pungent aromatics and tangy acidity make it unique. It is grown with success all over the world, but the best areas are listed above. For more details on sauvignon blanc, see page 98.

semillon / sem-ee-YAWN / **grape** / $$–$$$

HAPPIEST HOMES: Bordeaux, France; Australia

DEFINING AROMAS/FLAVORS: honey, wax, lanolin, fig

Semillon is most commonly found blended with sauvignon blanc in both the dry and sweet dessert wines of Bordeaux, France (most notably in the appellations of Pessac-Léognan, Graves, Entre-Deux-Mers, Sauternes, and Barsac). Semillon adds complexity to sauvignon blanc via aromatics and also texturally—semillon has a beautiful, almost oily mouthfeel and fuller body. The grape can be found (to a much lesser extent) in Australia, where it makes some wonderful dry and dessert wines.

Sherry / SHARE-ee / **appellation** / $$–$$$

LOCATION: southern Spain

GRAPES: palomino, muscat pedro ximénez

DEFINING AROMAS/FLAVORS: nuts, fig, molasses

Sherry is a very special fortified wine made only in the Jerez region of Spain. Styles range from bone-dry to sweet.

Soave / SWAH-vay / **appellation** / $–$$

LOCATION: northern Italy

GRAPES: predominantly garganega, with chardonnay, pinot bianco, and trebbiano di Soave

DEFINING AROMAS/FLAVORS: citrus, pear, mineral

Soave is a crisp, neutral Italian white. Many are nothing special, but high-quality producers are making dry, steely versions that can be excellent values. Look for wines labeled "Soave Classico" or "Soave Classico Superiore" as they will have more depth and elegance than most of the bulk wine labeled simply "Soave."

syrah/shiraz / sih-RAH & shi-RAHZ / **grape** / $-$$$$

HAPPIEST HOMES: Rhône Valley, France; Australia; California; Washington state

DEFINING AROMAS/FLAVORS: black fruit, pepper, jammed fruit, meat, bacon, leather

Syrah makes substantial, powerful, and complex wines with lots of tannin and color. Syrah grown in cool climates tends to have more peppery, leathery flavors whereas those grown in warmer climates ooze jammy, brambly fruit flavors.

Taurasi / tour-AH-zee / **appellation** / $$-$$$

LOCATION: southern Italy

GRAPE: aglianico

DEFINING AROMAS/FLAVORS: dark chocolate, prune, mineral, leather, tar

Taurasi is the home of southern Italy's most respected red wines. Not only are they extremely interesting to smell and taste—with deep, dark, brooding flavors—but their substantial tannin makes them long-lived.

tawny Port / TAW-nee port /

See Port.

tempranillo / tem-prah-NEE-yo / **grape** / $-$$$

HAPPIEST HOME: all over Spain

DEFINING AROMAS/FLAVORS: berries, plum, tobacco, leather, earth

Tempranillo is to Spain what sangiovese is to Italy—the quintessential red grape. It grows all over the country, but is most famous as a blending partner with grenache in the wines of Rioja and in the serious, staunch wines of Ribera del Duero.

Tokaji Aszú / toe-KY ah-ZOO / **type of wine/** $$$-$$$$

LOCATION: Hungary

GRAPES: furmint, hárslevelű, muscat, orémus

DEFINING AROMAS/FLAVORS: honey, tea, dried apricot, orange peel, peach

Lusciously sweet (but refreshingly tangy) Hungarian wine made from grapes affected with the "noble rot" (see page 151), Tokaji Aszú has a rich history and is considered one of the world's most beautiful, special wines. For more details, see page 152.

torrontés / tor-ON-tez / **grape** / $-$$

HAPPIEST HOME: Argentina

DEFINING AROMAS/FLAVORS: citrus, white flowers

A rising superstar in Argentina, torrontés makes wines that are highly floral, almost perfumish on the nose, which then surprise with loads of tangy citrus on the palate. Rarely expensive, torrontés offers good value for those looking for fun, interesting white wines.

Valpolicella / val-pole-ee-CHEL-ah / **appellation** / $-$$$

LOCATION: northern Italy

GRAPES: corvina, rondinella, molinara, negrara

DEFINING AROMAS/FLAVORS: dried cherry, grape, flowers, licorice

A lot of innocuous Valpolicella exists. However, from excellent producers, these red wines can be terrific, with rich, earthy flavors, delicate texture, and nice bright acidity that screams for Italian food pairings.

vernaccia di San Gimignano / ver-NACH-ah dee san-jam-in-YAH-no / **grape** and **appellation** / $-$$

LOCATION: Tuscany, Italy

GRAPE: vernaccia

DEFINING AROMAS/FLAVORS: pear, citrus, bitter almond, chamomile

The vernaccia grape, grown in the picturesque hillside town of San Gimignano, is a tangy wine that goes well with seafood of all sorts. Vernaccia di San Gimignano has a characteristic finish that is reminiscent of bitter almond.

Vinho Verde / VEE-no VAIR-day /**type of wine**/ $-$$

LOCATION: Portugal

GRAPES: many are permitted, the most common and highest quality is alvarinho (albariño)

DEFINING AROMAS/FLAVORS: peaches, flowers

Portugal's most popular white wine, Vinho Verde is meant to be consumed quickly after harvest, when the wine is young and vibrant. Most Vinho Verde has a light effervescence, which is due to the small dose of carbon dioxide added to the bottle just before it is encapsulated.

Vino Nobile di Montepulciano / VEE-no NO-bee-lay dee mon-teh-pull-chee-AH-no / **appellation** / $$-$$$

LOCATION: Tuscany, Italy

GRAPE: prugnolo gentile (a sangiovese clone)

DEFINING AROMAS/FLAVORS: dried cherry, earth, licorice, leather

The best Vino Nobile di Montepulciano is as noble tasting as its name. High acid and high tannin make for gripping wines with good aging potential.

viognier / vee-on-YAY / **grape** / $-$$$$

HAPPIEST HOMES: Rhône Valley, France; California

DEFINING AROMAS/FLAVORS: gardenia, honeysuckle, peach, apricot, citrus

Viognier smells exotic, with potent aromas of gardenias and honeysuckle, peaches and apricots. It makes a lush, full-bodied white with high alcohol.

Vouvray / voo-VRAY / **appellation** / $$-$$$$

LOCATION: Loire Valley, France

GRAPE: chenin blanc

DEFINING AROMAS/FLAVORS: honey, peach, mineral, earth

Vouvrays can be hard to navigate, since they range from dry to sweet and do not usually indicate anywhere on the label where on the spectrum they fall. (Vouvray fans might admit they enjoy the suspense of not knowing until they uncork the bottle.) Most have a high level of acidity and a touch of sweetness that comes across as fresh peachiness and honey.

zinfandel / ZIN-fan-del / **grape** / $-$$$

HAPPIEST HOME: California

DEFINING AROMAS/FLAVORS: jammy, brambly fruit, prune, raisin, chocolate, pepper, clove

Zinfandel is considered the "all-American" grape; it is most at home all over warm pockets of California. The grape makes red wines of varying quality, but no matter the origin or the price, it produces big, robust, fruit-driven wines. For more details on zinfandel, see page 119.

Index

A

B

D

E

H

I

J

K

L

M

R

S

T

U

V

W

Acknowledgments

Just as I hope to inspire your appetite for wine, there are many people who have inspired mine. A big, happy toast to all of those who've played an essential role in this book:

To Joy Sterling, who answered a letter which opened a door

To Paul Torres, who took a chance and changed the direction of my life

To Peter Neptune, who captivated me from the beginning

To Bob Bath, for your insight

To Cindy Nixon, for your generosity

To Karen MacNeil, for your encouragement and openness

To Kermit Lynch, for your inspiration and for believing in me

To Bob Lescher, for your enthusiasm and faith in my voice

To Bill LeBlond, for your support

To Sarah Billingsley, for your creativity, passion, and professionalism

To Jane Tunks, for your keen eye and thoughtful feedback

To my mom, who inspires in so many ways and who always wanted me to be a writer

To Teresa, who introduced me to California, to wine, and to living life to the fullest

To Bill, for your strong, steady support, and for putting up with the three of us

To Bourbon, constant companion and foot warmer

To Evan, my joy, and my first beautiful baby boy

To Harrison, my second, who patiently waited to be born until the week after I was finished writing this book

And finally, to Christian: This project was a long time in the making, but it never would have happened without you. You are the love of my life. Let's drink it in together.